AF248714

College of Commerce and Business Administration

The First 75 Years

The old Commerce School, Bidgood Hall, circa 1948.

College of Commerce and Business Administration

The First 75 Years

MORRIS MAYER

RICHARD MELANCON

College of Commerce and Business Administration
The University of Alabama

$\mathscr{D}$edication

It is a genuine pleasure to dedicate this record of the first seventy-five years of the College of Commerce and Business Administration to our friend and alumnus Osie P. Spencer, through whose generosity this volume has become a reality. Mr. Spencer is a modest man who loves our college and who enjoys remembering—the real basis for any history of this nature.

"It was always my dream," he explained during an interview, "to come to the University of Alabama. That dream became a reality in the fall of 1926 after I graduated from Troy (Alabama) High School. When I got to [the University of] Alabama I thought it was out of this world.

"I had forty dollars that my late brother, Burford Spencer, gave me. Burford was a graduate of the Commerce School [in 1923], and after graduation he worked for an accounting firm in Mobile, Alabama. While in school at the University he had worked at the Supe Store and had had good working relations with Mr. Bernard Ingram who was managing the store at that time. It was through this connection that I was given a job at the Supe Store also. I did all kinds of work, mostly soda fountain work, which began at 5:00 P.M. and ended at midnight. Except on nights when there was an A Club dance or other big dances that lasted later."

Mr. Spencer remembered most fondly Professor Daugherty who taught him labor. It was obvious during the interview that this teacher made a great impact. "He knew everything," Mr. Spencer said. "He was forceful and didn't take kindly to loafing." Mr. Spencer continued:

> I stayed out of school in 1927-28, which was when my father died. When I returned to school, Mr. Jeff Coleman was manager of the Supe Store and a new *big* store it was! My relationship with Mr. Coleman was great. He allowed me to do extra work, earning extra pay. He was a good man to work for.
>
> [When I graduated] in the spring of 1931, we learned what the depression was all about. One of my good friends in my class, who made the best grades, went to work for Goodyear, selling rubber heels in Brooklyn, New York, and earned $90 a month. The University offered me a job to remain at the Supe Store at $125 a month, which I accepted at once and appreciated. Everything went well. I enjoyed my work and was later promoted to the book department. By the end of the year I had saved a little money and Amy and I got married in December 1932.
>
> Thinking there was an opportunity to better [my] work situation, in 1940 I took managerial control of the Alabama Book Store, which proved to be reasonably successful, first as a partnership, later as a corporation. My partner at the time was Mr. Strickland who had a small store downtown. It was called Alabama Book Store [although it actually] had few books, and I wanted that

name. Dean Bidgood advised me at the time to avoid a lot of debt, and Mr. Jim Alston [for whose wife Alston Hall is named], president of the City National Bank [now First Alabama], was most helpful. From Alabama we ventured out to LSU, Atlanta, Georgia, Columbia, South Carolina, and another store that was not profitable. The Alabama Book Store is a separate entity now.

In discussing the reasons for his success, Mr. Spencer said hard work, paying bills on time, and loving what he did were the major factors. He retired from active participation in the business in 1970, and he and his wife live comfortably in Tuscaloosa.

We salute and praise one of our oldest living alumni.

Contents

List of Illustrations

Foreword

Compiling this history of the first seventy-five years of the College of Commerce and Business Administration was a strenuous and demanding task. It required the cooperation and commitment of many people. The authors have recognized many of those people in the acknowledgments. I add my thanks to theirs. The acknowledgments, however, do not include the names of two people without whom this history could not have been completed. They are, of course, the authors: Morris Mayer and Richard Melancon.

Morris Mayer's firsthand knowledge of the people and events that shaped C&BA's development is evident in every chapter. His personal reminiscences, which form an integral part of the latter half of the book, provide an informed perspective on C&BA that no outsider could ever attain. The college, the University, and not least of all the reader of this book owe much to this dedicated faculty member who even in retirement continues to serve his alma mater and professional home.

The C&BA history is a combination of an oral history and an archival history. Without Richard Melancon's excellent research skills and his love for seeking out details in university catalogs and some forty-eight dusty, uncataloged boxes of materials in the University Archives, this history could not have been attempted.

Within the pages of this book are recorded highlights of C&BA's first seventy-five years. The men and women whose words, personalities, aspirations, and achievements are captured herein are characteristic of the faculty, staff, and students who have graced our college—and of those who will come after us.

Barry Mason

Clock in front of Bashinsky Computer Center, 1994.

Preface

If ever there were a labor of love, this history of the first seventy-five years of the College of Commerce and Business Administration must qualify. For some years, the college administration has considered the opportunities that exist for pulling together a documented oral history–archival record of C&BA. Because I achieved emeritus status in August 1992 (and assumed I would have a lot of time on my hands) and because Richard Melancon, a recent Ph.D. in English with writing and research skills was available "for hire," the time for action seemed appropriate. The team became a reality in June 1993 when the two of us began our voyage through time. Seldom have two more different people worked so closely together for such an extended time. We hope the reader will agree that we have accomplished our common goal: to record for posterity the life of our college from 1919 to 1994.

As all writers and researchers do, we designed the inevitable outline. Ricky took off to immerse himself in C&BA lore in written form, found primarily in the Special Collections of the University. Perhaps the most time-consuming activity of all his investigatory efforts was compiling a detailed record of all faculty members who ever taught in our school, as well as tracing each career through time. My major value in the process has been a close relationship with C&BA—as student and faculty member—resulting in firsthand knowledge of the people and conditions that built, shaped, and sustained the culture that has created the great institution of today. Much of our information has come from oral histories. We have talked to alumni, faculty, and staff who remembered the heroes who had the vision and the friends who shared the educational experience.

For me it was a sentimental journey. When I heard former students and colleagues mention my mentors and respected teachers—later colleagues—I felt a rush of nostalgia for my lost youth. More important, however, was my pride in having been a part of the history and being able now to make sure that for all time we will have a record to cherish. You will read herein about such visionaries as Deans Lee Bidgood, S. Paul Garner, Bill Mitchell, and perhaps my closest colleague, Dean Barry Mason, as well as Professors Bonham, Holladay, Whitman, Alyea, Morley, and Hawley. I was fortunate indeed to know them. I am sad when I realize that my relationship with Professors Chapman and Knight was limited. During the process of investigation, it was enlightening and heartwarming to speak to a dear friend, Miriam Locke, as well as respected colleague James McMillan, who, unknown to me, served C&BA for many of its earliest years.

I am full of emotion as I sit in the beautiful Alston Hall and remember my many years in old Bidgood Hall. I see the magnificence of "the Commerce Building's" renovation and reflect on what the magnificent Bruno Library–Bashinsky Computer Center will mean to future generations who will love C&BA and the University of Alabama as I do. My father studied economics under Lee Bidgood and my daughter enjoyed management with Jim Cashman. When the next installment of this history is written, perhaps a fourth generation of my family will share in my devotion to this institution, which has been the focal point of my professional career.

My affiliation with the University and C&BA has been lengthy, encompassing my years as a student in the 1940s to my retirement from the faculty in 1992 and extending into the present with teaching assignments and the compilation of this history of the college. Following my service in World War II, I was an undergraduate at the University, graduating in 1949 with a B.S. in business administration. In 1955–56 I was a temporary faculty member, before taking a four-year leave of absence to obtain a doctorate from Ohio State University. The later decades—the sixties, seventies, eighties, and nineties—are those years when I served C&BA as a full-time, tenured faculty member. For many of those years I served as a departmental administrator. I was department chair from 1969 to 1974 and coordinator of the faculty of marketing from 1974 until my retirement in 1992, serving with Barry Mason and Ron Dulek.

I present this brief chronology of my involvement with C&BA because following chapter 4, which deals with the 1950s, the reader may notice a change in "tone." I am able to write about the more recent years—the decades covered in chapters 5, 6, and 7—because I was a part of the action, and I have a perspective that allows me to occasionally interject what I believe are meaningful asides. The basis for much of the information in those later chapters is the oral interviews conducted with alumni and faculty, most of whom are people I have known and worked with.

The oral part of this history was great fun for me. I found myself reliving much of my life in talking to old friends, former students, emeritus and active faculty and staff. To share the devotion for Alabama and C&BA with others has been a joy. We thank you all for the time and effort.

My coauthor, Richard Melancon, is a skilled researcher. He has, therefore, depended primarily on archival materials, especially letters and documents carefully accumulated by Dean Lee Bidgood over his long tenure, as the source of his discussions. In addition, the number of people available to discuss the early days of our history is limited. Seventy-five years is a long time!

So this history depends in the early years primarily on archival research, whereas later years rest more firmly on the oral history tradition. In the narrative portions of the book, all references to "I," "my," or "me" (that is, any first-person pronouns interjected into text that is not a transcription of an interview) refer to me, Morris Mayer. My coauthor and I are comfortable with the two approaches—the archival and the personal—and in fact believe the change in pace and tone will in the final analysis result in a more interesting document. We hope the reader will agree.

In the appendixes we have listed all those with whom we had oral history interviews. Similarly in the appendixes is a list of Alabama Hall of Fame inductees, colleagues who have been named to the C&BA Faculty Hall of Fame, Austin Cup winners, Board of Visitors members, a roster of all the faculty members who are a part of the history of C&BA, and other miscellaneous data.

We encourage you to look through the appendixes at the facts and figures gathered there. We will only celebrate the first seventy-five years once, and we want to include as many details and particulars as possible. An appendix is a wonderful depository for interesting things that no one tries to remember, but many of us like to have access to.

I could not have taken on this project without the "approval" of my real boss, Judy Mayer. She was available at all times to proofread, evaluate, critique, and just listen to my frustrations. She would say she didn't do anything, but I beg to differ. Thanks, dear.

Morris Mayer

Typical classroom, 1920s.

Acknowledgments

In a project of this magnitude many people are involved and should be acknowledged. The danger, of course, is that someone may be forgotten. We apologize at the outset for this possibility and ask for your understanding.

First of all we express our gratitude to Dean Barry Mason for supporting the project from inception to conclusion. His enthusiasm for the importance of the history was contagious. Tom Moore, the administrator of the project, was always available for consultation and assistance, as was Tony Linn.

When we agreed to write the history of C&BA, we had no clear idea of the tremendous task we were undertaking. Now, as the year of work comes to an end and we reflect on our accomplishment—and the many people who helped bring it to fruition—our thoughts come somewhat at random. The ordering of those acknowledged does not necessarily reflect their importance to the project.

Cathy Andreen has been of great assistance in discovering pictures, old and new, to enhance this history. Ricky Melancon's wife, Tami, has been invaluable in that effort as well. Morris Mayer's M.B.A. assistant Robin Jones helped preserve his sanity throughout the period of research and writing. His M.B.A. assistant Angie Penuel was of great help during the final stages of the project. He is forever grateful for their excellent assistance.

To provide perspective for the various decades of our history, Suzanne Wolfe's *Pictorial History of the University of Alabama* was indispensable. We acknowledge the work, which is a real treasure.

Sherry O'Brien of the Center for Business and Economic Research is largely responsible for the design and layout of the history. She is a pleasure to work with. We thank her, as well as Bill Gunther and Deborah Hamilton for assigning her to this job and supporting our efforts all the way.

Working closely with Sherry and the authors were Anne Gibbons, an efficient and dedicated editor whose work makes us all look better, and Anna Singer, whose expertise in matters of design, development, and production benefited all of us.

We acknowledge the contributions of all faculty members—past and present—to what and who we are. The roster of Austin Cup recipients in appendix C acknowledges the best of our graduates, who are indeed the pivotal focus of our work.

What would we have done without the assistance of Mary Ann Albright and Glender Leasor who listened to hours of interviews and transcribed them with loving care? Without dedicated secretarial assistance, an oral history cannot be transformed from mere memories into, well, history. We are grateful to the dean's office for allowing us access to this exceptional assistance.

Jan Pruitt Duvall was a source of great support when we needed her assistance. We are fortunate to have her at the University of Alabama.

Quotations from the letters of Dean Lee Bidgood and from those who corresponded with him were taken from the C&BA archives collection located in the William Stanley Hoole Special Collections Library at the University of Alabama. During the course of many hours spent rummaging through C&BA archives, Ricky came to know the fine group of people who work in the University's William Stanley Hoole Special Collections Library. We thank them for all their kindnesses during the past fourteen months.

Prof. Joyce Lamont, now Assistant Dean Emerita for Special Collections, is to be congratulated on assembling such a capable and helpful staff. We also thank her for granting the special permission necessary to check out some material germane to the project. University Archivist Dr. Jerry Oldshue was helpful in pointing out some important sources of information about the early years of C&BA and always had a smile and a hello. Clark Center, technical archivist, also offered suggestions and located material that made this a better work.

Andrea Watson, Special Collections Librarian for Reference Services, spent considerable time helping locate University catalogs and other reference materials. Library Assistant Hugh Terry, Library Clerk Kevin Ray, Frank Holifield, Tom Land, and Greg Mattison located and pulled box after box of archival records. Each of these people proved to be professional, efficient, and friendly. We thank them all for their assistance and support.

Sheryl Tubbs and Debbie Beck, receptionists in the office of the Graduate School, also deserve thanks for allowing us to photocopy information from the University catalogs.

We single out for thanks Paul Garner who became the real, living contact with our beginnings. His unselfish commitment of time was typical of his devotion to the college and the University. His knowledge is limitless.

College of Commerce and Business Administration

The First 75 Years

The world is talking about:

The Nineteenth Amendment to the Constitution, giving women the right to vote, is ratified. (August 26, 1920)

The last U.S. troops from World War I are withdrawn from Germany. (January 10, 1923)

President Harding dies of apoplexy; Calvin Coolidge is sworn in as the thirtieth president. (August 3, 1923)

U.S. Steel Corporation institutes the eight-hour work day. (August 13, 1923)

John T. Scopes, a teacher from Dayton, Tennessee, is arrested for teaching Darwin's Theory of Evolution. (May 5, 1925)

Charles Lindbergh flies his monoplane, the *Spirit of St. Louis,* from New York to Paris—the first solo Atlantic crossing. (May 21, 1927)

Amelia Earhart becomes the first woman to pilot a plane across the Atlantic. (May 25, 1928)

In the St. Valentine's Day Massacre, six Chicago gangsters are lined up against a wall and shot by a rival gang. (February 14, 1929)

Black Tuesday, the most catastrophic day in stock market history, heralds the Great Depression. (October 29, 1929)

The University is talking about:

The Amelia Gorgas Memorial, the first building constructed with Million Dollar Campaign funds, is built in 1925. It housed the University library from 1925 to 1939 and administrative offices from 1925 to 1970. It was renamed Carmichael Hall in 1971 and was used extensively by C&BA for some years.

Alabama football: the 1926 Rose Bowl—Alabama 20, Washington 19. The 1927 Rose Bowl ends in a tie—Alabama 7, Stanford 7.

College "hot buttons" during the twenties:

1922–23

- The specialized areas of study are accounting, banking and finance, business and law, commercial teaching, foreign trade and consular service, general business, manufacturing, public service, real estate and insurance, transportation, and wholesale and retail trade.

1923–24

- Master of Science in Commerce is awarded.
- Statistics splits from economics.

1924–25

- Graduate work now administered by the Graduate School.
- New program in merchandising is begun.

1925–26

- C&BA is now the largest of the University's professional schools.
- Manufacturing is replaced by production management.

1926–27

- Accounting becomes accounting and statistics.
- Public utilities is added to transportation.

1927–28

- Personnel is added to production management.
- Advertising becomes a major.

1928–29

- The college is recognized by the American Association of Collegiate Schools of Business (AACSB).

Chapter 1

The Roaring Twenties
The Era of Dean Lee Bidgood Begins

Faculty "shapers" of the C&BA culture:

Harry Bonham (1923)
Herman Chapman (1921)
James Holladay (1927)
Chester Knight (1923)
Leroy J. Nations (1926)
Marcus Whitman (1927)

Lee Bidgood.

Faculty and staff who helped define the C&BA culture. (*Front, left to right*) Sarah Rodgers, Marcus Whitman, Julia Jackson, James Holladay; *(second row)* unidentified student, Ed Austin; *(back row)* Burton Morley, Harry Bonham, H. H. Chapman, and Langston Hawley.

In Their Own Words

How fortunate we were to be able to talk with alumni of the twenties. It is easy to calculate that in 1994 these gentlemen were all in their nineties. They were also extremely alert and interested. Their wisdom and their continuing interest in their alma mater provide a significant beginning to this history.

Mortimer A. Cohen, who graduated in 1922, is a former judge and former president and chairman of the board of a bank. He remembered that Lee Bidgood was dean of the school and George Denny was president of the University and considers them very fine people. He remembered fondly Chester Knight and H. H. Chapman. One of his classmates was the late Ehney H. Camp, who became president of Liberty National Life Insurance Company and was a true and valued friend of the business school.

"[In my years at the Commerce School] the faculty were fine, wonderful men who had been college trained and most of them had a Ph.D. The business philosophy was sound. We were taught ethics. We were taught how to be good businessmen, how to be decent people, and how to be successful, but to be successful businessmen we had to be good citizens in the community. We had to be good neighbors. Our purpose in life was to succeed by being good to other

people, by being thrifty and useful in making a place for leadership and encouraging our people in our communities to go to college." This philosophy of the twenties recalled by one of our earliest graduates is as appropriate in 1994 as it was seventy years ago—and will be appropriate seventy years from now. We are grateful and proud of our heritage.

One of the University's and C&BA's most honored and beloved graduates is _Jeff Coleman_, Class of 1928.

> I visited Tuscaloosa in 1923 when I was working at the Boy Scout camp nearby, so I got to know a little about the Alabama campus, but I didn't know what I wanted to study. My older brother had transferred from a one-year normal school in Livingston [the Colemans' hometown] to the University's College of Arts and Sciences. I heard about the Commerce School, but I knew very little about the curriculum, in fact, I doubt if I knew what the word curriculum meant. I was very fortunate that we had the excellent professors whom Dean Bidgood had hired as he put together a business school faculty.
>
> I studied with Dean Bidgood when I was a freshman in 1924—imagine having Bidgood for Economics I and II. The class was held in Clark Hall.

Coleman remembered Professors Chapman (statistics) and Nations (advertising) from whom he learned a lot. Chester Knight was a young professor in accounting, and Coleman remembered having difficulty in that subject. He also recalled Professors Holladay (finance), Bonham (marketing), and Whitman (transportation). He was enthusiastic about the caliber of the faculty he had during the twenties.

After graduation, Dr. Denny convinced Coleman to remain at Alabama, and he became business manager of the Athletics Department (Coleman Coliseum is named for him). Shortly thereafter, Coleman was given the opportunity by Denny to buy an interest in the Supe Store and to manage it.

"I'm delighted that I've lived to see the Commerce School develop as it is today. I was just looking at all the buildings yesterday afternoon. They were working on the library, and it's remarkable. I was purchasing agent for all of the University while I was still business manager for athletics." He thought about how difficult it had been during the first renovation of Bidgood to outfit the building. "President Gallalee wanted to see everything that went on from everywhere; he wanted to see what we were going to buy [desks, chairs, waste baskets, file cabinets, and so on]." For example, Coleman wanted a ten-dollar waste basket to match the furniture, and Gallalee said no waste basket was worth more than two dollars. So he wouldn't approve the purchase. Coleman was frustrated, wanting all the furniture and accessories to match.

In 1954 Jeff Coleman gave up purchasing and athletics and became director of Alumni Affairs, a position he held for the next twenty years. As our interview drew to a close, Coleman remembered that Dean Bidgood had a book on his desk in which he wrote down the name of every Commerce graduate. This was long before computers. Sadly, Coleman said nobody knows where the book is.

Jackson Coley, a member of the Class of 1922, was proud to say:

> *I was very close to Dean Bidgood. He was my good friend as well as my mentor. In my senior year, I was one of his assistants. There were three of us. Alfred William Rose and Hugh Bradley were his other two assistants.*
>
> *We graded papers and also served as instructors in his small quiz sections where we would quiz students on Saturday mornings on the economics lectures he had made during the week. It meant a great deal to me. It got me accustomed to standing on my feet in front of people, which was later quite useful in my business career.*
>
> *He would do things that developed you. For example, one day he came in, said he had an appointment and wanted me to give an hour lecture on a certain topic to his lecture section of 150 students. I said that I had no time to prepare as the class started in fifteen minutes, and he told me that I was qualified and knew the material and I should do it. I don't know how good the lecture was, but I got through it.*
>
> *Dr. Bidgood had a very keen sense of humor. He was a quiet type, and he was extremely efficient. I felt very indebted to the college. Dr. Bidgood recommended me to Irving Stern, who was head of Stern, Agee, and Leach, for my first job, and I stuck there. I started as a "flunky"—I did what I had to do and I wound up as a partner. When we incorporated, I was one of the senior stockholders and executive vice-president.*

J. Clemson Duckworth (known as Clem to his friends) was asked by Dean Bidgood at the beginning of the 1925 school year to teach economics. An instructor had failed to show up and Duckworth was asked to teach for a semester, until someone else could be secured. He actually taught for the whole academic year—he was only seventeen or eighteen at the time.

Duckworth graduated in 1928, and Dean Bidgood told him that if he would come back and enter graduate school, he could have a teaching job for the next year. He took Bidgood's advice and returned to teach some classes in insurance. His family had been in the insurance business for many years, and he suspects that's the reason he agreed to do it. "I didn't make much money doing it. As I recall it was one hundred dollars for each semester. I had an office in the newly opened business school building, and I was very proud of that. I went out to Bidgood Hall recently to see if I could find my old office, but the interior has changed so much I couldn't find it. I have been close to the school through all of the changes that have been going on and I still have a great deal of respect for it."

William Jessup Sr., Class of 1929, was delighted to discuss the early days of the Commerce School. He told me that his father had said he would pay college expenses for one year.

> *And after that it was up to me. Thanks to Dean Bidgood and others, I was able to graduate. I was the dean's secretary for three years. Back in those days, no dean had a full-time secretary, and no dean had a telephone. So I worked four hours a day, except Saturday, [when] I worked two hours, and I took care of his correspondence. I could take shorthand too. Even President Denny had [only] a part-time secretary.*

taught me to write everything I knew on the exam papers, so the teacher can read what you know. I made 100 on his final exam [and] became his student assistant [grader], and he became my mentor, adviser, and lifelong friend. Mr. Bonham was in his office early every day and left very late every day to be accessible to students and colleagues."

Herman Hollis Chapman joined the C&BA faculty in the fall of 1921 as an assistant professor of business administration and head of the accounting courses. By the 1924–25 academic year he was also listed as the only instructor of business statistics. As the head of the course offerings in statistics for several years, Chapman oversaw the development of one of the Southeast's first collegiate programs in the subject. He also provided able and diligent assistance to Dean Bidgood in establishing a sound business library. In 1930 Chapman became the first director of the Bureau of Business Research and for the next twenty-one years supervised the collection and dissemination of vitally important quantitative information on the broad range of economic activity in the state. Harry A. Lipson described him as "a tall, gaunt, white-haired, mild-mannered scholar. Very patient in teaching precise numerical materials. As director of the Bureau of Business Research, he encouraged faculty members to publish their research findings. He edited and published my first monograph, *Accounting Materials for Retail Concerns,* in 1951 and nurtured scholarship and excellent teaching among his colleagues. Dignity personified."

James Holladay was born in Kentucky and earned degrees from Georgetown College, the University of Illinois, and the University of Iowa. He joined the C&BA faculty as professor of economics in 1927 as a specialist in banking and finance. When the school's Department of Finance was created in 1946, Dean Bidgood selected him to head it. He retired in 1964. Lipson recalled,

"Students called him 'The Little General.' [He was] a dapper dresser. His lectures opened up the monetary world for us as his well-planned lectures provided example after example to illustrate the principles he was trying to get across. A demanding but fair grader of student work."

Chester Knight, a 1925 graduate of C&BA, distinguished himself by winning the Jefferson Medal and being inducted into both Beta Gamma Sigma and Phi Beta Kappa. While a student he also embarked on what would prove to be his lifelong career. In 1923 he entered the C&BA faculty ranks as a part-time instructor of accounting, becoming an assistant professor of the subject in 1927. Lipson offered high praise for Knight's teaching abilities and service to Commerce students: "He had the knack for teaching why to use accounting principles and procedures in each situation rather than relying on rote memory. He had an uncanny ability to provide counsel and guidance to any student coming to him for financial assistance or personal advice." During his twenty-two-year career with C&BA, Knight rose to become head of the accounting department and one of the best-loved members of the Commerce faculty. A World War I veteran who was seriously wounded in combat, he was chosen in 1944 to represent World War II veterans who entered the University under the GI Bill. The Commerce School lost one of its most dedicated and admired members with Chester Knight's death in 1949. In a resolution adopted by the University's Board of Trustees, Dean Bidgood noted that Knight's "knowledge, vision, and energy were primarily responsible for the fact that when he met his last class in the University, the Department of Accounting . . . was the most important one in this region."

Leroy J. Nations joined the Commerce School faculty as an instructor in business English during the fall of 1926. This lover of

I remember that Iris Carmack worked for Dean Bidgood and also worked for Dr. Denny. I made $35 a month, which was pretty good for then. In my first three years I spent approximately $750 and the last year $1,000, and I lived comfortably. I also managed an apartment called Spanish Inn, across the street from the old SAE house.

In thinking about his professors, Jessup remembered Mr. Bonham, who taught marketing. He also remembered Mr. Nations, whose office he had to walk through on the way to Dean Bidgood's. "We started off in 1926 in Manley Hall. The accounting department was on the third floor of Garland Hall. We finally had an office in the new business building. If you walked in from the quad side of the building, Dean Bidgood's office was to the left at the end on the left-hand side."

Like most of his classmates, Jessup talked about how much the dean meant to him and how he respected Marcus Whitman, Chester Knight, and H. H. Chapman. He also recalled the Senior Tour (a graduation requirement) and remembered visiting the offices of the *Birmingham News*, Moore-Handley (hardware wholesaler), and TCI, where he watched them make a piece of rail.

Harvey "Red" Terrell, Class of 1927, is one of Alabama's most respected businessmen; he served the First National Bank of Birmingham in many capacities, including chief executive officer. In recalling his years at Alabama he said, "Dean Bidgood was a tremendous guy—I just can't recall all the things he meant to me and to the Commerce School. I also include Dr. Chapman as an instructor who meant a lot to me, and Mr. Bonham was a fabulous guy."

One of Terrell's happiest memories is his great success as an amateur tennis player for which he has been widely recognized.

In the Beginning

The fall of 1919 opened one of the most eventful academic years in the eighty-eight year history of the University of Alabama. The War to End All Wars had drawn to a close less than a year before the opening of the University's 1919–20 session. With the world now made safe for democracy, record numbers of students prepared to begin or resume their academic careers. Women, celebrating their twenty-fifth year as students at the University, made up a larger percentage of the enrollment than ever before; their numbers would continue to increase throughout the coming decade. Students enrolling in the fall of 1919 found a number of improvements in the University's dormitories and for the first time could rent furniture for their rooms. New and returning students also discovered changes in the University's course offerings.

The curriculum changes grew out of a detailed study of Alabama's educational system conducted earlier in the year by a panel of experts from the U.S. Bureau of Education. In their report to the state legislature in June 1919, the experts had recommended several modifications of the state's educational programs, including those at the Capstone of higher education. The legislature adopted the panel's recommendations, and University of Alabama president George H. Denny used the institution's student newspaper, the *Crimson White*, to introduce the new programs and departments to the community. In the July 10, 1919, issue President Denny wrote that the University was "already preparing to develop the new fields assigned to it" and stood poised for a "great era of expansion." Improvements were planned for the offerings in vocational education and in the engineering department, but Denny seemed especially excited about a recommendation that the authors of the educational survey had most strongly urged: the creation of a school of commerce at the University of Alabama.

The University had been offering courses for some time in areas that would later become central to the collegiate study of commerce and business administration. The earliest recorded economics classes at the University of Alabama were taught in 1898–99 by Prof. Thomas Chalmers McCorvey, an 1873 graduate who joined the faculty that same year as a professor and commandant of cadets. By the 1879–80 session, McCorvey was a professor of mental and moral philosophy in the School of Mental and Moral Philosophy and Political Economy.

In 1885–86 McCorvey took over a course of lectures formerly given by the president of the University on "the History and Science of Political Economy." Political economy became independent of moral and mental philosophy in 1888–89. By the academic year of 1898–99, the University's catalog listed an economics course, taught by McCorvey, which was designed "to give an outline of knowledge of the accepted theories in Economic Science." Students in the course would also learn to apply economic theories to "the social and political problems of the day." Lee Bidgood, the first dean of the University's School of Commerce and Business Administration, dubbed McCorvey "the pioneer in the field of social sciences here."

In the following years, McCorvey added courses, expanding the University's offerings into subject areas that would later become widely recognized fields of study for collegiate students of business and commerce. In the latter half of the 1903–4 academic year, Professor McCorvey offered a course on money, banking, and finance that introduced students to "the nature and uses of money and credit, and the general principles and practice of banking and finance." During the 1912–13 session, McCorvey began to instruct students in economic history.

By the second decade of the twentieth century, the University of Alabama provided for its students basic coursework in economics, with some attention to the fundamentals of finance. This foundation had taken many years to lay. Following the arrival in 1912 of Dr. George Hutcheson Denny as president, business education at the University experienced more rapid development. At first glance, the former professor of Latin and German at Washington and Lee University may have seemed an unlikely candidate to spur growth in a business education program and to preside over the founding of the state's first university-level school of business. However, as the president of Washington and Lee, he had overseen the founding of its school of business.

Actions following his arrival at the University suggest that Dr. Denny also wanted to establish a collegiate school of business in Alabama. Surprised to find that the University offered only a few economics courses, he asked the legislature for twenty-five hundred dollars to inaugurate a chair of economics and sociology. After receiving an appropriation for the new department, he

baseball taught several generations of Commerce students such subjects as freshman composition, business correspondence, and survey of British and American literature. He became the head of the special composition and literature sections designed for Commerce students. He also introduced the study of advertising to the campus, teaching Economics 125 for several years, in addition to courses on salesmanship and sales management. Because of Nations's versatility and dedication, Dean Bidgood came to regard him as one of the stalwart members of his faculty. On May 26, 1943, Dean Bidgood wrote to University dean of administration M. C. Huntley to submit the Commerce School budget and to recommend several faculty members for promotion. Bidgood described Nations as one of the "old guard" faculty members who "remained with us through all of the dark and unpromising days, and who really made a success of the attempt to build the Commerce School on this campus. . . . He is rather generally regarded as one of our better classroom teachers." Nations received his promotion to full professor in 1943 and joined the faculty of the Department of Marketing when it was created in 1946.

In his report to the University's president dated May 16, 1949, Dean Bidgood wrote, "It is with the deepest regret that I record the loss through illness of the services of Professor Leroy J. Nations. A member of our faculty for twenty-three years, he was one of the half-dozen pioneer teachers who gave the school its form, character, and ideals. It will be almost impossible to fill his place."

Marcus Whitman was hired as associate professor of economics in 1927, specializing in transportation. In his first semester, Whitman expanded the offerings in his area by adding courses in utilities and traffic management. Harry Lipson remembered that students called him "The Bantam Rooster." He further described him as "barrel-chested"

asked fellow Virginian Lee Bidgood, who held a master's degree from the University of Virginia, to head it as professor of economics. If Denny wanted a man committed to establishing a business school, he could not have made a more appropriate choice. Some years later, Bidgood admitted, "I was led to accept that position [as department head] largely because of the hope that the installation of a commerce school would soon follow that of the department of economics."

Bidgood did everything in his power to hasten the day when the University numbered a commerce school among its major divisions. He expanded the course offerings within the department. The 1914–15 University catalog listed five courses in the department: Elements of Economics, Economic History of the United States, American Tariff History, Corporation Finance, and Trusts. These courses proved an immediate success. In his report to the June 1914 annual meeting of the board of trustees, President Denny stated, "One year ago the trustees established an independent chair of economics and sociology. Professor Lee Bidgood . . . was asked to inaugurate the new courses. From the very beginning the classes have been large. The courses offered have been popular with all elements of the student body. . . . I am convinced that these courses will continue to grow in popularity from year to year. I am also convinced that the work done in this department will . . . more and more contribute to the higher social and economic life of Alabama."

The courses offered in economics remained popular over the next few years, and soon Professor Bidgood needed an assistant, Mr. Robert Messer, to help him meet the demand for the classes. By 1919 Denny felt that the unqualified success of the economics department and the changing nature of Alabama's economy justified establishing a full school of business at the University. In his report to the University Board of Trustees on May 26, 1919, he stated his case:

> It is the duty of the University to establish a school of business administration. Many of our young men are choosing business as their life career. This number will steadily increase. From business a large percentage of our taxes is collected. It is good political economy to organize a school of commerce. The next few years will witness an enormous expansion in both foreign and domestic commerce. This is a very real and vital demand for business training. The University can organize such a course far more economically than any other institution. We already offer courses in commercial law and in economics. These courses constitute the basis of the work now proposed. It is merely a question of adding special courses in banking, finance, commerce, accounting, and kindred subjects. We are asking the sum of $7,000 per annum to make possible these new courses and thus give to Alabama youth a better chance to fit themselves to meet the demands of the day in the business world. No better investment can be made by the state looking to its own material prosperity.

Perhaps Denny was privy to the conclusions reached by the federal team studying Alabama's educational system about that same time. In its final report, released to the state legislature in early June, the team urged the formation of a school of business in the state:

The increasing urbanization of [Alabama's] population means a relative increase in business and commercial organization. This has already become highly complicated in cities like Birmingham and Mobile. It is a thing of numerous potential ramifications. Alabama is also one of the gateways of foreign trade. To relate the industries of the State to foreign markets, to exploit these, and to stimulate the growth of the State's commercial enterprise with a view to meeting the conditions of these markets, are projects vital to the State's material progress. Modern business administration rests on the application of science to business problems. The best school for acquiring knowledge of it is no longer the school of experience. Business education is a university subject. The more progressive universities have recognized this fact and have provided special professional schools to give training in the sciences which underlie commerce and business. As yet the higher institutions of Alabama have been able to do nothing in this direction. The committee is convinced that a State which includes 2 percent of the total population of the United States, a State which possesses the great commercial prospects which have been indicated, can no longer afford to neglect this field of professional training.

The report writers continued: "Obviously the appropriate place for [the school's] development is at the University of Alabama. The ultimate extent of the undertaking cannot be determined without preliminary investigation. Such investigation it will be the province of the State council of education to make. On the basis of its findings the program of the university can be modified from time to time. A modest and safe beginning can be made, however, even in advance of the council's inquiries."

In words that must have rung sweetly in the ears of both President Denny and Professor Bidgood, the report concluded: "The committee judges that the budgetary requests of the university for the establishment of work in commerce should receive favorable action."

H.H. Chapman.

President Denny.

Dean Bidgood's office, 1928.

The panel's recommendations soon made headlines in the *Crimson White*. The June 19 issue proclaimed, "Many Improvements Soon to be Made at University," "New Courses to be Offered," and "Courses in Business Training, Banking, and Finance to be Given." In a statement, President Denny asked, "Are you interested in business training? Do you expect to be a businessman? We are organizing courses in commercial law, banking, finance, economics, etc., into a school of commerce or business administration. These courses are in great demand. They fit young men for business along large lines." In the July 10 *Crimson White* President Denny made clear to readers that the University was acting in accordance with the educational survey commission's report to meet "the rapidly developing need [for] college-trained businessmen [by] organizing a complete school of business. . . This field should prove attractive to young men who wish to become 'captains of industry' in Alabama."

On November 13, 1919, the *Crimson White* reported, "A School of Commerce and Business Administration has been added to the University of Alabama. Mr. Lee Bidgood, Professor of Economics, is dean of the new school." The writer pointed out that collegiate study of business administration had proven popular at "large Eastern universities," but "the University of Alabama is one of the Southern Colleges leading in establishing this modern school." The writer's assertion that the school would open "a new field of practical training for students who wish to enter the business world with chances of rising" clearly echoed sentiments expressed by both President Denny and the educational survey commission members, who had exhorted Alabama to begin educating its future business leaders in a university setting rather than depending on the more haphazard education gained from experience alone.

Bidgood's Goals for C&BA

As part of his 1944 report to the Alabama Educational Survey Commission, Dean Bidgood provided a brief history of the University's School of Commerce and Business Administration. As he recalled, "The School . . . originated primarily in a desire to give the youth of this region an opportunity to rise to responsible positions in commerce, industry, and finance. It was seen that the complexity of business had become so great that avenues of advancement were largely closed to those who had not received such preparation. A few who were wealthy sent their children to another part of the country to get an education in business. But the average youth of this state and of its neighboring states could not expect to do more than become clerks or laborers in the new industrial life."

Early in his administration, Dean Bidgood formulated ten objectives for the University of Alabama commerce school:

1. To give Alabama boys and girls a chance to prepare for careers in the service of business and industry, either as enterprisers or as employees;
2. To supply employers with professionally trained personnel, in all of the varied fields of commerce and business administration;

3. To pour into this state and region at least a small but steadily increasing stream of ambitious and venturesome young men and women, equipped with modern education in the techniques of business, who would establish enterprises of their own;
4. To make available a modern type of preparation for the study of law, a preparation which would enable its recipients to help guide the State of Alabama and its neighbors through the legal difficulties incident to the transition from an agricultural to an industrial economy;
5. To educate an adequate number of young people for genuinely professional service to our local, state, and national governments;
6. To prepare a small and select group for teaching business and commercial subjects;
7. To contribute to the inadequate but rapidly expanding body of knowledge available to businessmen and to teachers of business subjects;
8. To publish and disseminate business and economic information to the people of Alabama and to cooperate with other agencies engaged in that undertaking;
9. To contribute professional courses in business administration to curricula offered in conjunction with the university's technical schools;
10. To provide cultural courses in economics for all undergraduate divisions of the university.

Large lecture hall, 1928.

Accounting lab, 1928.

The Early Years

By November 1919 the committee on the commerce course had approved a proposed curriculum as well as lists of credit and noncredit courses for those already in the University who wished to enroll in the School of Commerce and Business Administration. The official enrollment of the first students took place at the opening of the second term in January 1920. Seventy-one men became the first group of students to enroll in the new School of Commerce and Business Administration at the University of Alabama. The University catalog for the academic year 1920–21 listed a department of accounting and economics in the section devoted to the Commerce School, as well as special course offerings in commercial law, English, mathematics, commercial geography, and salesmanship. Prof. Joannes M. van der Westhuyzen, who had arrived on campus in January 1920, headed the accounting department; he also taught the salesmanship course and a course in business statistics. Bidgood relied on instructors from other areas of the University to teach such courses as commercial law and mathematics, but as the school grew he would establish his own English and mathematics departments and offer special courses in other areas such as commercial Spanish.

The newly established Commerce School experienced growing pains during its earliest days. In his 1944 report to the state education commission, Bidgood observed that at first the school had only "the good wishes of the University as a whole, one office and one classroom in Morgan Hall, one teacher other than the Dean, and a student assistant or two." The faculty and students had no building to call their own and for several more years would meet in classrooms scattered about the campus. Until the fall of 1923, students had no areas of specialization from which to choose.

Mimeograph room, 1928.

Another problem that plagued Bidgood was keeping qualified faculty members. Professor van der Westhuyzen was apparently uncomfortable with conditions at the University and soon left. In 1921, however, Herman Hollis Chapman arrived to take charge of the accounting and statistic courses offered by the school. He was the first of the group of men Morris Mayer describes as the "shapers" of the Commerce School. Chapman early on proved himself an able assistant as Dean Bidgood worked toward achieving his goals.

The Business Library

One of Dean Bidgood's priorities for the school was establishing a library exclusively for the use of Commerce students. Chapman suggested that Bidgood follow the practice of the University of Michigan by setting up a room devoted to the purpose. In the University catalog for the academic year 1923–24, the following notice appeared: "A commodious reading room has been fitted up in Woods Hall for the use of students in the school of commerce and business administration in order to supplement the facilities offered by the University library. It is well furnished with tables and chairs; it contains duplicate copies of the most important books reserved for reference and parallel reading in the commerce courses, and it is supplied with business and financial magazines, and government bulletins on business and economic subjects."

In the unpublished memoirs of his years with C&BA, Chapman recalled that because his office was located above the reading room, he felt a certain responsibility for the facility and for finding ways of improving it. He allowed students to use some of his materials and convinced Bidgood to subscribe to various business and government publications that students would find helpful. By the 1925–26 academic year, the reading room was called the business library.

Early Physical Facilities and Equipment

The first commerce students did not have a central location at which to meet their classes. In fact, commerce classes for the first few years of the school's existence were held in various campus buildings, including Woods, Clark, Morgan, and Manly halls. The University catalog for the academic year 1922–23 contained the statement that "for recitation and lecture rooms the school uses any class rooms that are not otherwise used, in all of the university buildings." Such a situation no doubt frustrated students and faculty members who had to attend classes in scattered locations about the campus.

Despite the lack of a building to call its own, the school did its best to provide adequate equipment for its students in those rooms assigned to it. In the same catalog, the writer noted that "for accounting and statistics there are two fully equipped laboratories, one in Morgan Hall and one in Woods Hall. Each is furnished with tables and chairs for forty-two students. The tables are narrow, and students are seated on one side of them only, so that all face the front of the room. Every student has ample elbow room, and a drawer large enough for his books and practice set."

Catalogs also provide information about C&BA's early equipment. Prior to the 1922–23 academic term, no mention is made of any equipment. However, the catalog for that term records that the school owned two nine-bank adding machines and a Monroe computing machine, with additional machines being loaned by unspecified manufacturers. Model graphs and wall charts, "suitably framed," apparently constituted the school's visual aids. Printed resources available to commerce students included the Moody investment rating books, reference works used in actual businesses, textbooks used in higher education for business, and the Brookmire statistical and business forecasting service.

The Business Tour

Another component of Bidgood's plan to provide the best business education he could for his students was the annual senior class business tour, inaugurated in 1923. Initially, the class would visit several Birmingham businesses during the fall semester of its graduation year. The dean wanted his commerce students, many of whom came from less-industrialized areas of the state, to see major businesses putting into operation the theories, principles, and practices the class members had been learning about since their freshman year.

Birmingham-area businesses such as the Tennessee Coal, Iron, and Railroad Company, the First National Bank, the *Birmingham News*, and others welcomed the seniors and gave them guided tours of the enterprise. Any student who requested to be excused from the tour was required to give the dean a satisfactory reason. Those who were excused had to make a series of local visits and write a report of not less than three thousand words.

The 1928 senior trip was probably typical for those of the period. On October 22, 1928, the *Commerce Bulletin*, a weekly newsletter published during the school's early history, described the arrangements for transportation. The Senior Trip was scheduled for Thursday morning, "with the departure of the group on the 9:00 A.M. train from the A.G.S. station. Wednesday at 12 noon, Mr. Armistead, downtown ticket agent for the A.G.S., will appear in Dean

Bidgood's office with tickets for the group. Seniors will obtain their tickets there at that time upon payment of the fare of $3.05. The party will disembark Thursday morning at Phoenixville, where the first trip, one to the cement mill located there, will start the seniors on their tour of inspection."

The next week, the *Bulletin* provided additional details of the trip: "The accounting group was the guest of the Southern Bell Telephone and Telegraph Company at a luncheon on Friday at noon. Each senior received from Moore-Handley Hardware Company a very fine knife as a souvenir of the trip. At the commerce luncheon held Thursday night, the seniors had as their guests Col. J. C. Persons, President, American Traders National Bank, Mr. Sam Clabaugh, President, Protective Life Insurance Company, and Mr. Francis B. Latady, one of the leading accountants of the state."

A Controversy with Auburn

The following headline appeared in the *Montgomery Advertiser* on Sunday, October 5, 1924: "Auburn Alumni Body Endorses Commerce School—Three Hundred Members Attending College Home Coming Request Trustees to Take Early Action." The accompanying article contained a motion by Horace Turner that Alabama Polytechnic Institute (Auburn) establish a commerce school. According to the reporter at the scene, Turner argued that "the time had come for the establishment of a school of commerce in the South" and the place should be Auburn. Turner said, "I was astounded to know that we had no really outstanding school of commerce in the South. The educators whom I consulted referred me to the Wharton School of Commerce at the University of Pennsylvania as the logical place to send my son for commercial training."

Bidgood quickly responded to these statements in letters written to Judge William H. Samford, president of Auburn's alumni association. In his letter of October 8, 1924, Bidgood observed that the statements made by Turner "implied that there exists no outstanding school of commerce in Alabama or anywhere in the Southern states." The dean continued, "I take the liberty of stating the actual facts to you." Bidgood reminded Samford that a panel of "unbiased, nonpartisan experts" had recommended establishing a commerce school at the University of Alabama, a finding that the institutions of higher learning in the state—including Auburn—had endorsed. "No accusation," asserted Bidgood, "can be brought against the University that it has failed to carry out the recommendations of the survey of 1919, or the terms of the agreement made between the institutions of higher learning, by which it was given the exclusive duty of conducting a school of commerce in Alabama."

The Bureau of Personnel and Placement

High on Bidgood's list of priorities was finding Commerce School graduates jobs as soon as possible. In the early years, graduates of the school encountered some resistance from employers who felt that college-trained personnel would lack the necessary skills to become effective employees. In 1944, reflecting on the history of his school, Dean Bidgood admitted that many employers were at first reluctant to hire people with college training in business. Beginning in 1921 the dean contacted prospective employers annually on behalf of C&BA

graduates, seeking jobs for these students. Bidgood managed to convince initially reluctant business owners and employers that graduates of the University's Commerce School were worth considering when hiring time rolled around. Because the early C&BA graduating classes were quite small, Bidgood knew every student. Given the dean's reputation and numerous contacts, without doubt his personal recommendation helped many C&BA graduates find their first jobs.

As the number of graduates and the demand for them grew, Bidgood realized that a more formalized process of job placement was needed. In 1926 he established the Bureau of Personnel and Placement. He organized it, set up its files and procedures, and served as its first chairman. Under the system Bidgood devised, informational bulletins were sent to prospective employers, listing the more important information about students who were soon to graduate. The rapid growth in C&BA enrollment and graduates soon made Bidgood's direct supervision of the bureau impossible, and in 1928 Prof. Carroll R. Daugherty assumed the chairmanship of the placement bureau. He corresponded with several C&BA graduates, whose letters provide a glimpse into the working conditions early graduates of the Commerce School encountered. Bill Singleterry wrote his former professor on November 26, 1929, from Barrios, Guatemala:

> [United Fruit Company] treats its employees down here a whole lot better than those in the States. It maintains a hospital with a good staff and the slightest fever sends a person there. The living quarters are really a surprise [because] they are so good, and we have good meals at a big dining hall.
>
> Our pay at the start down here is $125.00 a month and after seven months we get a $15.00 raise. This is equal to a much higher salary back home because our only necessary expense [is] $30.00 for board, and $7.00 for laundry (which includes suits, trousers, etc.). . . . Some of the boys spend all their surplus cash on booze but although I was considered a roughneck I don't qualify there because I don't drink and don't intend to start now.

Singleterry described the entertainment and activities available to company employees and noted that his former teacher would find the workers' hours strange ("from 7 A.M. to 11 A.M. and from 1 P.M. to 4 P.M.," with a break for a siesta).

Daugherty chaired the placement bureau until 1931, when Prof. Burton R. Morley became chairman, holding the position for several years. In 1973 the placement bureau became part of the University's Office of Career Planning and Placement Service, whose facilities are located in Ferguson Center.

Student Organizations

Another important element of Bidgood's plan to create a cohesive commerce culture at the University of Alabama involved using student organizations to build camaraderie and to promote professional development among business students. During the first decade of the school's existence, several organizations were formed to achieve these goals.

Acting on the suggestion of H. H. Chapman, commerce students organized this club during the 1922–23 academic year. The Commerce Club sought to advance the purposes of the Commerce School by creating a spirit of good fellowship and a closer affiliation among students of the school. The first members instituted the Commerce Club banquet, a custom that continued for many years and provided an opportunity for current students, faculty, and alumni to meet for the exchange of experiences and ideas. The club also held biweekly meetings at which prominent business leaders would address the group. The Commerce Club was the only organization formed in the first decade of the school's existence that was open to all commerce students.

ALPHA DELTA SIGMA

A national advertising fraternity, Alpha Delta Sigma was founded at the University of Missouri in 1913. The local chapter, Paoli Smith, grew out of the Advertising Club, which had been formed in 1924 by ten C&BA upperclassmen. In 1926 the group changed its name to Theta Alpha Sigma, which functioned as a local advertising fraternity. The national fraternity of Alpha Delta Sigma admitted Theta Alpha Sigma to membership in the spring of 1927. Alpha Delta Sigma drew its members from journalism students and students in the Commerce School who expected to be connected with advertising work. It sought to foster a deeper interest in the profession of advertising, to be of material benefit to the School of Commerce and the University as a whole, and to examine developments in and to exchange ideas about the field of advertising.

ALPHA KAPPA PSI

This oldest of the professional commercial fraternities was created in 1904 at New York University. The University's chapter, Alpha Rho, was installed in 1924. The ideals of the fraternity included furthering the individual welfare of its members; supporting scientific research in the fields of commerce, accounts, and finance; educating the public to appreciate and demand higher ideals in the conduct of business; and promoting and advancing courses leading to degrees in business administration in institutions of collegiate rank. Soon after its formation, the Alpha Rho chapter began the annual practice of awarding a loving cup to the most outstanding student in the commerce school.

DELTA SIGMA PI

This international professional commerce fraternity originated at the New York School of Commerce in 1907. Since that time, it has encouraged the collegiate study of business, supported scholarship and the association of students for their mutual improvement, promoted closer affiliation between the commercial world and students of business, and encouraged higher ethical standards for the conduct of commerce. A local chapter had been active on the University campus for some time when the Alpha Sigma chapter was established in April 1926. The group soon began the practice of presenting a key to the senior with the highest academic standing.

Dean Lee Bidgood, Assoc. Prof. H. H. Chapman, and Asst. Prof. Arthur R. Upgren were largely responsible for organizing Sigma Eta, the local honorary commerce fraternity in September 1923. The object of the organization was to encourage an interest in higher scholarship and college activities among commerce and business administration students. Members, elected annually from the junior and senior classes, were chosen from the top quarter of their class and arranged according to scholarship; not more than one-fifth of any class could be chosen. Election to Sigma Eta depended on scholarship, leadership, and character. The organization presented Greek letter keys to those students selected. In 1931 Sigma Eta was admitted into Beta Gamma Sigma as the University's chapter of that most prestigious of commerce honorary societies.

PHI CHI THETA (CHI THETA)

Organized in the Commerce School in 1929, Chi Theta was a professional fraternity for women that undertook to foster the study of commerce by women and to further the interests of women in business. In 1936 the local chapter affiliated with Phi Chi Theta, the national organization. In that same year, the organization began presenting a scholarship to the female student who maintained the highest scholastic average during her first three years of resident work.

These organizations proved of inestimable value to the school's mission as defined by Dean Bidgood. Most of them preceded the opening of the Commerce Building and all provided opportunities for students to gather for the type of social companionship that not only relieves the stresses of academic study but also enhances that study by allowing for the free exchange and discussion of ideas. The Commerce Club's biweekly meetings, at which prominent business leaders usually spoke, allowed students to profit from the experiences of veteran practitioners of commerce and to compare the ideas and theories they read in textbooks and heard in lectures to what occurred in actual business practice. Bidgood recognized that the school's students would enter a professional world that could be unmerciful to the underprepared, so he gave his students as many opportunities as he could to learn from those with more experience.

Another means of building a sense of camaraderie among the Commerce School students was the adoption of a common insignia for all senior class members. From the *Commerce Bulletin*, February 13, 1928: "The Senior Class has inaugurated a new tradition for commerce men! Under the leadership of President H. K. Toenes, the class of '28 has adopted as their official insignia, which, incidentally, will be the insignia of all commerce seniors to come, dark blue sweaters with a ship of commerce in the center. The ship of commerce is a large representation of a clipper ship in white cutout, framed in a circle. Sail on, seniors! Just what THE BULLETIN was yelping for!!"

The Commerce Building

One of Dean Bidgood's dearest dreams began to be realized in 1926 when he received word that the University intended to construct a building to house the new School of Commerce. Dr. Herman Hollis Chapman, in a recollection

Typical classroom, 1928.

published in 1963 on the occasion of Dean Bidgood's death, recalled when University officials informed the dean that a commerce building would be the next major construction project undertaken on campus. Bidgood had, in Chapman's words, "rough floor plans and memoranda detailing his ideas of what was needed. Consequently, he was ready to begin work with the architects and engineers on plans and specifications." The Board of Trustees authorized the construction and furnishing of the Commerce Building in its September 1927 meeting.

According to the *Commerce Bulletin*, by October 1927 the building was underway. "There is only one thing in which the school of commerce is interested just now—the new commerce building, already started on the campus, between Morgan Hall and the Library [now Carmichael Hall]. This fine new building will embody many of the latest features of design and construction."

The *Bulletin* maintained a running commentary over the next several months as construction proceeded. By November 28, 1927, editor George Hoffman, an instructor in business English, could comment: "The Commerce Building, we note with pleasure, is now on the level. With its appearance from subterranean depths comes night-work under the bright electric lights. For the past week men have been working day and night on the foundations and first floor at the ground level."

Apparently, the eager commerce students and faculty found the pace of work on the building agonizingly slow, for the January 9, 1928, *Bulletin* noted, "The new building sprang up like a mushroom while we were gone. The old maxim that a watched pot never boils is evidently true. But there is a great deal of first floor in evidence, and the steel is up for the second. Even the pessimists now believe there will be a building. (A pessimist is a faculty member from any school other than Commerce)." Jokingly, the *Bulletin* announced: "We shall hold classes in the new commerce building on April First—1929. Yes, we have a COMMERCE SCHOOL."

Actually, those itching to occupy the new building did so before April Fool's Day 1929. An accelerated construction schedule for the summer enabled workers to complete their tasks in time for the opening of classes in the fall 1928 session.

The new Commerce Building was hailed as one of the most modern and most complete in the South (*Crimson White*, September 13, 1928). The new building was of southern colonial architecture with a portico of six massive limestone columns. Its face brick exterior was trimmed in limestone. The edifice consisted of three floors and a basement, which housed four classrooms and two offices. The first floor featured three classrooms and six offices, a conference room, and one large assembly room with a capacity of 224 people. The second floor contained six classrooms, four offices, a reading room, a book room, and one seminar room. The uppermost floor, the home of the accounting and statistics departments, consisted of one classroom, four offices, six laboratories, one seminar room, one stenography room, and one mimeographing room. The Commerce Building provided its faculty, staff, and students with a total of sixteen offices, fourteen classrooms, and fourteen multipurpose rooms for an approximate total cost of $230,000, including equipment.

The *Crimson White* offered its opinion that the interior of the new structure was more beautiful than the exterior. Inside were light-colored walls, concrete corridor floors covered with a new type of sound-deadening rubber, and classrooms with naturally finished maple floors and matching maple desks. The laboratories were furnished with oak tables. The woodwork throughout the building was specially sawn and fitted; stained in a combination brown-and-green color, it provided a pleasing, if unusual, contrast with the floors.

The dedication ceremony for the Commerce Building, held on Homecoming Saturday, October 20, 1928, reflected the significance of this new structure. At an informal reception the previous Friday night, lights illuminated the entire Commerce Building, and the public was invited to tour the structure. At the actual dedication ceremony, Dr. A. W. Rawles, dean of the School of Commerce and Finance at the University of Indiana, delivered the principal address, entitled "Some Problems in a University Training for Business," and Frank Maxwell Moody, president of the First National Bank of Tuskaloosa, presided over the festivities.

The ceremony received rave reviews. In the October 22, 1928, issue of the *Commerce Bulletin*, George Hoffman commented that "the reception and dedication fittingly capped the many affairs held at the University during Homecoming. The Library was most beautifully decorated by the ladies of the Commerce School, and the room's sharp corners and square dimensions were softened by the many flower vases. Dean Rawles gave a brief but interesting address before the building Saturday morning. His talk was planned to please the layman, rather than the technical business man or the theoretical-minded teacher. In such a moment it was a well-timed speech, and it struck the proper note in the group assembled to dedicate the building."

Accreditation by the AACSB

The later years of the 1920s were especially encouraging to C&BA faculty and students. In 1929, only one year after occupying its new building, the School of Commerce and Business Administration became the thirty-eighth school to earn admission into the American Association of Collegiate Schools of Business (AACSB).

The Bidgood Legacy

Lee Bidgood, the son of Willis and Belle Bidgood, was born on a farm in rural Norfolk, Virginia, in February 1884. After attending Churchland Academy, he attended the University of Virginia, earning his A.B. in 1905 and his master's the following year. In 1906 he accepted a position as head of the Department of History and Social Sciences at the State Normal School at Farmville, an appointment he held for three years. From 1909 to 1911, he served as a fellow in economics at the University of Wisconsin. He returned to his alma mater as an adjunct professor of economics for the 1911–12 term, then taught economics at the University of Wisconsin from 1912 to 1913.

Bidgood's decision to accept the position as first head of the University of Alabama's Department of Economics in 1913 changed the course of his life and of collegiate business education in the Southeast. From his initial appointment as C&BA dean in 1919 until his retirement in 1954, he oversaw the growth and development of what became the first nationally accredited collegiate business education program in Alabama. His influence, however, extended far beyond the confines of the University campus and the state's borders. He served on the boards of directors of many companies, both small and large. He also worked on behalf of civic and charitable organizations during his long, illustrious career. His many articles and speeches on university education for business helped to shape debate on the subject. His presidency of both Beta Gamma Sigma and the American Association of Collegiate Schools of Business testified to the esteem in which these two national organizations held Lee Bidgood.

At the time of his death in May 1963, Lee Bidgood left behind a legacy of achievement that few people could match. Individuals and institutions offered praise for this man who had taken the Commerce School from the days of scattered classes held in various rooms around campus to a nationally recognized school providing innovative training in all major fields of business and at degree levels from the baccalaureate to the doctorate. Given Bidgood's love of and devotion to his students and the cause of business education, perhaps the comment he would be proudest of is the tribute in the Alabama Business Hall of Fame: "Generations are being served by the institution and school that he founded, shaped, and nurtured. So also will those generations that follow."

The University's presidents:

George H. "Mike" Denny (retired, 1936)
Richard C. Foster (1937 until his sudden death in 1941)

The world is talking about:

Congress authorizes $230 million for a public works program. (March 31, 1930)

Congress passes the Glass-Steagall Act, authorizing the Federal Reserve bank to expand credit and release government gold to business interests, in an attempt to get money circulating. (February 27, 1932)

The Twenty-first Amendment, repealing Prohibition, goes into effect. (December 5, 1933)

Pres. Franklin D. Roosevelt signs the Social Security Act. (August 14, 1935)

Albert Einstein writes to President Roosevelt informing him that some sort of powerful bomb is feasible; this will lead to the Manhattan Project to develop the atomic bomb. (August 2, 1939)

The University is talking about:

New buildings are constructed in 1930—the women's gymnasium, named for dean of Arts and Sciences Charles H. Barnwell; an education building named for Bibb Graves, Alabama governor (1927–31, 1935–39); and the Alabama Union.

The University's 1931 Centennial Pageant is held; the *Alumni News* calls it "the most brilliant, beautiful and interest-compelling celebration ever witnessed in Alabama."

The School of Home Economics is organized; Agnes Ellen Harris serves as the first dean in 1931.

All-American basketball player Lindy Hood and his stripped-down Ford are news in 1932.

Alabama football: the 1931 Rose Bowl—Alabama 24, Washington State 0. Alabama defeats Stanford, 29 to 13, in the 1935 Rose Bowl.

Dr. Denny retires in 1936 and is awarded honorary title of chancellor; he is commended by the Board of Trustees as well as by many students, alumni, and state officials for his long and dedicated service to the University.

College "hot buttons" during the thirties:

1930
- The Bureau of Business Research is established with H. H. Chapman as director.

1932
- A two-year prelaw program is established.
- A six-year business and law combination is established.

1936
- Secretarial work becomes a major.

1937
- Statistics becomes a major.

1938
- A new wing is added to the Commerce Building.
- C&BA offers enough courses to allow a student to sit for the CPA exam in any state.

The Prewar Thirties
The Bidgood Era Continues

In Their Own Words

No great mathematical acumen is necessary to calculate that these alumni were at least eighty years old in 1994. Memories of the past came easier to some than to others, but all in this remarkable group offered some insight into our early history.

William Edward Bertkau, Class of 1934: "I attribute all or a good part of [my success] to the University. I still maintain a relationship [by giving] small amounts to the Alumni Fund, which Phillip Morris not only matches, but doubles. My life at Alabama was just plain great. I never joined a fraternity, and I lived with a Lutheran minister whom I just had a letter from yesterday. He is now in his nineties and just wrote me about losing his wife."

Bertkau described his trip from his home in New York to Tuscaloosa in 1930. "I went down to Savannah by ship, the old Savannah line, and the name of the ship was the *City of Birmingham.* I took the train from Savannah to Birmingham and took the 10:00 out of Birmingham; [that] was the Queen and Crescent Limited [that went] from Cincinnati to New Orleans on the old L&N. I got to Tuscaloosa at 11:32 at night. I remember all these things very well. . . . It was a hot night and the mosquitoes were all over the place."

Left to right: James McMillan, Miriam Locke, and Barry Mason at rededication of Bidgood Hall, 1994.

Munny Sokol *(left)* and Morris Mayer (John Robbins in background).

Reminiscences

Drs. Miriam Locke and James McMillan, both of whom earned their doctorates in English, taught freshman composition, business English, and literature courses in C&BA's Department of Business English during the 1930s and early 1940s. In separate interviews, these veteran University faculty members offered interesting perspectives on people and events in C&BA during their years of service.

On Dean Bidgood

Dr. Locke: His daughter was a friend of mine, and I was quite frequently there at dinner. It was so [delightful] to listen to that man talking to his children, particularly to Mary, who was as bright as she could be and an English major. They got into such [interesting] discussions, and Mrs. Bidgood was so dear. She was such a perfect little charming lady, and she would say, "I just don't always know what Mary and Lee are talking about." I knew him as a host and as a wonderful, loving father to his children.

Dr. McMillan: Dean Bidgood was not a business graduate himself. He was pretty widely educated; never [earned] a Ph.D. and didn't mind telling people that he didn't have it. Of course, it was less necessary in his day. He could be gruff, but he could also be kind and understanding. He was very sharp, very intelligent. When he held a meeting, it was all business. He brought up things, got decisions made, and dismissed it. There wasn't any long palavering.

McMillan offered additional thoughts on C&BA and its dean during those years he served as an instructor, assistant professor, and associate professor of business English. He noted that the departmental structure then was

In thinking about his professors, he remembered Larry Nations very favorably. Bertkau concluded, "I am a member of the New York Alabama National Alumni group; since my wife died, I have not been attending their activities. But I am still a member."

Young J. Boozer Jr., Class of 1936, set the tone of the interview when he said, "Everything good that has happened to me has had some kind of connection with the University." Young Boozer, who at eighty-one is indeed "young," was one of James McMillan's favorite students. And Boozer considers his former teacher as one of his good friends, in spite of Dr. McMillan's Auburn degree.

Young Boozer *(right)* with Jack Warner, first chairman of Board of Visitors.

Iris Carmack wearing the Commerce sweater, circa 1930.

Names such as Frank Moody, Munny Sokol, and Mel Allen are part of Young Boozer's memories. In describing his good friend Munny Sokol, he said, "He was the most considerate man I ever knew and he always had empathy for the other guy. He loved the Commerce School—just loved it." Young said another C&BA alum, Ernest Williams, was his best friend.

At the close of the interview, Boozer said with enthusiasm, "I love the Commerce School. You know that."

Iris Carmack, Class of 1930, reflected on his years at the Capstone:

> *My feelings about the University and the Commerce School relate mainly to people. Dean Bidgood had enormous impact on my life. He was a marvelous teacher. I was Dr. Denny's secretary, and I know how often Dean Bidgood visited Denny's office—he had an inside track to the president's office—a confidant. Dean Bidgood's classes were taught in Manley Hall because the Commerce Building had not been built at that time. I was also particularly fond of Lee Glover who cared about teaching—he was just ideal. I had great respect for Marcus Whitman and for Chester Knight whom I liked very much. I didn't know Professor Bonham well, but everyone who knew him thought highly of him. I still stay in touch with the college, and Dean Mason is doing a marvelous job.*

Harmon Looney, Class of 1933, lived on Thirteenth Street when cars were rare, and he did a lot of walking. He entered C&BA in prelaw. He drove around

less formal than in the post–World War II era. "In the catalog, you might see department this, that, or the other," he observed, "but I never attended a department meeting in my whole fifteen years in the School of Commerce." He attributed Dean Bidgood's creation of the school's own English, mathematics, and Spanish course offerings to the dean's determination to provide the best education he could for Commerce students. "He just thought that teachers who realized that [Commerce students] . . . were . . . in a professional school and were not aesthetes" would be best. McMillan also acknowledged Bidgood's perceptive foresight: "He saw way ahead that Spanish [would] be important for business students, and he knew that statistics was going to be, [too]."

On Teaching in C&BA

Dr. Locke: I [enjoyed] thoroughly my work and Dean Bidgood. The students had to take literature, one class. So I taught American literature. Dean Bidgood was a man of such [varied] interests. He was brought up in the humanities in Virginia, and he believed in students having a broad liberal education along with the specialized business courses. . . . Eventually, he let us teach something that was of particular interest. I wanted to teach the thirty brightest freshmen world literature instead of just regular freshman English. So we started out with that, and they were so thrilled! As one long-legged, blond boy on the front row said, "I never did know anything about this fellow Homer." And he was so excited to learn. That was an exceptional group of students. They were wonderful. Except so many of them were killed in the war; so many of them died.

Locke also pointed out that Dean Bidgood let the English instructors experiment with directed readings.

the campus on a Sunday in 1994 and reflected on the tremendous changes since the 1930s when there were few cars, few buildings, and not nearly as many students: "When I entered the University," he said, "we had only [about] four thousand students. I had three classes under Dean Bidgood. Chester Knight stands out in my memory because he was in the accounting department. Mr. Bonham was something—he really was. I think the accounting and economics courses were most valuable for me. I took a fancy to accounting, as it came naturally to me."

Looney went to Law School and was also working in the family grocery store (Bama Cash Grocery Company on University Avenue). Looney recalled that the dean of the Law School said to him, "I've watched you at your grocery store. You do a very good job down there. I trade with you. You know, I just believe you'd make a better groceryman than you would a lawyer." Looney said, "I get the hint, Dean. I don't think I'll be back next year." And he wasn't. In 1957 the family acquired the Piggly Wiggly franchise and moved the business downtown. In recalling friends from his C&BA days Looney remembered Dan Haughton (brother of long-time C&BA faculty member Sarah Rodgers and former president of Lockheed) and the late Beenie (Henry) Mize, a successful lawyer in Tuscaloosa.

Victor Hugo Marx Jr. attended the University from 1932 to 1935. Reminiscing about his teachers of sixty years ago, Marx recalled that Dean Bidgood was "smart, technically, but he was a hard man to get to know." He remembered fondly Marcus Whitman with whom he remained friends after leaving Alabama. Commenting on his peers, he mentioned Rankin Fite (a lawyer and a legislator), Fred Richard (from Demopolis, now an accountant in Montgomery), and Alan Gassenheimer (a retired businessman from Montgomery). Marx noted that his son, Hugo, graduated from the University in 1975 and is now a partner in the family business. The senior Marx said with sly humor that he only gave his son half the business so he couldn't fire his dad.

Max Sokol, Class of 1930, proclaimed, "I am really proud that the second member of the third generation of my family is now at Alabama in C&BA. First my brother, Munny [Morris], and me, then my son, Bruce, then his son and now his daughter." When asked what teachers he remembered fondly, he named Dean Bidgood, and Professors Larry Nations, James Holladay, Chester Knight, Harry Bonham, Herman Chapman, and Marcus Whitman, the "shapers" of CB&A's culture.

Osie Spencer graduated in 1931. He started his college career in 1926 with only forty dollars, which one of his brothers gave him. He said this was enough money to get to Tuscaloosa and that was about all. He dropped out of school for a year when his father died. He worked in the college bookstore, otherwise known as the Supe Store, during his student days, reporting to Jeff Coleman, who was the store manager. "Alabama and the Commerce School meant everything to me," Spencer said. "After graduating, I was offered a job in the Supe Store at $125 a month. You could get a good meal then for 35 cents. I stayed with the University until I started the Alabama Book Store in 1940." Spencer said that Carroll Daugherty influenced him more than any other teacher in C&BA.

Edward Turner, Class of 1939, talked about Commerce Day, which he remembered as a celebration. There were activities at the school during the day and a dance in the evening, perhaps at the Armory as Foster Auditorium had not been built according to Mr. Turner. (The Armory still stands on University Boulevard East in front of the motor pool and is, as of this writing, the home of the University of Alabama Press.)

In talking about his professors, Turner considered Bidgood first. He thought it interesting that the dean wore three pairs of glasses—not all at the same time—but one to read with, one for close work, and one for distance. He remembered Langston Hawley whom he described as

> *a nice, handsome fellow with a receding hair line that was premature, but he pushed his hair straight back. Very attractive. A large Roman nose. He knew how to deliver his material very well. He was formal, but he knew how to be cordial with the students so that they all loved him.*
>
> *Miriam Locke was a lovely, blond, attractive, beautiful lady. She was a great English teacher and everybody thought she was just wonderful. She stayed there a long time too, I understand.*

When Turner learned that Miriam Locke was alive and well and living in Tuscaloosa, he asked for her address so he could write her a card. What a pleasant by-product to an oral history!

The Decade Begins

By 1930 the School of Commerce and Business Administration was a growing, vibrant part of the University of Alabama's educational endeavor. With steadily increasing enrollments, a new building, a set of majors in place, and a faculty of dedicated, talented individuals to lead it, the school seemed well prepared for another decade of growth. C&BA enrollment would eventually be affected by the hard economic times of the Great Depression, but the decline was relatively short-lived and mild. A more serious problem would be the budget cutbacks that began to take place early in the 1930s. Despite these problems, however, the school would expand its faculty, increase its course offerings, and add to its physical facilities. It would also assume a leading role in gathering and publishing detailed information about economic activity in the state and region.

The Bureau of Business Research

One of the most significant developments that occurred early in the new decade was the establishment in November 1930 of the Bureau of Business Research within the school. In his unpublished memoir, "Of These Accomplishments I Take Pride," Prof. H. H. Chapman provided details about the creation of the Bureau, as it was commonly called until its redesignation as the Center for Business and Economic Research (CBER) in 1969. Chapman

Moving On

Locke and McMillan were
transferred out of the Commerce
School in the post–World War II
reorganization of the University's
administrative structure. Miriam
Locke moved to the College of Arts
and Sciences, under whose
jurisdiction all English courses
were placed. Jim McMillan oversaw
the formation of a Department of
Linguistics and was also appointed
the first director of the University of
Alabama Press. He moved to the
Department of English in 1962 as
its chairman, serving nine years in
that position. Both he and Locke
rendered exemplary service to the
University in their new posts, and
they remembered their years in
C&BA with fondness. "I had a very,

traced the genesis of the Bureau to Bidgood's days as a graduate student at the University of Wisconsin, where the future C&BA dean formulated, in Chapman's words, "a vision of a state university as being a servant of the people of the state—in providing inspiration and in being a service agency [for] making the state a better place in which to live." Bidgood found a kindred soul in Chapman, and both agreed that developing a program of economic research would benefit the Commerce School and the state of Alabama. Given the shared determination to act on their convictions, a business research bureau within C&BA seemed inevitable.

Competition with Auburn provided additional motivation for the creation of a business research bureau at the University of Alabama. According to Chapman, President Denny regarded Auburn's Bureau of Economic Research (created in the late 1920s) and its issuing of a monthly economic review as "an invasion of an area that belonged to the University, and [he] decided that this invasion should not go unchallenged." Chapman related the subsequent events: "[Denny] told Bidgood that he wanted a recommendation of what should be done. Dean Bidgood asked me to come up with a plan. I told the dean that if I was to undertake to direct a Bureau of Business Research I would want, as a minimum, a statistician to devote the major portion of his time to the work of the Bureau, a full-time librarian with sufficient training to manage the Business Library and to do reference work, a reduction in my teaching load so that I would have some time to work on Bureau projects, and enough clerical help to take care of typing reports and handling the correspondence that such an operation would require."

Professor Chapman recalled that Denny "basically" agreed to these requests, although he did not give Chapman enough money to hire "fully trained and experienced statisticians and librarians." The University president insisted on the publication of a monthly bulletin, gave Chapman a brief outline of what he wanted in it, and even named it—the *University of Alabama Business News*. Chapman wasted no time in assembling the personnel to undertake this newest mission of the School of Commerce and Business Administration. He hired as business librarian Julia Jackson, who served in that capacity until the early 1940s. Wendell Adamson became the Bureau's first statistician. A recent graduate of Indiana University and fresh from a stint with the Indiana state reference office, Adamson possessed what Chapman called "a brilliant mind" and was a tireless worker. Chapman credited Adamson with producing some of the Bureau's best work during its first decade.

The following announcement appeared in the University general catalog for 1930–31:

For several years, the School of Commerce and Business Administration has been adding to its research facilities by gradually building up a collection of informational material on business and economic subjects and by acquiring equipment to be used in doing research work. In the autumn of 1930, a bureau of business research was organized and a definite program of research work was projected.

The activities of the Bureau of Business Research may be classified into four main groups:

1. Building up the research facilities of the School of Commerce.
2. Rendering aid to members of the faculty of the school in any research projects in which they may be engaged either as a part of their instructional work or independently of such duties.
3. Carrying on specific research projects of its own.
4. Acting as an agent in the dissemination to students and to citizens of the state of the information which it has available.

The staff of the Bureau was given as Director H. H. Chapman, Statistician Wendell M. Adamson, Librarian Julia Jackson, Secretary Iris Martin, and Mimeographer Dorothy Church. The 1930–31 catalog also listed, for the first time, the members of the school's Committee on Research. Dean Bidgood headed the committee; Chapman, Holladay, Nations, and Edward W. Gregory, who taught sociology, were the committee members.

The December 15, 1930, issue of the *University of Alabama Business News* described the Bureau as "an integral part of the School of Commerce and Business Administration at the University of Alabama. Its function is to aid in the instructional work of the school and particularly to extend to the citizens of Alabama the facilities of the school. It welcomes opportunities for service." In the 1930s the Bureau fulfilled its responsibilities by gathering and publishing vital data on the various types of economic activities conducted in Alabama. Under the leadership of Professor Chapman, the Bureau built a reputation for producing accurate and useful data upon which businesses and individuals came to rely. By serving the state's people in this manner, the Bureau fulfilled its objectives.

Two Vital New Student Organizations

As he had in the previous decade, Bidgood continued his support of organizations that would strengthen the school by promoting camaraderie among the students and by encouraging above-average academic performance. He actively campaigned to have the local commerce honorary fraternity and the local women's professional sorority accepted into national chapters.

Beta Gamma Sigma

The following notice appeared in the January 5, 1931, *Commerce Bulletin:*

> Word has been received from Dr. W. D. Gordon, Grand President of Beta Gamma Sigma, that the local commerce honor fraternity, Sigma Eta, has been elected to membership in Beta Gamma Sigma. The chapter is to be installed by Professor John W. Jenkins, Grand Secretary-Treasurer, probably during the second week in February. This will be the thirty-third chapter of the fraternity. It will be known as the Alpha Chapter of Alabama. Beta Gamma Sigma is . . . recognized by the American Association of Collegiate Schools of Business as the official honor fraternity of the commerce schools, and it establishes chapters only in schools recognized by the association. Only seniors are eligible for membership, and not more than one-tenth of the graduating class can be elected. Sigma Eta

is indeed to be congratulated upon having met the high requirements of such a fraternity as Beta Gamma Sigma.

Charter faculty members of Beta Gamma Sigma's Alpha Chapter of Alabama were Dean Lee Bidgood, H. H. Chapman, Chester Knight, Lee Glover, H. D. Bonham, L. J. Nations, Harry V. Mitchell, and Ralph E. Adams, executive secretary of the University.

Student members were James J. Campbell Jr., J. W. Donahoo, Kenneth V. James, George L. Law, W. B. Howard, James L. Permutt, and James G. Stalcup.

On February 16, 1931, Bidgood wrote to W. E. Pickens Jr.: "Beta Gamma Sigma is installing a chapter here on March 4 or 5. That winds up the acquisition of all the different 'recognitions' that our school has sought."

Phi Chi Theta

On February 20, 1931, Bidgood wrote to the Grand Chapter of Phi Chi Theta, a national professional organization for women, in support of the local chapter's petition for national membership. He wrote that the sixteen students who presented the petition "are admirably representative of our best young women students. Their scholastic standing as a whole is excellent. No one of them is a weak student. You will notice that one has made no grade lower than A during the first semester of this year. This is a rare happening with us. Two or three others are not far behind."

Bidgood also praised the entrepreneurial spirit of these students. "These young women," he wrote, "have displayed distinct enterprise in forming and retaining the local group. Several of them show already qualities of leadership. The group is well represented in student activities." These women, he claimed, were "very helpful in all problems arising from the increased numbers of women students" in the 1920s. In conclusion, he assured the Grand Chapter that these women "would do you credit."

Despite Bidgood's assurances, the local chapter was not admitted into national membership in 1931. The national organization did install a chapter at the University in 1936.

Expansion of the Business Tour

Bidgood made modifications to the school's annual senior business tour during the decade. During the 1930s, business tours occurred in the spring rather than the fall semester. Also, as senior commerce classes grew larger, the seniors were divided into smaller groups, which visited businesses separately. In the late 1930s, groups went to different cities according to their majors. For example, in 1938 Birmingham was the destination for students majoring in accounting, advertising, merchandising, production and personnel, real estate, secretarial work, and statistics. Those majoring in banking-finance and transportation–public utilities, however, traveled to Mobile. Students in the third year of the business-law major and seniors in either the four-year prelaw or the public business majors took their tour in Montgomery.

Effects of the Great Depression

No educational institution can completely avoid the effects of an economic catastrophe that brings about a worldwide depression in which millions of people lose jobs. The depression exerted its influence on the future of the Commerce School and the University as a whole. Budget cuts became necessary, and enrollment dipped in the early years of the decade, although the slowdown was temporary. Inevitably, the budgetary reductions affected the quality of instruction at the institution. The student-faculty ratio began to climb, and by the end of the decade the University of Alabama had been placed on the "starred list" of the leading collegiate accreditation agency, which meant it faced the danger of losing its accreditation.

Enrollment

The onset of the Great Depression following the stock market crash of October 1929 initially did not halt a steady rise in C&BA enrollment. From June 1929 to June 1930, enrollment was 706, an increase of 58 students from the previous year. The first dip in C&BA enrollment occurred in the 1932–33 academic year, when only 727 students were enrolled, down from 843 in the previous year. Most people regard 1932 as the worst year of the Great Depression, and the enrollment pattern of C&BA reflects that fact. As early as the June 1933–June 1934 academic year, enrollment began to recover with a modest increase of 11 students. By the 1934–35 session the school enjoyed an increase of 147 students. The school's enrollment continued to grow throughout the remainder of the decade until a decline in the June 1939–June 1940 interval, perhaps accounted for by the increased demand for military draftees in the United States as a response to the conflict raging in Europe.

The depression, however, affected the University and C&BA in more areas than simply enrollment. Faculty and staff had to find ways to cope with salary and budget cuts during the 1930s as state appropriations for higher education fell. Dr. James McMillan, instructor in business English at the time, recalled that he married in 1932 and at the same time received a 10 percent cut in salary. Another 10 percent reduction followed the next year. Students at the Capstone had to face the prospect of higher tuition rates as their families dealt with the hardships brought on by unemployment and the other woes that accompanied the harsh economic downturn.

The plight of the University student particularly affected Dean Bidgood and moved him to write President Denny on August 11, 1932, using the situation of one C&BA student to argue against a proposed tuition increase. Perhaps no other single surviving document from Dean Bidgood so eloquently expresses his concern for students:

> Pursuing the line of thought expressed in our recent conversations and exchange of letters, I should like to call your attention to the case of a student who has been enrolled in the University, taking Commerce, this summer. The young man is named Troy Crawford. He is a country boy from Lamar County. After very interesting experiences and hard struggles, he finished high school, and got into the University this summer. When he registered for his course in

Commerce, I thought his situation an impossible one, and confidently expected he would soon quit. But he is still here, made a grade of A on his accounting course, and says that he is going to stick to it until he graduates.

The day he registered he told me that he had arrived with ninety cents in his pocket. He had no expectations of receiving any money whatever from home. He got Mr. Adams to defer his University fees, with the understanding that they would be paid gradually during the summer on the installment plan. He got a job on Mr. Hughes's campus gang, and has been mowing grass, chopping weeds, and the like, for three or four hours a day since he came. He told me last Saturday that he was applying all of his earnings from this campus labor to the payment of his fees, and expected to have them discharged by the end of the summer. I said, "Crawford, what have you been eating, and where do you sleep?" He explained that he had an uncle in Northport. The uncle is a casual laborer who came to Northport from Lamar County three years ago, and has had only odd jobs since. Now when Troy Crawford came from home, he brought from the farm a lot of vegetables and other foodstuffs which he had raised by his own labor while going to school. The uncle has had nothing at all to do for some time, so he has been letting Troy sleep at his house, and all of them have been living on the food that Troy brought and has had sent here from the farm. Troy further said that between the close of his high school and the opening of the University summer school he planted a little crop of foodstuffs, including an acre patch of potatoes from which he hopes to dig over one hundred bushels. Troy's plan was to go home about once a month and bring over a lot of those potatoes and other edibles during the winter, live with his uncle, and feed them all as payment. The only thing that is worrying him now is that the uncle is thinking of going back to the country, on account of lack of work in Northport. But Troy is trying to get a sweeping job, or some similar place, and stay on anyhow.

The point about Troy Crawford is that his case is exactly similar to about two hundred Alabama boys in the School of Commerce. Troy's ninety cents and potato patch make a little more dramatic story, but the conditions are essentially alike. Any attempt to finance the University of Alabama by a further increase in fees will absolutely close the door of hope to Troy Crawford and the others like him. It means that these ambitious, capable, and uncrushably hopeful fellows would be permanently cut off from a university education.

These are the young people whom Thomas Jefferson saw in his day when he demanded equality of opportunity and sought it through the medium of state-supported higher education. These are the young people whom the Constitutional Convention of Alabama, meeting at Huntsville more than a century ago, had in mind when they provided for the establishment of a state university. These are the ones for whom democracy has provided a door of opportunity for the exercise of their talents in the state-supported colleges of the land for these past three or four generations, and they are the ones to whom Alabama looks with hope for the progress of her people during the coming generation.

It seems to me that those who are responsible for the financial problems of Alabama at the present time might well consider Troy Crawford of Lamar County and the many hundreds of others like him.

Yours sincerely,
Lee Bidgood
Dean, School of Com. & Bus. Adm.

Entertainment during the Depression

Despite the hardships of the depression, Commerce students and faculty managed to keep up their spirits. One of the long-standing Commerce School events began in 1934 with the advent of expanded Commerce Day celebrations. Commerce Day had been a senior class day until C&BA student Paul Thomas proposed a day of programs in which all Commerce students would take part. In a March 2, 1934, letter from Dean Bidgood to Ed Austin, the dean wrote, "Our Senior Class plans to have its exercises on Friday, March 9, this year. They are planning something a little bit different and more distinctive, and Friday will be called'Commerce Day.'" The schedule of events published by the seniors provides details of the day's activities:

> Commerce Day Bulletin
> Commerce Day . . . . Friday, March 9th
>
> The plans of the Class of 1934 for Commerce Day have my hearty approval and encouragement. They will lend a new interest to university life, and we may hope that they will found a tradition by which this class will long be remembered.
> —Dean Lee Bidgood

HIGHLIGHTS OF COMMERCE DAY

10:00 A.M. All classes dismissed until 2:00 P.M. Senior Class Day exercises begin promptly in Morgan Hall, attendance being required of all Commerce students. A truly different program has been planned which will include a Senior Class skit, clever musical numbers, tapping exercises of Beta Gamma Sigma, the presentation of the Alpha Kappa Psi Medallion, and many other features of interest. Seniors are excused from classes all day.

1:00 to 4:00 P.M. The Commerce Building will be open for inspection. Plans have been arranged to demonstrate the facilities of the building, especially the laboratories of the Accounting and Statistics Departments. Come yourself and invite your friends.

9:00 [P.M.] to 1:00 A.M. The Commerce School "New Deal" dance will be held at the Attic, 2307 7th Street (downtown Tuscaloosa). This, the first Commerce dance, promises to be a huge success. Elaborate plans are being made for this unusually interesting function, including commerce organization leadouts. The Alabama Cavaliers will furnish the music. Paul Thomas has appointed the following committee to sell subscriptions for the dance:

> Pelham Durant
> Sam Neyman
> Russell Branscom
> Eugene Heilpern
> Pete Derzis
> Merrill Doss
> Paul Thomas
> George Ganster

These certificates, price fifty cents, will be exchanged on the night of the dance for tickets. Everyone in the Commerce School is urged to purchase his ticket just as soon as possible to prevent a last-minute rush. No individual profits whatsoever will be made from the dance. All money over expenses, if any, will go to the senior class toward their present which they will give to the School.

This is the first attempt of the Commerce School to stage a Commerce Day. Its success and continuance depend upon the cooperation of the entire student body.

Let's put it over big!

—The Publicity Committee
  Clarence Solnic
  Andrew Manning
  John Hundermark
  Pinkney Pruitt

Apparently, the 1934 Senior Class did indeed put the event over in a big way. Commerce Day thereafter became an annual celebration to commemorate the 1919 founding of C&BA. It continued to provide a mixture of academic and entertainment activities, as a description of the 1937 program indicates. Beta Gamma Sigma and Delta Sigma Pi presented awards. Phi Chi Theta tapped members. Entertainment for the day included "Bluin' the Blues," "Your Commerce School Hit Song," and "Where the Lazy River Goes By" as performed by the Cavaliers, as well as the annual senior skit. And, of course, everyone looked forward to the annual dance, which for the first time included decorations.

The senior trip to Mobile, 1930s.

The Senior Class of 1934 initiated what became a tradition in the school, just as Dean Bidgood had hoped. Over the years, the celebration underwent modifications, and it was briefly suspended during World War II, but Commerce Day continued to celebrate the establishment of C&BA until the University combined all such divisional ceremonies into Honors Day in the 1970s.

Members of previous C&BA classes also knew how to entertain themselves. The Class of 1928 ten-year reunion included entertaining roasts of its members delivered by L. A. Duncan, who lambasted several prominent C&BA alumni, all in the name of good fun.

Of Clemson Duckworth: "[He] was always interested in life insurance, making a very detailed study of its opportunities. He passed as a Baronet, married a wealthy widow from Cleveland, persuaded her to have herself insured for $10 million; unfortunately, she died, and now Clem is doing well. He was always a staunch believer in insurance."

Of Jefferson Jackson Coleman: "Next on my list is a man little known during his college career, quiet, unassuming, retiring, never one to make his own way or to push himself ahead; nevertheless, [he is] at the top of his chosen work, the only successor to C. C. Pyle—some of you will recall Jefferson Jackson Coleman."

Of Ehney Camp: "And now we come to a man who dreads what I have to say about him; he is grinning even now in his seat. If you watch, you can spot him where he sits. He knows that he is about to be accused. He knows that he is guilty and that what I am about to say is the adulterated truth. Were it possible, he would have joyously absented himself from this assembly, but he was forced by circumstance to attend. Listen while before your eyes I denounce him! I sincerely believe that I voice the sentiment of the Senior Class as a whole when I say that the man to whom we point as most outstanding among us, the man in our midst who during these fourteen years has accomplished most, is a man whom we all respect and honor—Mr. Ehney A. Camp."

Alumni at Work during the 1930s

A number of the school's alumni kept in touch with their former professors over the years, especially Dean Bidgood and Dr. Carroll R. Daugherty, director of placement from 1928 until 1931. These letters describe the working lives of some C&BA graduates and convey the sense of loyalty they felt toward the Commerce School.

Ted Leach, Class of 1927, wrote a letter that was printed in the April 7, 1930, *Commerce Bulletin.* Leach described his work with a bank in Tientsin, China, and his way of life. He wrote that he shared a twelve-room house with three other men, and they had eight servants who woke them up, laid out their clothes, and prepared their baths. He also described sights that no one back in Alabama was likely to see: "Imagine six half-dressed men pulling heavy loads of coal, flour, and other commodities down University Avenue[;] people would think they were ready for Dr. Bryce's [an insane asylum in Tuscaloosa], but it is [a] very common sight here as well as a thousand other things."

S. R. Gassenheimer wrote to Daugherty on September 29, 1930, to describe his sales training with Remington Rand Business Service:

[Whereas] in the plants our main job was to watch and learn [about] the construction of the products, we are now very actively engaged in finding out what they are for, how to use them, and why.

On the whole, I am thoroughly sold on Remington Rand, both the organization and its products, and want to thank you for the opportunity I now have, which you were so instrumental in helping me to get.

Remington Rand thought as highly of Mr. Gassenheimer as he did of them. A September 15, 1930, letter from W. L. Cornwell of the Sales Personnel Department informed Daugherty:

Mr. Gassenheimer has shown marked progress, and we are very hopeful that his connection with our organization will result in a happy connection for him and a mutually profitable arrangement for all.

We wish to assure you of our appreciation for the courtesy extended to us during our contacts last spring and we are hopeful that in another year an even larger number of desirable graduates may be secured from your university.

In an April 1936 letter to Dean Bidgood, Gus Connerth described his job in the plant intelligence division of the National Carbon Company:

It is our duty to meet secretly and present facts [about] standards of living of employees, also to bring forth suggestions and try to formulate plans of how to handle labor problems. For example, we have a man who is a perpetual father—in twenty-four years of married life he has become the father of seventeen children. He was given a job at $.63 an hour, but asked us for a raise to $.70. We investigated, found 8 sons of 18 or over, smoking and drinking, loafing on the father's weekly wage, making no attempt to get work. We had no alternative except to refuse the raise until these sons received some sort of wage. The old man was upset but soon brought these boys with him, one by one, and [they] were placed at temporary jobs. They received hard laboring jobs and the father got $.68. He has eight minor children at home and can give them a decent standard of living. With board and room paid to him by his 8 older boys his income is close to $60.00 a week now while it was only $26.00 before.

We also run across this [sort of] case. A man is hired for a special job. The A.F. of L. may be 100% organized in his department. He may refuse to become a member and his co-workers put him on "the island." This is a term used by laborites meaning that union men will have nothing to do with the man, have nothing to say to him, and will refuse to eat with him. We must manipulate our puppets so that the [ill will] is broken and in such a way that everyone is satisfied.

A New Crop of Faculty Members

In the later years of the decade, the University continued to suffer from the effects of budgetary cuts made during the depths of the Depression. Despite a 1937 adjustment, faculty salaries still remained below the minimum standards set by the Southern Association of Colleges and Secondary Schools. The library and laboratories lacked the personnel and equipment to carry out their educational missions adequately. Because enrollment had climbed following the 1933–34 academic session without an accompanying increase in faculty, the student-to-faculty ratio had risen to an unacceptable level. The University's expenditure per student was the lowest among the region's twenty-four major state-supported institutions of higher learning. As a result of these conditions, in 1939 the association placed the University on its starred list, which meant an institution was in danger of losing its accreditation.

Fortunately, the Capstone had an eloquent and persuasive champion in Pres. Richard Clarke Foster, who appealed to the legislature for help in forestalling the University's imminent loss of accreditation. The lawmakers responded to Foster's plea with additional funding. Armed with this money, Foster implemented steps designed to enhance the University's ability to perform its missions. In addition to buying new equipment and making curricular changes, he formed a research fund committee and approved the hiring of thirty-four new faculty members.

C&BA faculty members played prominent roles in the rejuvenation of University programs at the end of the 1930s. Dean Bidgood sat on the Research Fund Committee, and several C&BA faculty members received grants that enabled them to earn their doctorates. Bidgood's school also received an infusion of new blood with the hiring of more than a dozen new instructors and professors in 1939. Included in this group were Frank E. Dykema, Charles L. Seebeck Jr., and Edward H. Anderson, scholars and educators who would influence the future development of C&BA and the University.

One 1939 faculty prospect whom Dean Bidgood recruited quite diligently was S. Paul Garner. In a July 25, 1939, letter to Prof. Chester Knight, Bidgood, discussing possible new faculty members, wrote, "The best man in sight now seems to be S. Paul Garner, a tar-heel from Winston-Salem. . . . Garner is quite young, physically very impressive, strikingly pleasant, and has a nice wife who is also an M.A. of Duke." Bidgood noted that the other candidates for the accounting position in the Commerce School did not "have either [Garner's] brilliance or his personality." Through his many contacts, the dean had also discovered that Garner was "an unusually good teacher" in whom several universities were interested. Bidgood wrote to Knight that Garner was already collaborating to write a cost accounting text for a major publisher, and he had "passed a brilliant examination for his Ph.D. and made the C.P.A. at the first crack."

In a second letter to Chester Knight two days later, Dean Bidgood referred to a "merry war" that almost broke out between his school and Mississippi State over Garner. Everything had now been smoothed over, however, and Dean Bowen of Mississippi State assured Bidgood that Garner would be "a treasure" if the Commerce School got him.

Former dean Paul Garner reminisced about the events of 1939. He recalled that while still at the University of Texas he received employment offers from the University of Alabama; Baylor University in Waco, Texas; and Mississippi State University. The University of Texas Business School also wanted him and his wife to remain there if he found no attractive job offers. According to Dean Garner, "We visited with the officials at Baylor University, Mississippi State University, and also the University of Alabama shortly afterward. The salaries offered were within 10 to 15 percent of [each other], with Alabama's being the largest [salary]. Since both of us really wanted to move back closer to our relatives in Mississippi [his wife's home state] and North Carolina [his home state], we favored the Alabama location. In addition, the visit to Alabama for the interview was very expertly handled, and there were several attractive opportunities presented by the faculty and administrative officers in addition to the larger salary. Therefore, in evaluating the three opportunities, the choice of Alabama was comparatively easy."

The University of Alabama Commerce School did indeed get Garner, and the caliber of his service to the institution, state, and even the nation has proven him to be the treasure Dean Bowen predicted him to be more than fifty-five years ago.

A New Wing for the Commerce Building

When Paul Garner visited for his initial interview with Dean Bidgood, one of their stops was the much-needed addition to the Commerce Building. The 1928 structure had been designed to accommodate 1,000 students. By the 1935–36 session, however, 1,007 men and women were registered as Commerce students, and by 1938–39 more than 1,200 students were straining the school's physical facilities. Clearly the school needed more space, and plans were drawn to expand the Commerce Building by adding a new wing to the original structure. In September 1939 the new addition to the Commerce Building opened, physical testimony to the school's successes during its first two decades of operation.

Paul Garner provided additional details about the expansion and about his visit to it with Dean Bidgood. He recalled that the new wing was subsidized by the Work Progress Administration, established by Pres. Franklin Roosevelt to alleviate the severe unemployment problems of the depression. Garner remembered vividly his guided tour of the structure:

> When [I] came [to] interview, Dean Bidgood took me to that part of the new building instead of going to the front part first. He was proud of getting that addition to the Commerce Building. The wing held the business library, the Bureau of Business Research, and down on the ground level floor, in the basement, a machine room where people could go and [use] various bookkeeping machines, adding machines, and so on. Then they had a relatively large room for mimeographing. The next floor held the Bureau of Business Research. The next floor above that was the periodical room and the reference library room.
>
> The top floor, and he took me there first, had a relatively large open space in the center, and there were six modest-sized rooms, maybe 8-by-12 feet, around the walls, each one with a window, and he had the architect design those for faculty members to be assigned on a yearly basis who wanted to get away to write articles or books. He knew I had a textbook in progress, and he said, "You will be assigned one of those, the first person." I wrote the first textbook that I published in the first room on the right. Later on, when we began to develop more faculty needs and were able to [fill the faculty positions], they became faculty offices instead of being used for the purpose Dean Bidgood had them designed for. Incidentally, he told me one time after I assumed the job that he didn't like the idea of using them for faculty offices; they should have been used for the purpose he thought best. When he was working with a project that dealt with economic and social issues, he used one of those rooms. In later years [the area] was converted into the accounting department headquarters.

Garner pointed out that the building addition cost more than one hundred thousand dollars to construct. "It was a lot of money," he commented, "but the library was the primary purpose for the new wing. Dean Bidgood was determined to have adequate space for the library. That was one of his pride and joys."

Business Research and Military Defense

Following the Nazi invasion of Poland in September 1939, Bidgood perceived a shift in the relationship between collegiate schools of business and the federal government. Thus far the 1930s had seen a cooperative effort between business schools and the government to combat unemployment during the depression; now Bidgood realized that national defense would be the keystone of the relationship between the two. In a series of letters written to several members of Congress and military officials in the months following the aggression, Bidgood argued that economic mobilization was as urgent as military mobilization in an emergency situation. He felt that business schools, particularly their research bureaus, could play an important role in national defense preparation.

In a letter to Maj. Rufus Boylan, dated October 3, 1939, Bidgood offered the services of the University's Bureau of Business Research to the military, arguing that "recent events in Europe suggest that perhaps economic mobilization may be as necessary for national defense as purely military mobilization." He suggested that the Bureau could be "a source of economic information for Alabama and for the Southeast," pointing out that it had "the largest collections of economic data in the Southeast." Bidgood also gave a résumé of the Bureau's associations with several federal agencies during the past three or four years, including the Department of Labor, the Works Progress Administration, and the National Emergency Council. He noted that the Bureau also worked with the U.S. Engineer Office of the War Department on two canal projects, "but so far the agencies entrusted with economic phases of the national defense have not made use of the Bureau."

On October 9, 1939, Bidgood wrote again to Major Boylan:

> The Conference of State University Schools of Business has a committee on cooperation with the United States Department of Commerce, of which I happen to be chairman at this time, which committee is meeting with the Department in Washington the latter part of this week. I expect to suggest that the committee and our conferees in the Department of Commerce consider suggesting to the proper authorities in the War and Navy Departments the fact that extensive collections of economic information exist in the files of a good many state bureaus of business research in different parts of the country, which in many cases contain information that cannot be procured in Washington.

Bidgood seemed genuinely confused about and annoyed at the apparent reluctance of defense officials to make use of his bureau's data and expertise in preparing the nation for the possibility of war. Within a little more than two years, the Commerce School and other divisions of the University would find themselves preparing for little else.

The world is talking about:

The Selective Service Bill becomes law, mandating compulsory registration for all males between the ages of twenty-one and thirty-five. (September 16, 1940)

The Japanese attack Pearl Harbor. (December 7, 1941)

Germany and Italy declare war on the United States. (December 22, 1941)

Gasoline rationing is extended throughout the country. (December 1, 1942)

D-Day—the largest invasion in history—is marked by epic movements and individual heroism. (June 6, 1944)

President Roosevelt signs the Servicemen's Readjustment Act (the GI Bill). (June 22, 1944)

President Roosevelt is inaugurated for an unprecedented fourth term. (January 20, 1945)

The Japanese surrender is signed on the USS *Missouri* in Tokyo Bay, signaling the end of World War II. (September 2, 1945)

The United Nations comes into existence. (October 24, 1945)

An executive order signed by President Truman bars segregation in the armed forces and calls for an end to racial segregation in federal employment. (July 26, 1948)

The University is talking about:

Maj. Charles W. Davis, Class of 1940 and pitcher for the 1939 Crimson Tide baseball team, is awarded the Congressional Medal of Honor for his actions on January 12 and 13, 1943, on Guadalcanal Island.

Nancy Batson, a licensed pilot by the time she graduated from the University in 1941, ferries B-24 and B-26 planes from the factory to designated airfields and ports of embarkation as a member of the Women's Auxiliary Ferry Squadron.

After "scouring attics, basements, and all kinds of junk heaps," reports the *Crimson White* in the fall of 1942, "Bama students attended the 'A' Club Scrap Dance . . . and dumped more than twenty tons of metal at the door of Foster Auditorium."

Alabama football: the Crimson Tide wins the 1942 Cotton Bowl and the 1943 Orange Bowl. During the 1943–44 academic year the team is disbanded because most of Alabama's able-bodied men are in the armed service.

The number of men enrolled as regular students declines during the war years; women's enrollment rises steadily. During calendar year 1944, the University confers degrees on 152 men and 241 women.

In 1946 President Paty tells the trustees that "the students who came to us from the armed forces, in general, have shown themselves to be the best students we have ever had."

The University Club officially opens on February 23, 1947.

Chapter 3

War and Peace: The Forties
The Bidgood Era Continues

In Their Own Words

Students

Ray Baker, Class of 1949:

> *Reflecting back on my time at the University, I have great memories, and I have enjoyed a good success in business because of the education I got. I came to Alabama after World War II when there was a substantial influx of GIs. With the GI Bill I think we got seventy-five dollars a month, and that was pretty good then. As I remember, typically the classes were seventy-five to one hundred people. Because of that we didn't have real close relationships with faculty [members]. I do remember Dr. Paustian, my economics teacher, who was very inspirational to me.*
>
> *One of the highlights of my college years was playing in the Million Dollar Band under Colonel Butler, truly a legendary figure. I don't think I have ever known anybody who could motivate people like he could.*

Baker described himself as an entrepreneur.

Allene Burbank (nee Smith), Class of 1941: "All my statistical knowledge came from Alabama except for the year I got my M.B.A. at Northwestern. The adviser at Northwestern was very ill, so I got my M.B.A. in marketing research. I was very well prepared by Alabama to go to Northwestern. I had no academic problems."

In describing Dean Bidgood, Burbank said

> *He was as warm as he could be inside, but he liked to put on a big, gruff attitude outside. There were many students, especially when they first came to school, who were terrified of him. I think he liked me because I wasn't terrified of him. He helped me so much. He offered me a teaching job. In college teaching nobody trains you. You just go into the classroom and start. Dean Bidgood was a great help in that first year I was teaching. I was really very fond of him.*
>
> *We understood that Mr. Bonham, who taught marketing, had been a professional boxer; he had a sense of humor and we felt he was mortal. Some professors didn't seem mortal at first. And Mr. Bonham knew so much. He never had any notes. He would sit down, put his feet up on the desk, and just start talking, with that big cigar in his mouth.*

Burbank also remembered Chester Knight fondly. Although Miriam Locke was not one of her instructors, she was important to Burbank because of her assistance in obtaining the scholarship that made the Northwestern master's

College "hot buttons" during the forties:

1940

- The curricula expands with the addition of courses in commercial art and in secretarial work.

1941

- The University goes on the quarter system.

1943

- A new curriculum offering, social administration, is added.

1944

- The M.B.A. degree is offered, making two graduate degrees available; the other is the master's in C&BA.
- The commercial art curriculum is dropped.

1947

- The "modern" departments are formed.

1949

- The University returns to the semester system.
- Curriculum VII for college graduates is introduced.

Chester Knight at graduation, 1940.

Military training group, circa 1944.

degree possible. Burbank volunteered a comment on the current administration, saying how impressed she is with Dean Barry Mason, whom she has met in Nashville at alumni luncheons, and what he is doing for the college.

Margaret Carpenter, who graduated in 1944, loved the fine arts. But when her father asked her how she expected to make a living in that, she went to see Dean Bidgood and told him that she wanted to be a commercial artist. Although the University didn't offer a way to do it, the dean said not to worry, he would design a curriculum for her. And he did. As a matter of fact, the curriculum was in the catalog for two years. "He had me walking all the way across the quadrangle to engineering to make mechanical drawings," said Carpenter.
Recalling Larry Nations, Carpenter said

> *I still have this recurring dream that I'm sure has some horrible meaning. In the dream I'm on my way to Mr. Nations's advertising exam and I haven't attended class the entire semester, and I mean I just wake up in a cold sweat!*
>
> *But I made good grades. I am chairman of the Board of Education in Montgomery County now, and I spoke recently to a whole auditorium full of high school kids. I told them they must pay attention to what they are doing and [learning], even [though they might] think they will never use [the information]. They just might. I had no idea of running a business, but I've been running one for thirty years now. All I wanted to do was to be an artist and [it never occurred to me] that one day I would be running a business.*
>
> *My husband and I started Compose-It in our dining room. He was running it. He was selling. I was on the drawing board doing all the creative design and having a great time. He had a heart attack and died. We had three little boys, and we had invested in equipment, so I had to start running the business. I wasn't as prepared as I should have been. If I had known I was going to do what I had to do, I would have approached school a lot differently. That's what I was trying to tell those [high school] kids—you never know and you had better pay attention.*

During the interview I found out a lot about Margaret Carpenter. She is a dynamo who pays her civic dues, and then some. She'll be the first woman chair of the Chamber of Commerce after she completes her Board of Education service. She is on the Executive Committee of the Alabama Shakespeare Festival and has been chairman of the Committee of 100. Her roots at the University run deep. She and her sister, Libby Anderson Cater, have left a legacy here that is enviable.

Laura Cooper (known as Grace Jones except to her college classmates), Class of 1949, was a classmate of mine. She and I agreed on our mutual love for our University and college. A self-described career homemaker, Cooper still sees the good friends she made at college. She says "Miss Commerce," Betty Joyce Cain (nee Mills), is a neighbor and they still laugh about Cain's recognition at Commerce Day in the late 1940s. Another friend, Ellen Crowe Smith, has her own accounting business.
Cooper said twelve of her Alabama friends meet the first Thursday of each month for lunch at someone's home. Most of their husbands are Alabama graduates as well, all now living in Birmingham. What a good example of

the president, to come to Alabama as the major speaker during Retailing Day. Later, Hal's daughter came to major in marketing at the University, and Louise and I became good friends.

I also remember a woman named Virginia Glass who served on the planning committee. I think she was from Fayette or Gordo. I wonder whatever happened to Virginia Glass?

On Temporary Housing: There were nice trees over behind Smith Hall, and the area was called Smith Woods. There were old barracks [in Smith Woods] used for classrooms because we outgrew ourselves. We grew so rapidly because the GI Bill made it possible for people like me to come back to school. I think I had a class over there. They taught freshman classes there, and you felt like you were in a barrack. I don't remember when they were torn down, but I would say it was some time in the fifties.

At the same time [the University] owned Northington campus, which used to be an army hospital. Part of it was used for University classes and for married student apartments. I had dozens of student friends who lived at Northington campus, and the apartments were absolutely awful. Living there was the lowest possible kind of living you could imagine. Some of the girls tried to fix them up, but it was pretty awful. I can remember going over for dinner at this friend's house and they were most apologetic because of the ambience, which simply didn't exist.

I also remember that there was another bunch of army barracks used for married student housing where the Law School is now. That area was called Bakersfield. I don't think there were any classes there.

I haven't mentioned Ridgecrest. Ridgecrest was north of the

networking! Three of Cooper's sons and one daughter-in-law are Alabama C&BA graduates. During our conversation she remembered Bert Morley, Frank Dykema, and Ed Austin.

Faculty

R. Murray Havens graciously wrote some of his reflections of the early days in a letter in November 1993. Following are excerpts from that communication:

> *I corresponded with Dean Bidgood about the possibility of coming to Alabama in the summer of 1945 while I was in the army in Germany. At the time I was the officer in charge of the University of Heidelberg. Dean Bidgood was an economist by training and emphasized the role he thought economics should play in the curriculum of C&BA. It was his belief in the central role of economics in business training that attracted me to the University. I had been teaching accounting at Duke University, but I was very interested in shifting into the teaching of advanced and graduate economic theory.*

In the early years of C&BA Dean Bidgood had insisted that each faculty member teach one course in elementary economics, but the growth of the college had made this no longer feasible. As a student of Murray Havens in 1946, I can attest to the fact that he is a "professor's professor." How fortunate we all are that Dean Bidgood provided him the environment in which he could spend a career.

Minnie C. Miles came to Alabama in 1942 and was hired by Dean Bidgood. "I heard that Alabama had a vacancy in the secretarial department so I applied for that position. The dean called me and said the job was filled before my application came, but he noted that I had a background in management and that there was a vacancy in that area because a faculty member was away (this was during World War II). I was delighted to consider it. And that's how I came [to the University]."

When asked about her relationship with Dean Bidgood, Miles responded:

> *My relationship with the dean was good. A lot of people were afraid of him. In my second year, he asked me if I would take over the Placement Bureau if I had a reduced teaching load. I told Dean Bidgood that I had been away from Alabama and had lost contact with the business people. He said that I'd soon learn them. I said there were other faculty members who had been at Alabama all the time and knew the business people, so why should I do it? He said, "I'll tell you why. Of all the faculty members who wrote recommendations for students, you did the best job and I think you should take the position." Well, you really didn't argue with the dean if he thought you should do something. So I did it.*

Minnie Miles remembers that when she came to the Commerce School, Louise Clymer and Mary Woeber were the only two other women in the school. In her reminiscences of the faculty members on board when she arrived who contributed most to the mission of the college, the following were mentioned: Marcus Whitman, Langston Hawley, Harry Bonham, H. H. Chapman, and Chester Knight—some classic names of our history. Miles's admiration for these remarkable men was clear.

men's dormitories on McCrory Drive. They were barracks left over from the war, and they were also used for married student housing. So many of the students were married at that time. Either [the men] were married during their service time or they got married right after. I was one of the rare unmarried students, as a matter of fact. Well, that may be a little overstated because there were plenty of single guys. Not many women, though. The women that were in the Commerce School at that time were primarily in secretarial administration.

On C&BA Instructors: I guess in some ways I am uniquely qualified to discuss our great teachers [because they were] still here when I came back. As a teacher myself, I think I can look back with objectivity. First of all, Harry Bonham was my mentor. I don't know how we got to be so close, but I got to know him [because I was] a major in advertising and selling at the time, and he was head of that area. I had him for a course, [which I think was] purchasing. He sat at the desk and was very informal and put his feet up on the desk. In fact, he put his feet up on his desk when he went into his office. And he always had a cigar in his mouth, and he was very, very thoughtful. He had those tiny little eyes that penetrated [you] when he talked to you, but he was the warmest, most genuine man I probably ever knew. And something about him made me believe that I wanted to be a teacher someday. At that time, when I was an undergraduate, it was unheard of that I might want to be a teacher, but as I think back in retrospect, Harry Bonham was the kind of person I wanted to be.

My first adviser was Larry Nations. I was crazy about Larry Nations, but he wasn't as warm as Harry Bonham to me. After

When asked how she would like to be remembered, she replied without hesitation: "That I lived for my students. I always felt students came first. Without students we would have no university." As one of her students in the forties, I confirm her commitment and thank her for being a role model for me.

The War Years and Beyond

The 1940s proved to be as turbulent a decade for C&BA as it was for the entire world. Most college-age men were drafted for military service during World War II, and the school's enrollment began to decline as a result. Perhaps the scarcity of students was fortunate, because so many C&BA faculty members were doing their part to win the war that not too many remained to teach. The postwar period led to a different sort of stress as returning GIs flocked to colleges and universities to take advantage of Pres. Franklin Roosevelt's GI Bill. The swelling enrollments strained physical facilities and faculty resources across the nation before subsiding in 1949. Through all these events, Dean Bidgood and his faculty struggled to maintain their equilibrium.

The University and C&BA as Wartime Training Areas

Even prior to the attack on Pearl Harbor, Dean Bidgood and other officials were considering what role business schools could play in preparing the nation for war. In a June 24, 1941, letter, W. Mackenzie Stevens, secretary of the National Conference of State University Schools of Business, wrote to his colleagues in collegiate business education: "Some problems of national defense involving economic and business research can be carried out much more effectively as well as more economically by decentralized research organizations in each state (cooperating with one another and with government departments) than they can by a centralized governmental agency operating in or from Washington. For these problems, personnel, facilities, and money can be most effectually applied in a decentralized organization of this sort—and the state university schools of business with their specialized personnel are ideally situated to perform this cooperative function."

Despite the hopes of both Stevens and Dean Bidgood, the federal government seems not to have relied on the bureaus of business research to the degree these men wished.

At the same time, the federal government was busy expanding national defense training operations that already existed. The following notice appeared in the National University Extension Association Bulletin in September 1941:

> The Engineering, Science, and Management Defense Training Program of the United States Office of Education—The new appropriation provides for the offering, in addition to courses in engineering, of courses in chemistry, physics, and production supervision (accounting, industrial management, personnel management, statistics, transportation, and employment management). The purpose of this program is to meet training needs in defense industries and in army camps. Emphasis is being given to in-service courses that are based upon actual demands either for the up-grading of men already employed or for the training of those who may be placed immediately upon completion of the courses. Hence, a large part of this program is extension class work and should be

Nations became ill. Ed Austin was my adviser, and we became very good friends. In fact, years later I became his boss. Ed Austin was a rare individual. He never got [an advanced] degree and was not a particularly stimulating teacher, but he was very student-oriented. . . . He established the Austin Cup for the outstanding graduating senior. It was called the Austin '25 cup in reference to his graduation year. The recipient was elected by the faculty, and the award is still given today, but we don't give a cup. After he passed away we tried to get the family interested in funding a cup, but they declined, so now we give a plaque, which we still call a cup. (I think that's odd, but it seems typical somehow of a university.)

I was crazy about Marcus Whitman, although I never had him as a teacher. I had Constantin, who taught me transportation, and he was a magnificent teacher. I kept in touch with him over the years. I would often see him at conferences.

One person who was very influential in my life wasn't even a full-time teacher: Winnie Breene. She taught me retailing. It was really her alerting me to the possibility of getting a master's degree in retailing that changed my life. She talked about having her master's from Northwestern and suggested that I might want to talk to a new young man who had just come aboard the [UA] faculty named Harry Lipson. Harry had gotten a similar degree from Northwestern in retailing and had come here to teach. I got to know Harry very well. We became very dear friends.

Murray Havens was [another] superb teacher. He had just had a remarkable experience with the Office of Price Administration or something and he was really a magnificent teacher. I enjoyed his course as much as any. I also

administered by established extension divisions or organized and developed in cooperation with them.

The University's Commerce School played an important role in administering the training called for in the program. Dean Lee Bidgood was a member of the University's National Defense Council of Engineering, Science, and Management Defense Training (ESMDT) Program. Prof. E. H. Anderson was in charge of the management courses taught in the program, and in April 1944 he was named state supervisor for ESMWT (the program's designation as of July 1, 1942). For the first two years, Dr. Paul Garner directed the program's accounting courses, which were held in Birmingham.

Another national defense project that the University supported was the Advanced Quartermaster ROTC Unit. Plans for this unit were announced in the February 16, 1942, *Commerce Bulletin*:

> Word has been received from the Fourth Corps Area that a military instructor in quartermaster work will be sent to the University as soon as possible, and the unit will consist of fifty persons during the present semester, and of 100 persons beginning next semester.
>
> It is suggested that all students who wish to be enrolled in the quartermaster advanced ROTC unit apply to Colonel Carpenter at once. It will be borne in mind that this unit is exactly similar to the other three advanced units now on campus. To get in, a student must have completed basic military training, and must have at least junior standing at the present time. Membership in the quartermaster unit is restricted to Commerce students, just as membership in the engineering unit is restricted to engineering students.

According to the University catalog for the academic year 1942–43, the successful completion of this program led to the commissioning of participants as second lieutenants, Reserve Quartermaster Corps.

The Army Specialized Training Program (ASTP) also operated on campus during the war years. According to an August 30, 1943, booklet, "The Army Specialized Training Program was organized by the War Department in collaboration with civilian educators. To direct the program the Army Specialized Training Division was established 18 December 1942."

In the same document, Gen. George C. Marshall, the U.S. Army's chief of staff, described the program: "The Army has been increasingly handicapped by a shortage of men possessing desirable combinations of intelligence, aptitude, education, and training in fields such as medicine, engineering, languages, science, mathematics, and psychology, who are qualified for service as officers of the Army. With the establishment of the minimum Selective Service age of 18, the Army was compelled to assure itself that there would be no interruption in the flow of professionally and technically trained men who have hitherto been provided in regular increments by American colleges and universities."

Lt. Gen. Lesley J. McNair, Commanding General of the Army Ground Forces, added, "The speed of modern warfare demands leadership that can accelerate our operations by rapidity of thought and by the application of the most expeditious means known to modern science. Intelligent men who have been

enjoyed a business law class taught by Clinton McGee, who had been involved in the Nuremberg trials. [His teaching method] really got my interest up.

On Teaching: I taught economics in a summer quarter at the Mobile extension center after I got my undergraduate degree. In 1955 I returned to the University to take care of Austin's position because he went away on a Fulbright. I first taught in advertising and promotion. When I walked into Bidgood Hall in 1955, Harry Bonham asked, "Well, where are you going to get your Ph.D.?" This was before I even knew whether I liked teaching. After I got my Ph.D. and came back to teach in 1960, Harry Lipson said, "I am going to let you teach retailing. You have got all the abilities, you have had a retailing career, and you love the subject, so I am giving it up and letting you have it." That changed the direction of my academic career.

When I came back in 1955 I taught five courses with four preparations. I am rather amazed sometimes when I think how difficult it is to find somebody who will teach twelve semester hours today. But the difference really was we were not expected to do research. We were . . . very committed to teaching. Dean Bidgood laid the groundwork for the emphasis on serving students.

On Dean Bidgood: I never had the pleasure of having him teach me, but my father had studied under him right after World War I. [After I enrolled in the University] my father told me, "You go into Dean Bidgood's office and introduce yourself because I want you to give him my regards." I said, "Oh, my God, me go into Dean Bidgood's office? I am scared to death. Who would ever go into that office unarmed?" But I screwed my courage up and one day went in to ask to see him. [The secretary] said for me to go

trained to think and who can apply scientific knowledge to the everyday problems in combat are urgently needed in the leadership of our combat units."

Specialized Training and Reassignment (STAR) units were "established at specified colleges and universities for the purpose of receiving, housing, classifying, and instructing soldiers selected as generally qualified for the ASTP"

Civilian educational authorities were responsible for all instruction conducted under the ASTP program. Although no specific commerce or business administration courses were in the booklet, C&BA instructors in mathematics and geography were called upon to teach those subjects to army personnel.

A September 29, 1943, letter from Brig. Gen. Joe N. Dalton to University president R. R. Paty gave some idea of the scope of the ASTP program: "Instruction under the ASTP has been in progress for six months. More than 100,000 soldiers have been selected and assigned to courses on college campuses. During this trying period of rapid growth and adjustment, the War Department has greatly appreciated the cooperative spirit and sustained effectiveness of college administrative officers and faculties in the team job of putting the program into operation."

Wartime Disruptions

Even before U.S. entry into World War II, the conflict began to affect universities and colleges. According to Dean Bidgood's 1944 report to the Alabama Educational Survey Commission, by November 1940 national guard units were putting some men on active duty, and selective service calls went out soon afterward. C&BA enrollment data reflect these events. For the June 1939 to June 1940 period, enrollment stood at 1,230. The next year 1,131 students registered in the school; in the next session (by which time the nation had entered the war) the number had declined to 959. This trend continued until the 1943–44 academic year, when only 360 students (144 men and 216 women) registered for classes.

The senior business tour, an integral part of Dean Bidgood's educational program for nearly twenty years, was suspended because of a lack of students and teachers, as well as because of security concerns. The Commerce Association disbanded temporarily, leading to the cancellation of Commerce Day for at least one year, but both returned after the war.

Faculty members left the school to serve their country in various ways. Several instructors joined the military services, and one, Russell C. Johnson, was reported as missing in action. Others served in a civilian capacity. H. H. Chapman became chief of the Program Policy Division, Fats and Oils Branch, in the Food Distribution Administration of the War Food Administration; Harry Bonham was named his assistant chief. (James McMillan remembered that Chapman and Bonham were called the "fat and oil boys" because of these assignments). Burton Morley took a post as the Gulf area director for the War Manpower Commission, and Paul Alyea was a senior price analyst with the Office of Price Administration. Several other faculty members held positions as government analysts and instructors in military detachments.

on in. I walked in and he looked at me as I walked in the door. He said, "Your name is 'Meyer,' from Demopolis." I said, "Dean Bidgood, how did you know? I never met you." He said, "You look just like your father did. Well, it's good to meet you." I stood there wondering what to say next.

From that point on he always spoke to me. He called me 'Meyer' because he always called my father that, and Dean Bidgood never would change. [In later years], I found him to be a sweet, kind, gentle man, [but] I had been so frightened of him when he was in the big chair.

On His Career at the University: Thinking about Dean Bidgood makes me realize what Alabama has meant to me. There is really nothing I have done in my life that I can't trace back to something that [was connected to] the University of Alabama. I feel that it's been second only to my family. The University of Alabama is just part of my life.

Those faculty members who remained on campus also served the war effort. In his report to the president for 1942–43, Dean Bidgood cited Professor Holladay for his work to develop an insurance plan for University employees and Professor Knight for "tactful, tireless, and successful [leadership]" in his role as chairman of the University Committee on War Information and Service. (Knight later joined Holladay to create the University's retirement plan). The dean recognized Professors Anderson and Garner for their leadership in the ESMDT and ESMWT program. (Garner would also later contribute his expertise to the Office of Price Administration in Montgomery). Bidgood expressed his appreciation to James McMillan for serving as acting director of the Bureau of Business Research in Chapman's absence and for taking charge of civilian instruction for the aircrew unit. Later, McMillan headed the ASTP Reserve program.

Dean Lee Bidgood served as chairman of the Investigation and Procurement of Training Programs for the Armed Forces Committee, which was charged with ascertaining the kinds of training needed in the various branches of the armed forces and then securing the right for the University to offer those programs for which it could qualify. Bidgood also held positions with the War Information and Service Committee and the National Defense Council.

The dean also helped the war effort in smaller, quieter ways. Col. Francis T. Spaulding of the Army Education Branch, Morale Services Division, wrote to President Paty on June 19, 1944:

> The War Department is making available to American prisoners in Germany many of the educational facilities available to other military and naval personnel through the United States Armed Forces Institute. The provision of material to relieve monotony and help the men prepare themselves constructively for their return to the United States is extremely important. . . . Many of these men are now indicating a desire to study specific subjects, perhaps continuing courses interrupted by the war. One such request from a man who desires to undertake further study in your institution is described in the enclosed communication. . . If you have textbooks, lesson outlines, or examinations which you would like to have sent to this man, you will find in the enclosed letter from Dr. David R. Porter suggestions regarding the ways in which War Prisoners' Aid is finding it possible to facilitate censoring, shipment, etc.

The soldier in question was Lt. Alfred D. Blair, at the time being held prisoner in Stalag Luft III, Germany. He had attended the Commerce School in 1936–37, and he wished to continue his studies in economics.

Bidgood wrote to Porter on June 30, 1944, that he was "delighted" to send Lieutenant Blair the Extension Division correspondence courses in the subjects requested (except for geography in Europe, for which there was none) as well as the textbooks used and the examinations given in each course. "This is the first case of this kind which we have handled," Bidgood wrote, "and I beg for your patience and assistance for doing it right." He concluded, "We are very grateful for this opportunity to be of service to Lt. Blair and will welcome all similar chances to help our prisoners of war who are former students of this institution."

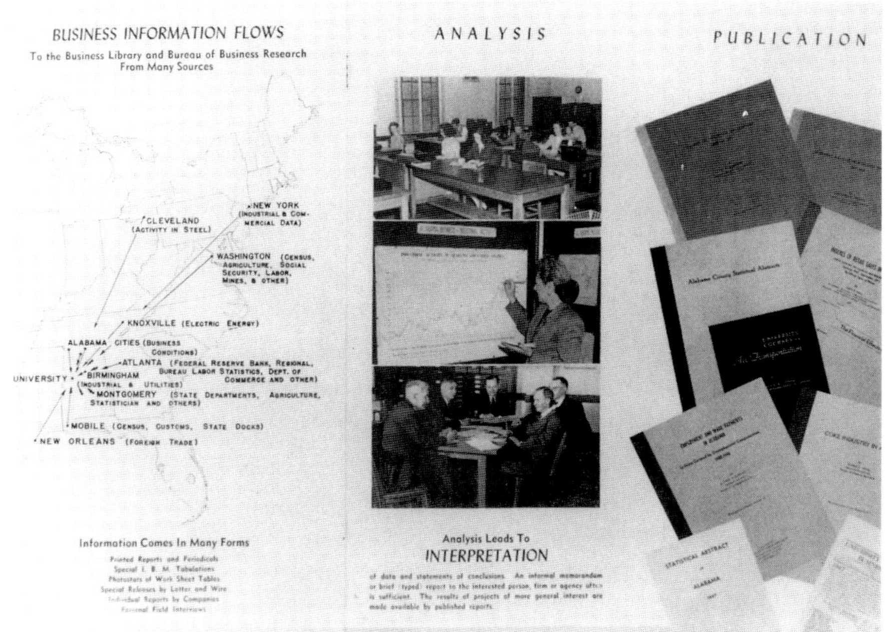

Business information flows, circa 1948.

The Bureau of Business Research

Enrollment and instruction were not the only areas of the school affected by the war effort. Bidgood wrote in his 1944 educational report that the research activity of the Bureau of Business Research was "sharply curtailed" by World War II. The director, statistician, and business analyst left to take jobs with government agencies, and censorship closed down several sources of information. Despite these difficulties, the staff of the Bureau did its best to compile and publish valuable information on economic activity in the state. Mrs. Lillian C. Hinton, who joined the Bureau in June 1941 and served as an analyst until late 1945, pointed out that Bidgood and Chapman had worked

Bureau of Business Research exhibit in the forties.

Many alumni letters to Dean Bidgood and other C&BA faculty members described how graduates' lives were influenced by the professors they met at the University, but few went so far as to credit the dean or his staff with influencing the rebuilding of a nation's economy. But Lt. Col. Dwight M. Wilhelm (Class of 1923) did exactly that in an April 23, 1946, letter to his former dean. He wrote: "A little over one year ago, it was my good fortune to see you at a meeting of the Selma Kiwanis Club, where you made the feature address. At that time I was stationed at Craig Field as Director of Administration and Services. Shortly after that time I was transferred. I have thought you might be interested to know my next assignments, since the instruction I received under you has not only played a great part in my civilian and Army work, but your teachings have had a part in the recon- struction of Korea."

By October 1945, Wilhelm was Chief of the Bureau of Industry in Seoul, Korea, charged with rebuilding Korea's industrial infrastructure, which had been left in a state of chaos following the withdrawal of the Japanese occupation forces earlier in the

hard to let business people in the state know what the Commerce School was doing and how the Bureau could help business owners by studying market conditions, population changes, and so forth. According to Mrs. Hinton, Dr. Chapman insisted upon "excellence and correctness" in the Bureau's work, setting a high standard for himself as well as his staff members. She recalled that he often said, "If [people] find an error in any of our statistics, they'll doubt everything else that we publish."

The remaining Bureau staff tried to maintain Dr. Chapman's high standards. Mrs. Hinton remembered that it was a struggle during the war years to publish the *University of Alabama Business News* because of the Bureau's limited budget. However, staff members had just experienced the depression, she remarked, so they "knew the value of a dollar." Through frugal expenditure of the resources available to them, the Bureau staff not only put out the *Business News*, but in 1943 published the first *Alabama County Statistical Abstracts*. Mrs. Hinton regarded this as a valuable source of data for businesses; the volume gathered together in one place essential data on each county and presented it in a useful form. According to her, the information contained in the abstract enabled businesses to make more informed decisions about their future plans.

Mrs. Hinton also participated with Allene Smith in collecting data for the first detailed study of retail sales in Alabama, a task that required them to examine state sales tax receipts in Montgomery. Mrs. Hinton recalled the strictures imposed under wartime conditions. "We had a very low per diem [allowance]," she pointed out, "so we wouldn't eat much breakfast or lunch. We would try to save up for a good dinner at the hotel." The results of these two women's investigations were published in the *Business News*, and as far as Mrs. Hinton knew they represented the most thorough study of retail sales published at that time.

The Bureau was fortunate to have such well-trained staff members as Lillian Hinton and others who contributed to the war effort by doing important work of their own. Acting Director McMillan, a trained linguist, had to rely on other staff members' expertise in statistical analysis. "I would get up the figures," Mrs. Hinton said, "[because] I knew all the sources." She would create the indexes that provided information on manufacturing and industrial activity in the state, and Acting Director McMillan would edit the material. Despite the hardships brought on by the war, the Bureau continued to fulfill the roles assigned to it in its original mission statement.

Two Faculty Members Recall V-J Day

Former dean Paul Garner arrived in Tuscaloosa on September 1, 1939, and listened to the news of Germany's invasion on the radio as he unpacked in his new home. He also recalled the end of the war: "I remember I was teaching class on the third floor of Bidgood [Hall] and we heard whistles sounding and Denny Chimes started chiming, and we wondered what it was. I sent somebody out to ask, and [we learned that] Japan had surrendered. That was in August [1945], of course. So, I went back to the classroom and said that we would adjourn."

Another C&BA professor was in Washington when the news of Japan's surrender was announced. Harry D. Bonham informed his dean of the reaction in an August 15, 1945, letter: "Last evening was quite an occasion here in Washington. I was just passing the Washington Post building when the loudspeaker boomed out the news. I followed the early crowd to 1600 Penn. Avenue and was fortunate to be close when the President came out and walked down close to the fence and around the flower bed and then made his speech. Then the crowd took over. Washington was very subdued and quiet this morning, however."

The Post–World War II Environment

The Enrollment Boom: "The Atmosphere Is Very Different"

Following the Allied victory in 1945 and the demobilization of military personnel, college and university campuses experienced severe overcrowding as former servicemen and women decided to take advantage of their educational benefits under the GI Bill. A May 20, 1946, letter from Bidgood to Catherine Zanthos revealed some details about the campus situation following the end of World War II. Bidgood wrote, "This campus is a regular meeting place now of former students. It looks like old times except that everybody is about five years older. Somehow the atmosphere is very different. Everybody in the faculty has worked very hard and is tired. We expect to have to operate at full swing for an indefinite number of years. For example, we have over 1,100 students in the Commerce School now and expect at least that number during the summer quarter."

The University took measures to curb applications, but the enrollment continued to swell. Bidgood wrote to Robert Vincent Zacher on October 7, 1946: "We have registered 2,182 students in the School of Commerce and Business Administration thus far, plus 46 graduate students in business administration. The total University enrollment is something over 8,500 though we have been restricting admissions entirely to former students with good grades, and residents of Alabama. We have appointed a number of teachers in the School of Commerce and Business Administration and are looking for more all the time, as our enrollment grows steadily from quarter to quarter."

The Campus Housing Shortage

Colleges and universities were woefully unprepared to house the veterans who crowded into them following the end of the war. The federal government tried to help by donating hundreds of war-surplus buildings to colleges and converting them into dormitories. At the University, more than six hundred families were placed in temporary housing at Ridgecrest, Riverside, and Alavet apartments. The University also used Northington General Hospital, given to it by the federal government, as supplementary housing for veterans.

Even these efforts, however, could not guarantee each student would find a place to live. Dean Bidgood's February 21, 1947, letter to Mrs. W. H. Thomas of Gadsden indicated just how acute the housing shortage was:

> We have contacted the Office of the Dean of Students, Dean N. B. Hendrix, who is in charge of the pre-fabricated apartments. That office tells us that your son is 1,170 on the waiting list for an apartment. . . . This means that it will be

year. Considering the monumental task that faced him and the shortage of personnel to do the job, Wilhelm felt that he had made substantial progress. "I now have the supervision of industry divided according to Machinery, Electricity, Chemistry, Textile, Processed Foods, Paper and Publishing, and the Zaibatsu Industries," he informed Bidgood. "That includes everything from production of toothpicks to airplanes and locomotives." Wilhelm attributed his success to what he had learned from Bidgood more than twenty years earlier. "Many times I have had to grope for ideas, and your own words still are fresh in my mind, and they have helped me greatly. Perhaps this might be of interest to some of your present students."

at least a year and a half before he can hope to get into one of the pre-fabricated buildings. . . .

I wish that we had a lot more pre-fabricated apartments and more room in town. But the Federal Government has done as well by us as by any of the universities in letting us have pre-fabricated buildings, and building has progressed in Tuscaloosa as fast as in any city in Alabama recently. The trouble is that we just have so many married students.

Cramped Quarters in the Commerce Building

Dormitory rooms were not the only space in short supply. More classroom space was needed to take care of the increasing number of students. In 1947 U.S. colleges tried to accommodate 2,338,000 students in facilities that had previously been crowded with 1,350,000 students.

Bidgood realized early in the postwar period that the increase in his school's enrollment was placing an enormous strain on its physical facilities, a strain that demanded a permanent solution. Bidgood had wanted to complete the Commerce Building's original plan, and he recognized now an opportunity to press for his desire. He wrote to Dr. B. R. Morley, Dr. E. H. Anderson, Dr. S. Paul Garner, and Miss Mary A. Woeber on February 6, 1946:

> We have no idea as to when the University can construct the addition to the Commerce Building. But it is urgently and immediately needed, and we should make our plans as soon as possible to indicate what use we desire to make of the space.
>
> I shall greatly appreciate your serving as a Building Committee, to develop these plans. A separate Committee on Equipment is being appointed. Dr. Anderson has agreed to accept the chairmanship of this Committee. In order to keep the two committees in constant touch, I am asking Dr. Anderson to serve as a member of the Building Committee and Dr. Morley to serve as a member of the Equipment Committee.

Bidgood's committee members went to work on their assignment. They evaluated the present use of the Commerce Building, the use of Smith Woods's temporary classrooms, and the need for additional office and library space. After studying the data, the committee members concluded that "the evidence here presented substantially supports the immediate need for the construction of the proposed wing. The present building, in spite of a high degree of utilization, is greatly inadequate. The temporary structures now being used cannot last long and certainly do not represent good classroom and laboratory housing. The extremely crowded conditions in regard to offices under which the staff is now operating require immediate attention. Unless the present stack capacity is increased, the Business Library will definitely not be able to use materials which should be preserved and be available for use."

By August 18, 1948, the dean had before him "tentative plans" for using the space in the new wing. In a letter written on that date, he requested that the Building Committee "assemble and brief the available information showing the need for the new addition, and the urgent character of that need." Furthermore, he wrote, "I would like you as a committee or perhaps through a sub-committee of your membership to lay this need before the president of the University."

Bidgood's request for completion of the Commerce Building's original floor plan came at a propitious moment in the University's history. By the spring of 1948 more than nine thousand students were crammed onto a campus designed for only sixty-five hundred. Pres. John M. Gallalee, former director of technical staff for the Alabama State Building Commission, placed the expansion of campus facilities as his first priority. Under his leadership, the University embarked on a building program in 1948 that continued for five years. The University announced that the expansion of the Commerce Building would be included in the building program during the January 1950 Commerce Day ceremonies.

A report in the September 25, 1949, *Atlanta Journal,* headlined "Southeast Warned of Educational Slums," made clear how well advised Gallalee's decision to undertake a building program was. According to the article, "In a lengthy report on college building needs, the United States Office of Education reported greater needs exist in Georgia, Florida, Alabama, Mississippi, Tennessee, North Carolina, and South Carolina." Southeastern colleges were expected to experience a 59 percent increase in student enrollment, whereas the nationwide increase was predicted to be only 32.8 percent. A 60.5 percent increase would occur in Alabama. According to the report, the University of Alabama had earmarked $3,151,630 for long-term construction to accommodate its share of the increased student population.

Too Few Business Teachers

The need for adequately trained business educators was especially acute during the mid-1940s. As early as his 1946–47 annual report to the president, Bidgood decried the poor facilities for graduate work in business administration nationwide and especially in the South. He felt that the University was obligated to do what it could to remedy the situation. "We must maintain and improve our work for the master's degrees in business administration," he wrote, "and should inaugurate immediately work leading to the Ph.D. degree. Unless we do so, we cannot do our part to staff southern schools of business or to meet the growing demand of southern business firms for personnel with advanced training. Most important of all, most of our own choice youth will be cut off from admission to advanced training in this field unless we provide it."

As early as 1945, Bidgood had expanded his school's graduate offerings. Former dean Paul Garner recalled that following the influx of GIs into the school, Dean Bidgood "seized the opportunity to look into graduate work. There were very few M.B.A. programs in the Southeast. So he sensed an opportunity to pioneer it and offer an M.B.A." In an April 12, 1948, letter to President Gallalee, Bidgood described the school's newest graduate degree and its difference from the more traditional master's:

> In 1945 a second professional Master's degree was added, the Master of Business Administration (M.B.A.). The M.S. in C&BA is now open only to graduates of a professional school of business which holds membership in the American Association of Collegiate Schools of Business, the standardizing agency. It is a one-year degree, that is, requires nine months' work. The M.B.A. is open to graduates of all standard institutions other than the above. It is a

two-year degree, that is, requires eighteen months. The M.S. in C.&B.A. is a second professional degree; the M.B.A. is a first professional degree in Business Administration. In addition to an A.B. or other degree, the M.B.A. requires for entrance that the candidate have completed elementary economics, and if he wishes to major in accounting he must also have completed elementary accounting before being admitted to graduate work.

The school's graduate degree programs were meeting with success, Bidgood reported to Gallalee in the same letter. "Both M.S. and M.B.A. students have increased greatly in number since 1945, though we have restricted admission to Alabama students, students from neighboring southern states, a few Regular Army officers, and alumni of the University of Alabama. During the academic year 1946–47, there were 75 different students enrolled during one or more quarters in graduate study in Business Administration. They included graduates of twenty-two different institutions. This year there are more students and more institutions are represented."

Another indication of an increased interest in graduate studies on the part of students was the January 1947 establishment of the Commerce Graduate Association. The organization's purpose was stated as: (1) promoting discussion of, interest in, and solutions to problems of graduates in business administration; (2) promoting the study and discussion of business and economic problems; and (3) promoting a closer fellowship among graduate students in business administration. Membership was open to all graduates pursuing the M.S. or M.B.A. degree.

Bidgood also did what he could to encourage former Commerce students to pursue the Ph.D. For example, he wrote to Donald B. Tuson on February 6, 1948: "It is true that the Master's degree plus a C.P.A. is generally accepted for advancement to the higher [academic] ranks, but I think after the present acute personnel shortage is over and normal competition is restored . . . the ambitious man should have a doctorate."

Maintaining Contact with C&BA Students

As head of the Commerce School, Dean Bidgood had pursued a personal involvement with the school's students and alumni. The rapid enrollment increase during the postwar period threatened this type of contact between the dean and his students. The dean could still personally see to it that a co-ed received her *Corolla* or advise a mother that her son's job prospects would not be better if he studied shorthand and typing instead of accounting, but with as many as twenty-four hundred students enrolled in the school, such personal attention was becoming more difficult to give.

This situation irked the dean. In order to develop a means of keeping in touch with student concerns, Bidgood drew a lesson from his past experience as a student. While attending the University of Wisconsin as a graduate student, Bidgood had served as a student representative on a conference committee created to provide a means for students and faculty to discuss problems that arose on the campus. He now announced the formation of a similar conference committee to increase contact between the students and the faculty of the

Commerce School. On November 12, 1948, Bidgood sent a memorandum to faculty members he hoped would serve on the committee:

> For twenty years in the history of this school I knew every senior in it, and a diminishing majority of the other students. The growth of numbers and the multiplication of other duties, particularly the procurement of faculty and caring for their problems, has made this acquaintanceship impossible.
>
> For some time it has seemed to me that a regular channel ought to be set up for student opinion to reach the administrative officers of this division. To that end I am inviting you, the elected representatives of the Commerce students, the administrative officers of this school, and the elected representatives of the Commerce faculty on the University Council, to meet with me as a Conference Committee.
>
> This group will have no powers as a body though all of its members have responsibilities and authority in their respective offices or jobs. I would like for us to meet for the first time on November 15, at 4:00 P.M., in Room 310, General Library.

The committee consisted of seven student officers of the school and seven faculty members, who were to meet regularly to discuss student and faculty concerns. Student members were Russell Terry, Commerce Association president; Theo Mitchelson, representative of the student government council; James Battles, senior class president; Marilyn Moses, Commerce Graduate Association president; Robert Owen, junior class president; Jessie Wilson, sophomore class president; and James Brice, freshman class president. Dean Bidgood served as chairman of the committee. Other faculty members who served on the board were H. H. Chapman, Bureau of Business Research director; B. R. Morley, Bureau of Personnel and Placement director; E. H. Anderson, Graduate Division director; W. C. Flewellen Jr., assistant to the dean; Alice Kingery, business librarian; Marcus Whitman, commerce faculty representative

Four commerce leaders attend dedication of Alumni Hall, 1949 (4th from left, Dean Bidgood; 5th, Dean Garner; 6th, Paul Paustian; 9th, Harry Bonham).

on the University Council; and Howard Folts, Commerce Extension Service acting director.

Other University officials expressed enthusiasm for Dean Bidgood's action. In a November 15, 1948, letter to Bidgood, Noble B. Hendrix, dean of students, wrote, "I believe the plan you have proposed to institute has great possibilities of benefit and I will be greatly interested in the outcome as it begins to operate."

Hendrix continued: "It has been evident to me for years that the School of Commerce and Business Administration has a great asset in the spirit of confidence, loyalty, and pride which so high a proportion of your students exhibit toward the school, the faculty, and the dean. I believe that the proposed student-faculty-administration committee will afford regular and recognized channels for more effective use of this spirit in furthering the essential goals of the school. It is not needed, according to my observation, to build spirit, but to give a better channel for the expression of a very fine spirit already in existence."

The Deaths of Two C&BA Shapers

The year 1949 was marred by the deaths of two long-time faculty members who had assisted Bidgood in the early days of the Commerce School. In an April 25, 1949, letter, Bidgood wrote to Mr. Clemens B. Thomas: "Leroy Nations had a cerebral hemorrhage the last day of 1948, and has been completely incapacitated ever since. His speech organs and his right side are paralyzed." The long-time advertising and business English teacher never recovered from his illness. In Bidgood's annual report to the University president dated May 16, 1949, he reported with regret the death of L. J. Nations, a member of the group of men whom Bidgood regarded as "seers of a kind."

The University community was soon saddened again by the death of Chester Knight. Regrets about his death and praise for his life's accomplishments came from several quarters. Dean Bidgood wrote a personal tribute for the University's Board of Trustees in which he lauded Knight as a pioneer in accounting education. "The public recognition of accounting as a learned profession was greatly accelerated by his work," Bidgood wrote. He further praised Knight as "an accountant of distinction, a classroom teacher of superior order, a scholar, a highly competent and constructive administrator, and a gallant soldier, but above all, a true and great friend."

Former University president and chancellor George H. Denny also wrote in praise of Knight:

> Since 1912 I have followed the careers of each member of our official University family. I can think of not a single one who, in his or her particular sphere, has served the University with greater loyalty and efficiency than has Chester Knight. He was an outstanding teacher and an excellent administrator. He was a great and loyal spirit. The University must not fail at this hour to do appropriate honor to his memory. . . .
>
> Now that he has been cut down in his prime, what are we going to do about it? My suggestion is that, through the Loyalty Fund and under the leadership of Dean Bidgood, who has built on the Alabama campus what is recognized over the country as the greatest school of Commerce south of Philadelphia, all of us who love the University shall fall in line and erect a suitable memorial to our

fellow alumnus and friend, who surely deserves to be named in any competently selected list of the ten most interested, useful, and loyal Alabama alumni of the past quarter-century.

The *Quarterly Review* of Theta Xi also honored Knight by dedicating its August 1949 issue to him and presenting a summary of his involvement with the fraternity. Soon after Knight joined the C&BA faculty, the article stated:

> He became a member of Tau Omega Chi, a local fraternity on the campus, and worked hard for this colony to receive its charter from Theta Xi. He was initiated as a charter member of Alpha Lambda of Theta Xi in 1932. From 1932 until the summer of 1948 he was Alpha Lambda's delegate to the Grand Lodge.
>
> Brother Knight was faculty adviser to Alpha Lambda and also to Alpha Delta Pi sorority. In his capacity as chapter adviser and as Brother and friend, he helped us considerably with the reactivation of Alpha Lambda in 1946. Brother Knight was also a member of the following honorary scholastic organizations: Phi Eta Sigma, Beta Gamma Sigma, Alpha Kappa Psi, and Phi Beta Kappa.

Dean Bidgood's letter of August 27, 1949, expressed his appreciation to the chapter for its tribute. "We have all suffered a great loss in the death of Professor Knight," the dean wrote. "Several memorials, including your dedication, have been published or are in preparation. But the most important memorial to him is the recollection of him existing in the minds of those who knew him."

Student Activities

The Commerce Association 1949–50 report to Dean Bidgood mentioned a new tradition it had established. "On May 14, 1949, the first annual Commerce Spring Frolics was held. . . . Mr. A. E. Hohenberg of Memphis gave the principal address, and awards from the various professional fraternities were presented. This was followed in the afternoon by a student-faculty softball game, which was won by the student team, 15–14. The night activities consisted of a smoker in Morgan Auditorium, at which professional fraternities presented humorous skits, and Miss Executive Secretary of Commerce School was chosen."

One of C&BA's oldest traditions, Commerce Day, underwent some changes at the end of the decade as well. Planners added a career fair to the schedule of events to enable graduating students to meet prospective employers and hear speeches about their chosen careers.

Beta Alpha Psi

This national accounting fraternity established a University chapter in the fall of 1948. The purpose of the fraternity was "to encourage and foster the ideal of service as the basis of the accounting profession; to promote the study of accounting and its high ethical standards; to act as a medium between professional men, instructors, students, and others who are interested in the development of the study or profession of accounting; and to develop high moral, scholastic, and professional attainments in its members." Members were required to be upperclass students with a B average in accounting and a C average in all other courses.

The University's presidents:

John M. Gallalee (1948–53)
Lee Bidgood (interim president, July and August 1953)
Oliver Cromwell Carmichael (1953–57)
James H. Newman (interim president, calendar year 1957)
Frank A. Rose (1958–69)

The world is talking about:

U.S. ground troops are sent to South Korea by President Truman. (June 30, 1950)

Dwight D. Eisenhower is elected president. (November 4, 1952)

A vaccine for polio is found and tested. (1954)

Brown vs. *Board of Education* finds racial discrimination in American public schools unconstitutional, rejecting the 1896 Supreme Court ruling of "separate but equal." (May 17, 1954)

In Montgomery, Alabama, Rosa Parks defies a city segregation ordinance by refusing to give up her bus seat to a white man. The ensuing boycott, led by Martin Luther King Jr. and others, leads to a Supreme Court decision declaring the ordinance unconstitutional. (December 1, 1955)

Alaska is admitted as the nation's forty-ninth state. (January 3, 1959)

New York governor Nelson Rockefeller proposes a system of compulsory fallout shelters for homes and other buildings to save millions from death or injury by radioactive fallout in the event of a nuclear attack. (July 6, 1959)

Hawaii brings the total number of states to fifty. (August 21, 1959)

The University is talking about:

The popular and widely traveled Alabama Cavaliers earn a reputation as "the name band of all collegiate orchestras" and are in great demand for dances throughout the region.

UA debate coach Annabel Dunham Hagood establishes one of the top debating programs in the United States. Under her guidance, Alabama teams win an exceptional number of debate titles and become national debate champions in 1949 and 1955.

Alabama's 1956 basketball team, coached by Johnny Dee, produces the Crimson Tide's first SEC championship since 1934.

In 1956, the year of the University's 125th anniversary, Autherine Lucy (Foster) becomes the first African American student to be admitted to the University of Alabama. She attends classes for three days. The events that occurred during those days, as well as the events that followed, form one of the saddest episodes in the institution's history.

The campus humor magazine *Rammer Jammer* ceases publication in 1956; the *Mahout* (meaning "driver of elephants") takes its place.

The Music and Speech Building (now called the Rowand-Johnson Building) opens in 1957 and houses the theater, later named for Marian Gallaway, director of theater from 1948 until her retirement in 1973.

The lodge at Ann Jordan Farm and more than 4,600 acres of property are given to the University by Sidney A. Mitchell. In 1957 an additional 350 acres of adjoining land are donated.

In 1958 Paul "Bear" Bryant returns to his alma mater as head coach and director of athletics.

Chapter 4

Business Booms: The Fifties
The End of the Bidgood Years
The Garner Era Begins

Faculty "enhancers" of the C&BA culture:

Wilson T. Ashby (1956)[*]
Arnold L. Barrett (1957)
William R. Bennett (1950)
Frederic A. Brett (1957)[*]
J. D. Corriher (1956)
Dale Cramer (1958)
V. Victor Harrison (1956)
Charles M. Hewitt (1950)
Paul F. Huddleston (1959)[*]
Harold D. Janes (1958)[*]
Morris L. Mayer (1955)
Dorothy C. Menning
   (Wilkinson) (1952)
Donald Mills (1956)
Henry B. Moore (1951)
Ernest F. Patterson (1950)
Clarence A. Spencer Jr. (1959)
Sue Waddell (1959)[*]
Alma B. Weber (1955)[*]
Percy B. Yeargan (1957)
Cecil M. Youngson (1955)

[*] Deceased as of 1994

In Their Own Words

Students

Frank Bromberg Jr., Class of 1954, was eager to share his strong feelings for his alma mater. He said that he met many of the people who are now leading the state of Alabama at the University of Alabama's business school and has known them for virtually a lifetime. "There isn't a town in Alabama where I don't know someone in a social or business way who is also a leader in that city—a lifetime network was formed at the University. I think the network of friends from the business school even overshadows the wonderful education I received."

Bromberg went on to say that it is more than a network; it is the power structure of the state. "Many of the political leaders of the state, most of whom were in C&BA when I was there, from the governor's office to people like the late federal judge Bob Vance, Congressman Jack Edwards, and all the Oliver Delchamps business types, passed through the doors of Bidgood Hall."

Frank Bromberg is proud of the fact that his three sons and his daughter are all C&BA graduates.

Jack R. Brunson, Class of 1953, said "I feel that the University—the College of Commerce and Business Administration—gave me a firm foundation in fundamental business practices. I achieved the proper outlook and perspective, which enabled me to operate in the world of business." In reflecting on professors he had, Jack remembered Jim Constantin whom he considered to be down to earth, matter of fact, and a person on whom one could rely.

Emory Folmar, Class of 1951, wrote in a letter:

> As a 1951 graduate of the University of Alabama College of Commerce and Business Administration, I look back to my days there as a time of learning and a time of fun.
>
> The education I received was both technical and broad. Such courses as accounting, finance, business law, and economics taught me the fundamentals of business. I have used [these skills] in the business world and in the mayor's office. Other courses such as speech and debate and business writing taught me how to think and communicate. These skills are used daily. I think my education at the University of Alabama was sound, meaningful, and prepared me for the business world and for the office I now hold.

Jim Nabors, class of 1953, one of our most famous graduates.

William R. (Bill) Bennett, a man of many dimensions.

College "hot buttons" during the fifties:

1950

- The Commerce Building is named Bidgood Hall in honor of C&BA dean Lee Bidgood.

1952

- The Secretarial Work Curriculum becomes Secretarial Administration.

1953

- The Alabama Research Council is established in the fall.

1954

- S. Paul Garner is appointed dean upon the retirement of Dean Lee Bidgood.

1955

- The Graduate School adopts Plans I and II (thesis).

1957

- The master's in C&BA is renamed M.S.C. (Master of Science in Commerce).

Lowell Friedman felt strongly that he has a message for the young people of today. In the 1950s, he says, he was stupid not to take school seriously.

Lowell Friedman is a successful businessman who wishes he had somehow done it all just a little differently.

Wallace Malone Jr., Class of 1957, transferred to Alabama after a year at another institution because of the excellent reputation of the University's business school. He remembers some outstanding teachers, and was especially complimentary about the strength of the accounting courses and teachers. "If I had to pick out one course, probably accounting has served me better than any other single course although all of them contributed—statistics, business law, money and banking, transportation, marketing, and insurance all fit in very well."

Malone singled out Dean Flewellen (assistant dean under Paul Garner) as a superior administrator who rendered the college a great service. He also got to know Dean Bidgood who was a personal friend of Wallace Malone's father. He used to go every now and then to have lunch with Dean Bidgood.

"Deans Garner and Flewellen," said Malone, "served the University and the college enormously well. I came to find out later that our business school is as good as there is anywhere. It may not have the reputation of the Harvards, Penns, Stanfords, and so on, but as far as the quality is concerned—I know because I got an M.B.A. from the University of Pennsylvania with its big reputation and my classmates were from Ivy League undergraduate programs, and with my Alabama degree, I did as well or better than any of them."

Faculty

Surely no other faculty member could represent the 1950s with more authority than *William R. Bennett*, professor emeritus. Most of our colleagues from that period are no longer with us, but under any conditions, Bill Bennett would be the most commanding spokesman for that time. He has had a most distinguished career and is still active on campus. The following excerpts from an interview with Bennett, capture much of his dedication and sincerity.

He noted that in the 1950s many business courses had been very descriptive, a point brought out strongly in "the reports." The Ford Foundation sponsored summer seminars at such institutions as Harvard, Williamstown, and Carnegie Tech to orient business faculties in the quantitative and behavioral science areas, thus moving from the purely descriptive to the analytical and decision oriented.

> [The reports] told us that we ought to make the business school academically respectable and that the way to do that was to emphasize the behavioral and quantitative areas of study and that we all ought to take courses or do whatever we had to do to learn these things. At the summer seminars we were with professors from all over the country, and a major point of discussion at that time was what to do about responding to the reports. Of course being at the high-level seminars was a very specific response. On our own campus we spent a lot of time in committees and meetings discussing how to respond.

When Bill Bennett arrived at Alabama in 1950 he joined the shapers and builders of our culture as a colleague—he mentioned Professors Bonham, Holladay, Whitman, Alyea, and Chapman. Chester Knight had died, but Lee Bidgood was still dean when Bennett came to C&BA.

Professor Bennett made his earliest mark at Alabama in the personal sales area of marketing. I asked how he developed an interest in salesmanship.

> When I got to Illinois [to pursue a Ph.D.], I was a graduate assistant and somebody asked me if I had any experience in selling. I said that I had. They immediately assigned me to Frank Beach [the "dean" of salesmanship academicians], and I became one of his assistants. I taught courses in sales, and Frank convinced me that salesmanship was an important area and one that we should pay more attention to. So I got interested.
>
> When I got to Alabama I started out teaching Marketing 53 [the basic marketing principles course, now MKT 300] and the basic advertising course. No one wanted to teach the sales course, so I took it on.

About four years later, Bill Bennett established his Sales Laboratory, which gained national repute and began a long academic career in salesmanship for Bennett.

During his long tenure at Alabama, Bennett not only taught salesmanship and other marketing courses, he served as director of the Graduate Division (1963–71) with Dean Paul Garner and then as associate dean under Jack Fielden. In the last phase of his career, he became the champion of international business. In recognition of his contributions to the field, the Bill Bennett International Trade Center was dedicated at his retirement in 1983.

Bennett admits that he originally came to the University of Alabama as a faculty member because he was a native Alabamian and wanted to get back to his roots. No one, particularly Bill Bennett, would have predicted such a productive and satisfactory career.

The following words from a professor of the era are unusual because the words are those of an author of this history. I, *Morris L. Mayer*, apologize for including myself, but I hope that after reading my comments, you will understand why I did.

Like Bill Bennett, I am a native Alabamian, born in Demopolis in 1925 into a retail family that owned a department store, Mayer Brothers. The "brothers" were my grandfather, Morris, and his two brothers, all of whom were German Jewish émigrés. My grandfather, the oldest, arrived in the United States shortly after the Civil War. The story of how he got to Gainesville, Alabama, is typical of many of that time—a relative or friend from "the old country" served as "sponsor." In my grandfather's case, a fourteen-year-old boy worked as a peddler en route from New York to the sponsor's home (which happened to be Uniontown, Alabama) and arrived with enough money to start a business. My grandfather studied the area and decided that being on a river was critically important, so he decided to start his store in Gainesville on the Tombigbee River. After several successful years, he was able to bring his brothers (and later a sister) to Gainesville to work with him in the store.

A fire destroyed the store, and the brothers thought that if being on one river was good, being on two would be better. So the Mayer brothers left Gainesville for Demopolis at the confluence of the Tombigbee and Black Warrior rivers.

The store flourished and by the time of my birth was being run by my father, Lehman (who attended the University of Alabama and studied under Dean Bidgood following service in World War I), and his two brothers-in-law. I was enchanted with the store and decided early on that someday I would certainly be the Merchant Prince of West Alabama.

My princedom was not to be. Mayer Brothers survived the depression, but failed in 1939. A major category of merchandise was a wholesale grocery department that catered to the business and personal needs of local farmers. A common operating procedure of the time was "advancing." Merchants granted credit in advance of the harvest period, expecting to be paid when the crops were in. Although they didn't know the term cash flow in the thirties, after a couple of poor harvests and no payment, Mayer Brothers was doomed by negative cash flow.

I survived. I served in World War II, got a bachelor's in business administration from C&BA, a master's in retailing from New York University, and found myself in Chicago as a buyer for a regional department store chain. In the summer of 1955 Prof. Harry Bonham called me and told me that Prof. Ed Austin was going on a Fulbright to India. Could I come to Alabama and teach Mr. Austin's courses? (I had been Ed Austin's grader as an undergraduate.) How could I turn down my mentor? I accepted his offer, taught during the academic year 1955–56, went to Ohio State (at Mr. Bonham's urging) for four years and received a doctorate, returned to Alabama in 1960, and retired in 1992 after a career that I enjoyed more than I can express.

I am in the unique position of having known all the shapers and builders of our culture while a student in the 1940s and a teacher in the mid-fifties. I have known all our deans—Bidgood, Garner, Fielden, Mitchell, Petersen, and Mason. I have known virtually every faculty member who has taught in our college. I feel fortunate and very proud that most of my working life has been spent at the University of Alabama.

people who worked there. Dr. [John] Gallalee was president, and when they had those budget meetings Dean Bidgood would fight for his faculty. He would never back down, and he got what he asked for."

When Dean Bidgood was asked to serve as interim president following Dr. Gallalee's retirement in the summer of 1953, Warren accompanied him on his new assignment. "It was in July and August that we were there," she said. "Mary Emily Keaton had been Dr. Gallalee's secretary. She had one of those little student desks (you know, with the lower part in the middle), a manual typewriter, and a straight chair. I said to Dean Bidgood, 'Look at this. I haven't typed on a manual typewriter since I was in high school, and I can't sit in this chair.' I had a really nice desk, an electric typewriter, and a comfortable chair over in the [Commerce School]. So he said, 'Well, bring your typewriter and chair, and we'll get you a desk.' And that's what he did.

"I knew [Bidgood's presidency] was going to be temporary, but I never thought about what I would do after that. The University [named him president] as a courtesy to him, I believe. He was so highly regarded and well thought of. They wanted to recognize him in that way because he just had another year [left to work]. He was sixty-nine when we moved over there."

As anyone who knew Dean Bidgood well could testify, he was not the type of person to hold a position, even a temporary one, without leaving his mark on it. Warren recalled one change the dean made in the president's office. "While he was dean of Commerce, sometimes in the morning he would say, 'Miss Warren, would you take this over to Dr. Gallalee?' The first time I did it, I went over, [and], well, the door to the president's office was locked. So I went across the hall to Billy Adams's office and I said, 'Dean Adams, I have something for

Dr. Gallalee. Would you mind if I used your phone to call?' So I called over there, and Mary Emily said, 'We'll open the door at ten o'clock.' I went back and said to Dean Bidgood, 'I couldn't get in. I'll have to go back.' That happened several times. I would go over at 10:00, the door would be locked again, I would call, and Mary Emily would say, 'We'll open the door at 11:00.' So, Dean Bidgood didn't say a word about that, but when we moved over there he had that beautiful wooden door removed and another door put up with a glass [window] in it.

"He had that door put up with glass, and we had a shade to pull down that said the lunch hour is 12:00 to whatever the time was. So it looked like a grocery store. But he told me, 'I want people to know that the president's office is open and they are welcome to come in at any time.'"

After Oliver Carmichael became University president in September 1953, Dean Bidgood asked him whether he intended to hire a new secretary. Dr. Carmichael replied, "No, I don't, but Miss Warren looks awfully young." Warren was somewhat taken aback by the comment, she recalled. "I was twenty-six years old and had been working for eight years, so I thought I was a grown-up person." Despite President Carmichael's comment, Warren stayed on as his secretary and found him to be a "marvelous" person to work for. Dean Bidgood was also pleased that she remained with President Carmichael. "You know," he confessed to her at one time, "leaving you in the president's office is the best thing I've ever done."

From time to time, her former boss would stop by to chat, "if he was in a good mood." He would often give her advice. "He told me one time that I should paint my bedroom green because that was a soothing color to wake up to. Another time he told me that he was worried about me because I was so frail. He told me I should eat

Growth and Transition

C&BA found itself in an enviable position in the early years of the decade. With the crush of World War II veterans now over, the school enjoyed a much more favorable student-to-faculty ratio. According to the *University of Alabama Business News* for August 15, 1952, "For the past two years our ratio of teachers to students has been highly satisfactory, and it will be even better next year. The individual student is receiving more attention than in any previous session other than the war years 1943–45. Few schools of business have so large a faculty in proportion to student enrollment."

Although the enrollment in the decade was more stable, C&BA underwent one of its most significant changes during the period, one that everyone realized would inevitably occur. Dean Bidgood would have to retire by 1954 at the latest, when he would reach the mandatory retirement age of seventy. The impending retirement of the only dean the school had ever known led many to consider how best to honor Bidgood's thirty-five years of service to C&BA and to assess his impact on the development of collegiate business education in the state.

Bidgood Hall

In late 1949 the Commerce Association proposed one means of honoring the dean's meritorious service to his school and University. On October 10, Melvin Weber, the association's president, wrote to the University's Board of Trustees:

"The Commerce Association of the University of Alabama, by and through its duly authorized Executive Council, does hereby respectfully petition you, subject to approval by the State Legislature, to name the present Commerce Building on the campus of the University 'Bidgood Hall' in honor of Dr. Lee Bidgood, who, for the past thirty years, has served this institution with outstanding ability, loyalty, and devotion as dean of the School of Commerce and Business Administration."

The Commerce Association petition had widespread support among alumni of the school as well as others who recognized the many positive contributions Dean Bidgood had made over the years to the cause of business education both within the state and the nation. By early 1950 newspapers in the area began carrying stories about the movement to have the Commerce Building named after C&BA's founding dean. *The Tuscaloosa News* reported in its January 20, 1950, edition: "The trustees have approved the petition, but final action will be left to the next session of the state legislature since a public building cannot be named after a living person except through a joint resolution by the legislature." At the Commerce Day ceremonies held in January 1950, the addition to and the naming of the Commerce Building were announced.

Former C&BA students seemed thrilled about the idea of naming the building after their dean. Doris and Robert Morrow wrote Bidgood on January 21: "Bob and I (both '42) count as the high point among our courses the War Economics class we had with you in the spring of 1942. Along with all Commerce alumni—but largely as a result of that course—we have the highest regard for you. It was, therefore, especially pleasant for us to read in the *Birmingham News* yesterday of the contemplated change of the Commerce

Building's name. It has our heartiest approval and is, as a matter of fact, long overdue."

A. C. Silverman echoed the Morrows's sentiments in his January 24 letter. "I was thrilled with the announcement that the Commerce Building at the University of Alabama was to be named for you," he wrote.

> Surely there is so much of you in it already that it was only logical that such public recognition be made.
>
> As you well know, the passing years tend to further mellow my feeling toward the University and particularly the Commerce School, and it is inevitable that those thoughts always embody some pleasant memory concerning you.
>
> May I wish for you and yours a continuation of the happiness that must come from such a well-earned recognition.

References to Lee Bidgood Hall in the University catalogs, letters, and other materials published soon after the Commerce Day announcement suggest that many people would think of the building as Bidgood Hall regardless of whether the legislature approved the name change. The official dedication of the Commerce Building as Lee Bidgood Hall took place February 15, 1952, during the Commerce Day celebration. The January 15 *Crimson White* previewed the upcoming festivities for its readers: "Plans for the day, which will also commemorate the 32nd anniversary of the School of Commerce, include a luncheon, [the] dedication of Bidgood Hall, and a dance in Foster [Auditorium]. Outstanding business and industrial leaders from the state have been invited to attend the ceremonies."

The February 12 issue of the college newspaper gave additional information about the events planned for Commerce Day. Arthur V. Wiebel, president of the TCI division of United States Steel Company, was scheduled to speak at 11:30 in Foster Auditorium. At 2:45, the dedication of the Commerce Building would take place, with University president John M. Gallalee officiating.

Accounts of the actual dedication appeared in the February 19 *Crimson White* and the February 16 *Tuscaloosa News*. According to the *News* account, Gallalee told those assembled, "The University does great honor to itself in naming this building Lee Bidgood Hall." Bidgood, "greatly embarrassed" by the proceedings, remarked, "Buildings are only as useful as the people in them. May truth be taught in this building and [may] that truth make our children free." The *Crimson White* reported that President Gallalee's address "was the story of Dean Lee Bidgood's life and his work for the University. Dean Bidgood made a formal acceptance, saying, 'The school is no more than the students in it.'"

Dean Bidgood's Achievements

As alumni and friends of the Commerce School realized that Dean Bidgood would soon have to step down from his position, many praised the dean who had played a leading role in establishing a nationally recognized program of collegiate education for business in Alabama. Brewer Dixon wrote on September 4, 1950, to Dean James H. Newman, University dean of administration: "This School of Commerce as we all know ranks among the very first in the land, and the members of the University Board and the entire alumni

oatmeal for breakfast every morning."

Warren called to mind other details about the dean's personality as she looked back on her years with him. Bidgood often relied upon the counsel of Prof. Harry D. Bonham, and Professors Chapman and Knight were two of his "favorites." She considered the dean a southern gentleman of the old school who walked to and from work each day, never failing to tip his hat to each woman he met on his way. She remembered with some sadness that C&BA was such an integral part of the dean's adult life that he really did not want to retire in 1954.

"I was devoted to Dean Bidgood and enjoyed working for him," Warren concluded. Apparently she found working for other University leaders generally agreeable as well; except for one brief intermission, she worked for University presidents until 1980.

are justly proud of it. As we all know, Dean Bidgood is one of the truly great educators of our time, and already the graduates of his School of Commerce have left their imprint on the business and economic life not only of this country but elsewhere in the world."

G. P. Brock, vice-president and general manager of the Gulf, Mobile, and Ohio Railroad Company, offered a brief character sketch of the dean while commending him for his achievements. On September 19, 1950, he wrote to Bidgood:

> I have read every word and figure several times [in the C&BA progress report Bidgood had sent him]. I think it characterizes the man—the man who built the University's School of Commerce and Business Administration. It is modest and a little short of wonderful, and while the quantity is there, and bespeaks of itself, the quality aspect is forceful.
>
> Your quiet determination to do well whatever you do is showing up in production, income, and happiness all over the State.
>
> The method you have of keeping in touch with the alumni will not only help the school, but will continue to make it less difficult for John Gallalee to make the work of both of you more effective.

Bidgood himself seemed to be in a mood to review the progress of the Commerce School. Typically, he gave much of the credit for the school's growth and development to its students. In an August 25, 1950, letter to Mortimer A. Cohen (Class of 1922), he wrote:

> We would never have made any headway at all with the School of Commerce and Business Administration if the first few crops of graduates had not averaged well and included some outstanding men. You did not have the opportunity that the young people have now. But you learned something anyway. The idea of what constitutes a good education in the business administration field has changed and advanced a lot all over the country. Accrediting standards have advanced enormously since I have been in contact with them.
>
> Due largely to the fact that we were turning out a good product with little or nothing other than capable young minds to work with, we have been able to grow gradually and steadily through the years. What our people should realize is that this school has advanced its relative position enormously.
>
> We watch very closely what other institutions are doing, especially in new ideas in teaching techniques. No catalogue of a business school goes over my desk without being carefully analyzed, especially as to faculty. The big difference between the situation now and 25 years ago, though, is that our school at present is itself so extensively used as a standard of comparison, even more in the north than in the south.

Bidgood identified another strength of the Commerce School that had helped it prosper over the years. In an October 1, 1951, letter to Mervyn Sterne, prominent Birmingham banker and investor, Bidgood explained what the guiding philosophy of the Commerce School had been during his tenure:

> Through the years, our emphasis has been mainly on the fundamentals, and so far as there has been any shift in the last two decades, the shift has also been in that direction. One good and sufficient reason is that three questionnaires,

sent out several years apart to our alumni, have developed the fact that within two years after graduation a majority of the graduates are not working in the field in which they majored. . . . These facts indicate to us that we should give a thin specialization, on the undergraduate level, and devote the great bulk of the student's time to the fundamentals that we call the "core" courses. In the last few years, this has become the official policy of . . . the [AACSB]. Our school and the Harvard Business School, so unlike in other respects, were perhaps the principal pioneers in this development. When the [AACSB] adopted as one of its standards of membership the principle that every student in every member school should receive instruction in accounting, business law, business statistics, economics, finance, management, and marketing, we had for a number of years organized our school so that each of these seven fields was served by a distinct department, and every student had to take one or more courses in each of these departments.

Bidgood pointed out that the advice of business people had also guided the practice of the school. Businesses could teach their employees any procedures peculiar to their affairs, Bidgood said. They needed collegiate business school graduates with firm foundations in the fundamentals and principles of a subject. Bidgood admitted, however, that more specialized and "semi-vocational" courses were offered in the University's extension centers.

The New Addition to the Commerce Building

President Gallalee's 1950 Commerce Day announcement that an addition to the Commerce Building was in the planning stages must have greatly pleased Bidgood. The new addition was something Dean Bidgood had been calling for since 1946, when the postwar enrollment boom strained the school's physical facilities, and now he would witness the completion of the structure while still serving as C&BA dean.

This new addition caused almost as much excitement as the construction of the original building had. The October 17, 1950, *Crimson White* carried a front-page photograph of the work in progress. The newspaper quoted Dean Bidgood as saying, "We won't need Smith Woods." In Bidgood's words, the two separate additions under construction would complete the original floor plan of the structure and make the building "look like an H with two crossbars in the center."

By the summer of 1951 construction was well underway on the new addition. Bidgood wrote to Mr. James C. Ingram in June of that year: "The two additions to the building are well along and completion is hoped for by September 1. The addition on the north side will increase our business library stackroom by about 150 percent and give us about 30 carrels for graduate students. The southwestern addition will increase our laboratory and classroom space by about two-thirds, and double the number of available offices. We will have one of the largest and best-appointed commerce buildings in the country when the work is completed."

Local news media provided more details about the expansion. According to a June 27 article in the *Birmingham News,* "When the new four-floor wing of Lee Bidgood Hall is completed at the University of Alabama, the School of Commerce and Business Administration will have a building and facilities worth

the building of large electronic computers and were using them for scientific and mathematical applications. The UA professors noted, however, that the leading business schools were "doing nothing" in the way of offering credit courses in EDP.

Dean Garner (who had become dean upon Bidgood's retirement) and Dr. Chapman encouraged Professor Moore to develop an introductory course in EDP that would be of interest not only to students in C&BA but also to other University students, especially those in engineering and mathematics. All these men recognized the great potential for electronic computers in business and the need to introduce business students to this developing field.

The new course was offered in the spring of 1957 and generated substantial interest and enthusiasm among students. Although the University did not acquire a computer (the Univac Solid State 80) until three years later, teaching the principles of EDP, programming, and applications proved feasible. The course was designed to remove some of the mystery from these "giant brains" and to emphasize the important role of intelligent, educated human beings in managing and controlling these man-made wonders.

more than $1,000,000 at today's prices, according to the office of Prof. Fred R. Maxwell, university consulting engineer.

"The addition will cost approximately $313,000. Completion is expected in November. An additional 36,032 square feet of space will be added to the existing 61,882 square feet, according to figures compiled by Dr. Burton R. Morley, professor of management and director of the Bureau of Personnel and Placement."

The new addition was completed in the fall of 1951, and Dean Bidgood was no doubt gratified that the Commerce Building had been completed as its designers had intended while he still led the school.

Expanded Academic Offerings: The Ph.D.

The post–World War II enrollment boom led to an increased emphasis on graduate education by most University divisions, including C&BA. Yet, not one of the GIs who attended the University in the immediate postwar period could earn a Ph.D. in any subject. That situation changed in the early 1950s. On June 5, 1950, President Gallalee reported to the University Board of Trustees that work leading to the Ph.D. would be offered in the next school year "in a limited number of departments." The departments he specified were Arts and Sciences, Chemistry, Commerce, and Education, with an Ed.D. degree also being given in education. Once again, Bidgood was fortunate enough to witness a milestone in the history of his school and University while serving as dean.

In a June 18, 1951, letter to Mr. James C. Ingram in Bangkok, Thailand, Bidgood wrote, "The Ph.D. work seems to be getting off to a pretty good start. We don't have many students, but they are rather strong people, holding rank in their respective institutions up to that of associate professor."

One of these strong C&BA Ph.D. candidates was Catherine E. Miles, who would make University history as the first woman to earn a doctorate from the institution (in August 1953). Her dissertation was entitled "Wartime 'Twilight' Reserves in Industrial Accounting: Their Background and Use."

New Student Organizations

The Propeller Club

Several organizations devoted to specialized areas of business study were formed during the early years of the decade. In the spring of 1950, a chapter of the Propeller Club was formed for those students interested in the maritime transportation industry. According to Bidgood's 1949–50 annual report to the president, the Propeller Club was a "national organization of ocean-shipping executives with student 'harbors' in universities that offer instruction in water transportation."

Soon after its establishment, members participated in an educational trip to Mobile that was regarded as a success by all concerned. Bidgood wrote to Mr. W. H. Hagan, manager of the Lykes Brothers Steamship Company, on May 9, 1950: "Dr. Constantin has just been telling me about the pleasant and profitable trip which the members of our local Propeller Club made to Mobile. . . . Without direct, continued contacts with steamship and port officials, I do not think that we can succeed very well with our venture into the field of water transportation. . . . I hope you can be in Tuscaloosa on Monday, May 22, when we have our next convocation of the school . . . and when our local Propeller Club hopes to receive its charter."

Officials in the shipping industry welcomed the organization and wished it well. James E. May, commercial representative of the Alabama Dry Dock and Shipbuilding Company, wrote to Dean Bidgood on May 19, 1950: "Please believe me it was a real pleasure for members of the Propeller Club of the Port of Mobile to receive Dr. Constantin, Dr. Whitman, and the fine group of young men they brought here for a tour of our port. . . .

"We congratulate you . . . and your worthy faculty members for this type of extracurricular work. It is our hope that the Propeller Club of the Port of the University of Alabama will become a virile activity in your school."

Chi Alpha Phi

In the spring of 1951, a group of business statistics students in the Commerce School created Chi Alpha Phi. The group wanted "to bring together in one body students, faculty members, and others who are interested in the application of statistical methods in the various fields of social and physical sciences, and to serve the University by undertaking feasible projects, within the realm of statistics, that may be requested by the faculty, administration, or the Student Government Association."

A New Director for the Bureau of Business Research

The following announcement, made in 1951, introduced the University community to the new director of the Bureau and acknowledged the accomplishments of outgoing director H. H. Chapman:

> Mr. Henry B. Moore became director of the Bureau of Business Research, replacing Dr. H. H. Chapman. . . . This change is an event of considerable importance both in the economic history and in the educational history of Alabama.
>
> Dr. Herman Hollis Chapman was the first director of the Bureau of Business Research and held that position for 21 years, 1930–51. He planned the scope of the Bureau's work, defined its aims, developed its techniques, gathered its staff, led it, and directly performed a large part of its work. When he undertook to organize the Bureau, he was professor of accounting and statistics and head of that department. A few years later, his work was made somewhat more manageable by dividing the combined department into a department of accounting and one of business statistics. Dr. Chapman stayed with statistics.
>
> As the work of both the research organization and the instructional department grew in magnitude, the task of heading the two became steadily more burdensome. . . . A decision was made to [have] a new person take over the directorship. A search . . . covering a period of more than six months, resulted in the selection of Henry B. Moore. . . .
>
> Mr. Moore is a native of Kentucky, a graduate of the University of Kentucky and of the Harvard Business School. He has taught at the University of Georgia, the Carnegie Institute of Technology, and as an evening lecturer at George Washington University and at Southern Methodist University. His last

exclusively teaching assignment was as associate professor in the University of Kentucky, 1937–42.

Mr. Moore's contacts with business have always been close, and his personal experience in business has been considerable. He was assistant manager of the Garrard Mills, Lancaster, Kentucky, from 1926–28, statistician of the Technical Market Service, Detroit, Michigan, in 1931, and director of research of Braniff Airways [in] Dallas, Texas, 1943–45. He has had extensive experience as a business consultant.

In the field of government, Mr. Moore served from 1934 to 1937 as Assistant Chief of the Marketing Research Division in the Bureau of Foreign and Domestic Commerce in the United States Department of Commerce. In 1942–43, he was Principal Industrial Economist in charge of the field offices in the United States Department of Labor Statistics. He is the author of a number of research bulletins and monographs.

From 1946 until he resigned to come to Alabama, Mr. Moore was director of the Bureau of Business Research of the University of Colorado. Concurrently he held the rank of professor in the faculty of that university. His work in Colorado has attracted favorable attention among persons interested in business research in many parts of the nation. . . .

In his two decades of directing the Bureau, Dr. Chapman [did] not merely maintain a service, [he also] created an institution of importance in the economic and intellectual life of the state. At the same time, he developed one of the most important departments of business statistics in the United States. Now he will be able to concentrate on his work for that department, and on his personal research and writing. The appointment of Mr. Moore to the directorship of the Bureau of Business Research . . . is a guarantee that the work of the Bureau will continue to go forward.

The Alabama Business Research Council

In his annual report to the University's president for the 1952–53 academic year, Bidgood described a new C&BA research endeavor. The Alabama Business Research Council was formed in 1953 with the help of a joint grant from the Committee for Economic Development and the Fund for Adult Education. Forty-four business executives representing twenty-three of Alabama's leading business concerns and seven representatives from the faculty of the school composed the council. It was divided into two committees: the Business Executives' Advisory Committee, made up of the chief executives of twenty-one leading Alabama business concerns, and the Business Executives' Research Committee, composed of other executives from the twenty-one firms as well as representatives from two additional firms. The Council cooperated closely with the Alabama Department of Industrial Relations.

The C&BA self-study report published in 1963 provided additional details about the Council and its goals:

> In the early years of this Council, financial aid was furnished by the Committee for Economic Development and the Ford Foundation. Beginning in 1960 Alabama business firms became the sole sponsors of the Council. The objectives of the Alabama Business Research Council [include]: [developing] effective ways in which a work and research team can bring together, through cooperating studies, facts and materials which will be useful in formulating policies bearing on the solution of economic problems; [maintaining] a research group which will

conduct studies and report on problems which affect the economy of the region; [developing and encouraging] a closer relationship between faculty and staff members of the University and business leaders over the State; and [learning] how a group of this type can help to increase public understanding of the economy in which we live.

The 1963 self-study report gave a summary of the research the Council had generated over its first decade of existence. "In carrying out the objectives of the Council, six research studies have been published thus far and a seventh one is [almost] complete. These studies have been widely used throughout the region. Fifteen faculty members have obtained much research experience in connection with the preparation of the published reports of the Council. In summary, it is believed that this is one of the most fruitful research efforts of the school during its forty-five years of existence."

Former dean Paul Garner also recalled details about the Council.

> *For a while it operated ad hoc, with the assistance of Dr. Chapman, his staff, business people, and some faculty members. The business people were highly involved in it—Alabama Power Company in particular. They agreed to pay a certain amount of dues and support funds for clerical assistance. Graduate students worked with [the Council as well]. As I remember, they had some doctoral candidates working for them, too. They published several small books about their findings and recommendations. . . . A lot of enthusiasm was developed [for it]. After Dean Bidgood retired, they invited him to join the Council as its Executive Director. [When I became dean] I met with them from time to time as I was able. It was a very worthwhile endeavor and lasted for several years.*

C&BA "Sales Laboratory" Makes National News

The June 1954 *NSE* [National Sales Executives] *News* carried a story headlined "NSE to Aid in Setting Up Sales Labs Using U. of Alabama Course as Model." The accompanying article gave a brief history of the program's development. According to the article, "The Alabama course, which began with the modest title of 'Economics 19' in 1922, has mushroomed into an entire area of study covering 18 semester hours and including such subjects as salesmanship, advanced selling, sales management, advertising, and marketing research."

A description of how the laboratory operated followed: "The Alabama program goes beyond the normal classroom discussion of the principles of selling. It attempts to give the student practical work in actual sales presentations. These classroom presentations are recorded on a tape or wire. Later they are played back to the student at a critique period where shortcomings and techniques are corrected and discussed. To this is added training in the preparation of sales manuals and in the use of materials in the sales laboratory such as sound slides, sales films, manuals, bulletins and advertising portfolios, and other modern sales training devices."

Dr. William R. Bennett, who taught the sales course, assessed the benefits of the course and associated laboratory work: "The student who participates will have some grasp of the basic techniques of business, which consist of all marketing courses and related subjects [such] as accounting, statistics, economics, and research methods. This does not imply that the student whose primary interest is in selling will be a certified public accountant, a qualified statistician, a professional economist, or researcher. But he will be aware of these areas and their relationship to distribution."

Dr. Harry Bonham, head of the marketing department, under whose control the program operated, said that the program had been developed in close cooperation with the Birmingham Sales Executive Club. The national recognition accorded this program provided convincing evidence that C&BA was on the cutting edge of developments in the field of marketing.

Bidgood Retires

Lee Bidgood stepped down as C&BA dean on June 30, 1954, after having held the position for thirty-five years. He had started teaching class in rooms for which no other use could be found; upon the dean's retirement, the school possessed one of the Southeast's finest buildings devoted to the study of business. In the early days, faculty members who would remain at the school were few and far between; by 1954 many faculty members had national reputations or were well on the way toward earning them. The school had started out offering a generalized course of study in business; by 1954 a student could choose to pursue degrees, including the Ph.D., in most of the major fields of business. Dean Bidgood had led C&BA through the Great Depression, World War II and its stressful aftermath, and the Korean Conflict. Through all these adversities, the school continued to produce a loyal group of well-trained graduates, many of whom went on to successful business careers in Alabama, the nation, and the world.

In his final report to the president as C&BA dean, Bidgood mentioned another noteworthy accomplishment of the school. Historically, collegiate business education departments suffered from high faculty turnover rates. Dean Bidgood pointed out that from 1919 until 1954, the school had lost only three faculty members who held the rank of full professor: Carroll R. Daugherty had resigned in 1931, and L. J. Nations and Chester Knight had died in 1949. Bidgood continued, "With the retirement on June 30, 1954, of the writer of this report, the number becomes four. In view of the many news stories, magazine articles, speeches, reports, and books that have been written about the loss of the South's top teaching talent to other parts of the country, the success of this school in retaining its highest-ranking teachers is worthy of some attention."

All these accomplishments and many others required team effort, and C&BA was fortunate to have Lee Bidgood as the leader of its team for so many years.

S. Paul Garner Named Dean

C&BA was also fortunate to find a worthy successor to Dean Bidgood already among its ranks. Following Lee Bidgood's retirement, Dr. S. Paul Garner became the second C&BA dean.

Dr. Garner had become an indispensable asset to the C&BA faculty since joining it in 1939. He had helped the World War II effort through his service to both the ESMWT program and to the Office of Price Administration in Montgomery. He had participated in the Federal Tax Clinics started in 1947 by the Alabama Society of Certified Public Accountants and C&BA. Following

Professor Knight's untimely death, he was appointed chairman of the accounting department, a post in which he served until 1954.

In addition to these achievements, Dr. Garner had been elected to a one-year term as president of the ten-thousand-member American Accounting Association in September 1950. According to the *Birmingham Post-Herald* of September 22, Dr. Garner was only the second person from the Southeast to be elected to the office in thirty-two years. The same article mentioned that Dr. Garner was also the secretary-treasurer of the Alabama Society of Certified Public Accountants and a member of the American Institute of Accountants. Dr. Garner had served as a member of the Standard Ratings Committee of the American Accounting Association and as editor for the teachers' clinic of the *Accounting Review*. In addition, he was a member of Beta Gamma Sigma, Phi Beta Kappa, Alpha Kappa Psi, Beta Alpha Psi, and Omicron Delta Kappa.

The new dean brought a keen interest in other countries and cultures, which had been piqued by his sixth-grade geography teacher. In 1932, with his newly earned bachelor's in economics (with minors in languages and physics) from Duke University, Paul Garner had taken five hundred dollars in savings and treated himself to a European trip. By 1954 he had expanded his national and international contacts considerably. The July 6, 1954, *Crimson White* article announcing his appointment as dean described him as "a man who has travelled widely, visiting over 250 colleges and universities in all 48 states, Canada, Mexico City, and Europe, studying administrative and educational problems." The former dean has continued to travel, and by 1994 had compiled a list of over five thousand friends in more than 125 countries. Because of his wide contacts, many refer to him as the University's unofficial "Ambassador to the World."

Dr. Garner had already established himself as a prominent scholar in his field before he became C&BA dean. As the *Crimson White* article noted: "He is the author of several accounting books widely used in American universities. This spring, notice came that a work on cost accounting that he coauthored with Prof. Newlove of the U. of Texas had been translated into Spanish and was being circulated in Latin America and Spain." Over the next few decades, Dean Garner would author or coauthor nine textbooks and write more than fifty articles that would appear in more than forty-nine professional journals in twelve languages. His revised dissertation, *The Evolution of Cost Accounting to 1925* (first published in 1954), was translated into Japanese and Chinese, and in 1991 was cited as a significant milestone in international accounting literature.

Dr. Garner had also distinguished himself through service to his local community. He had acted as an adviser to the City of Tuscaloosa on financial and fiscal affairs for several years. He was on the Board of Deacons of the First Baptist Church and for two years served as adviser to the Baptist Student Union at the University. He would eventually serve on the boards of four local businesses, something he would urge his faculty members to do so that they might acquire working experience in the business world.

As dean, Dr. Garner emphasized graduate studies, especially the new doctoral program. He also worked to develop the global dimensions of business education, a task for which his growing network of international contacts had well prepared him. Dean Garner's successes in these two areas of endeavor were especially gratifying to him.

The former dean commented on other pleasures he had had during his career.

> *Another positive experience has been observing the successes of hundreds of students that were in my classes, and those that I observed during my years as dean of C&BA. The implied dividend from this has been heartwarming. . . . It has also been a source of great satisfaction that the physical facilities of the college have been greatly expanded [and are now] second to none in the southland.*
>
> *I feel most fortunate that I have been allotted a time span [to serve] more than two-thirds of the entire life of C&BA. While many of my colleagues who came with me at the time that I was initially employed, and in later years, have regretfully been lost through untimely deaths, I have found my relationships over the two and one-half score of years to be satisfying and heartwarming. I am grateful for this opportunity to assist many young people in their career [and] educational objectives, and I look forward to continuing these efforts in the years ahead.*

The 1950s saw continued development of C&BA physical facilities, academic offerings, and student organizations. Under the leadership of Dean Paul Garner, the odds were in favor of continued growth and development. A talented and well-qualified leader would be essential, for soon after Dean Garner assumed office, two important assessments of collegiate business education touched off a debate about whether collegiate schools of business were adequately preparing their graduates for business careers. The debate, occasioned by *The Education of American Businessmen* (Frank C. Pierson et al.) and *Higher Education for Business* (Robert A. Gordon and James E. Howell), hinted that the 1960s would be a decade of change for collegiate business education. In a sense, the debate that surrounded these two studies foreshadowed the turbulent events that would rock the nation in the coming decade. Dean Paul Garner and the school would maintain a relatively steady course despite the societal disruptions surrounding them.

Aerial photo of Bidgood Hall showing 1951 addition.

The University's presidents:

Frank A. Rose (1958–69)
David Mathews (1969–80)

The world is talking about:

Forty-three-year-old John F. Kennedy is elected president, the first Roman Catholic and the youngest man ever elected. (November 8, 1960)

President Kennedy creates the Peace Corps. (March 1, 1961)

A five-foot-high wall is erected between East and West Berlin by the Communist regime in East Germany. (August 1961)

In a 6-to-1 decision based on the First Amendment, the Supreme Court rules that the reciting of an official prayer in New York State public schools is unconstitutional. (June 25, 1962)

Alabama's governor George Wallace defies a presidential order to allow registration of two black students at the University of Alabama. Kennedy federalizes the Alabama National Guard and Wallace steps aside from his position in front of Foster Auditorium. (June 11, 1963)

Martin Luther King delivers his "I have a dream" speech at the Lincoln Memorial in Washington, D.C. (August 28, 1963)

The "hot line," a direct communications link between Moscow and Washington, becomes operational. (August 30, 1963)

Pres. John Kennedy is fatally wounded in Dallas by assassin Lee Harvey Oswald. (November 22, 1963)

President Johnson signs the Civil Rights Act of 1964, banning racial and religious discrimination in many spheres, including public accommodations. (July 2, 1964)

The advent of a new fashion craze begins in London: the miniskirt. (1965)

The five-day Selma-to-Montgomery civil rights march begins. (March 21, 1965)

A series of nationwide anti–Vietnam War demonstrations begin in California with a march of ten thousand people from Berkeley to the Oakland army base. (October 1965)

Martin Luther King Jr., Nobel Prize-winner and nonviolent civil rights activist, is assassinated in Memphis, Tennessee. (April 4, 1968)

Sen. Robert F. Kennedy, campaigning for the Democratic presidential nomination, is fatally wounded after a campaign speech in Los Angeles. (June 5, 1968)

Richard M. Nixon is elected president. (November 5, 1968)

Astronaut Neil Armstrong, commander of the Apollo II mission, becomes the first man to set foot on the moon, declaring it "one small step for [a] man, one giant leap for mankind." (July 20, 1969)

A three-day rock concert is held at a farm in Bethel, New York. It will become known simply as Woodstock. (August 1969)

The University is talking about:

Pug's, a favorite college hangout for nearly forty years, closes.

Students are politically and socially motivated. Controversy is common.

In an era of dramatic campus growth, new buildings include Rose Administration, Tutwiler Hall, a seven-story addition to the Amelia Gayle Gorgas Library, Tommye Rose Towers (named in honor of President Rose's wife), the student health center (later named Russell Student Health Center in honor of a University trustee and his wife), Gordon Palmer Hall (named for a University trustee), Memorial Coliseum (later named for C&BA alumnus Jeff Coleman), ten Hoor Hall (named for long-time A&S dean), Mary Burke (named for a dean of women) and Martha Parham (named for a long-time member of the housing staff), Paty Hall (named for President Paty), and Paul W. Bryant Athletic Residence Hall.

Little Bohemia (Little Bo), a snack bar on the ground floor of Woods Hall, remains popular well into the decade.

On June 11, 1963, two black students, Vivian J. Malone and James A. Hood, enroll at the University of Alabama. Vivian Malone receives her degree from C&BA in 1965.

Chapter 5

Building and Enhancing a Reputation: The Sixties

The Garner Era Continues

Faculty "enhancers" of the C&BA culture:

Eric Baklanoff (1969)
A. Lee Cobb (1964)
John S. Evans (1968)
Hazel F. "Toppy" Ezell (1969)
    (hired as temporary instructor)
Albert E. Drake (1966)
Mary Fish (1966)
W. Baker Flowers (1963)
Robert J. Freeman (1965)
William Gunther (1968)
Charles Leathers (1968)
Betty Loomis (1966)
J. Barry Mason (1967)
John Mason (1968)
Joseph Mellichamp (1969)
John Moeller (1966)[*]
Charles Thomas Moore (1962)[*]
Thomas D. Moore (1965)
J. Donald Phillips (1965)
Frank E. Ryerson (1962)
Edward M. Smith (1964)
Allan Spritzer (1968)
A. J. Strickland III (1969)
Robert B. Sweeney (1960)
Arthur Thompson (1967)
J. F. Vallery Jr. (1966)

(*Note:* This list includes only faculty members who remained with C&BA at least ten years.)

[*] Deceased as of 1994

In Their Own Words

Students

Starting in 1962, *Hazel F. "Toppy" Ezell* began a relationship with Alabama and C&BA that has spanned more than three decades and three degrees (B.S., M.A., and Ph.D.), and an enviable role as teacher of thousands of students. She says that her life literally began on the University of Alabama campus, as she was born in the old Druid City Hospital, which was then on the site where the Russell Student Health Center is today.

In thinking about the early 1960s, Ezell said:

> *I had a strong interest in business because of my father (a local businessman), but at that point in time when a woman thought about opportunities in business she aspired to be an executive secretary. You didn't think about being a manager. So I entered the secretarial administration program.*
>
> *We had to take practically the same courses that a lot of the general business students took with the exception of our concentration in the secretarial classes. The options for women were so limited then, that to protect myself, I took a lot of additional work in the College of Education. If I couldn't get a job as a secretary, the only other thing for a woman to do was to teach.*

Ezell married during her sophomore year, and her memories of the undergraduate years consist of going to class, working twenty to thirty hours a week, studying, keeping house, and taking care of a child.

> *Because of that schedule, I was not in as many activities as I might have liked. I was in Secretarial Science, Phi Chi Theta [women's professional organization], and National Collegiate Association for Secretaries. I think that one of the things that made receiving the Austin Cup [awarded to the outstanding senior student elected by faculty] so special for me, was that I think most of the winners in the past had been people who had [participated in a lot of extracurricular activities] on campus. I remember the award was presented at commencement in those days and the ceremony was held outside. I was so pregnant with Deana [my second child] that my doctor didn't want me to go to graduation. So Dean Garner, Mr. and Mrs. Poe [registrar of C&BA], and my family had a small private ceremony right in front of Bidgood Hall. That was kind of fun.*

Reflecting on his education at Bidgood Hall, *Mickey Gee*, who earned a B.S. in 1968 and an M.A. in 1969, wrote the following, entitled "Those Steps":

Commerce department heads, 1969: *(top to bottom)* John Gill, Business Statistics; Morris Mayer, Marketing; Langston Hawley, Management; Marcus Whitman, Finance; John Moeller, Business Law; A. J. Penz, Accounting; Dale Cramer, Economics; and Wilson Ashby, Office Administration.

College "hot buttons" during the sixties:

1960
- Options in finance are banking, transportation, public utilities; real estate is returned to the curriculum.
- Marketing now offers options.

1961
- Graduate program offers M.A., in addition to M.S.C. and M.B.A..

1963
- Graduate programs at master's level fully accredited by AACSB.

1966
- Clothing and textiles merchandising becomes an option under marketing.
- Department of Secretarial Studies is renamed Office Management.
- Social administration is no longer offered as a major.
- An M.B.A. in international business is offered.

1968
- Teacher's certification in secretarial administration is offered.
- An Educational Specialists Degree is available for students.

1969
- School of Commerce and Business Administration becomes a college (C&BA).
- Graduate School of Business is created.

Hazel F. (Toppy) Ezell receives the 1967 Austin Cup from Dean Garner as Professor Austin looks on.

I remember those steps the first day I came to Bidgood Hall. They were long and steep and seemed to go up forever. I did not know anyone, and I was sure no one wanted to know me. I picked up one foot and started up. My gait was slow and uncertain and there was no rhythm, just anxiety and one foot following the other.

I did not know that day, but a long and slow, ever-increasing process was starting. My goal was to graduate. As I, day by day, climbed those steps, I felt my footing becoming more secure. I stopped and talked. I knew people by name, not just other students making the climb. Time would pass and days would be spent standing at the bottom of those steps talking, not just talking, but making friends, creating a common bond that carries on even today.

The steps of Bidgood are worn [or were until the renovation]. They are tested in many ways and stand the wear of time. I left those steps many years ago. My goal was achieved, my gait was quicker, my rhythm more sure, but more importantly, I left my footprint for others to follow. I learned my goal was education and that I must work on that goal each day. I found I had many friends who had helped to wear those steps. These are friends who have gone before me and are yet to come. They are my fellow students and they are my teachers. They are all who have come to love and trust our University of Alabama.

Few days go by that I do not meet a person who has climbed our steps. Fewer days pass that I fail to remember my first uncertain climb and my pledge to myself that if I ever made it to the top I would help others and I would always be loyal to our university, which gave us more than a degree. It gave us friends, memories, and an everlasting desire for education. I hope those steps will always be possible to climb. As one foot follows another, so will our finest history and traditions again be worn just a little deeper into each of those steps.

Wayne Gillis began his college career in Arts and Sciences, but transferred to C&BA, which he says was the best move he ever made. When asked why he transferred, he responded:

My father-in-law had a chain of jewelry stores and wanted me to go into that business. He had no one in marketing at the time. He wanted me to head up the marketing effort.

So I went to the business school, got a degree in 1969, and went into business with him. Because of what was probably naive pride, I decided I didn't want to work for my father-in-law and I went to work as a delivery boy for the advertising agency I was working with [at the jewelry stores]. Quite frankly, my experience and the knowledge I got from accounting and marketing from the Commerce School has probably helped me more than anything in my business career. It helped me understand one thing that a lot of kids don't get out of school, and it's called cash flow. I started my own business in 1973—this is my twentieth year in business.

When asked whom he remembered from his college days, Wayne mentioned me (Morris Mayer), and "Bob Sweeney [in accounting] who could write and erase at the same time, and Barry Mason. He hasn't changed a bit as far as I'm concerned. He's doing a beautiful job [as dean]. I was very impressed to hear Barry say that you folks are bringing kids in now and teaching them something about ethics and are also teaching them how to take notes. I can't stress how important that is—how to listen and jot down the right things and how to stay

with it, all at the same time. It will follow you all through life." Wayne Gillis also stressed the importance of networking and how through the "Alabama experience" you know people of all ages and walks of life.

In 1963 *Dot Martin* graduated from C&BA with a major in Secretarial Administration. "Being a woman in Secretarial Administration [traditionally a female area] was not unusual, but if I had been in any other major, it would have been strange. We got a general business degree, and my peers in my major generally took all the same classes, even outside those in the secretarial area, so we might have had some 25 percent of my classes comprised of women."

Dot Martin remembers her senior professors—Wilson Ashby, department head; Sue Waddell; and Martha Petit. She commented that in the early 1960s it never crossed her mind that any career other than secretarial existed for women in business: "I don't think females were advised of other career opportunities except perhaps some in accounting, marketing, and management. Dr. Minnie Miles in management always encouraged women to do something different. In those days discrimination wasn't an issue for female students."

In reviewing her career, she noted that she took a secretarial position in Atlanta for three years, came back to Tuscaloosa, got a job in Academic Affairs with Alex Pow, and has been in that office ever since. In the early 1990s she was appointed assistant vice-president of Academic Affairs. She moved out of secretarial work into administrative responsibilities when Willard Grey passed away in 1973, and she worked with Charley Scott who had come to Academic Affairs from the Graduate School. He delegated budget responsibilities to her. As she assumed more responsibilities, additional business education was deemed necessary by Dr. Roger Sayers, then vice-president of Academic Affairs. In 1986 Martin was a member of the first Executive M.B.A. class at Alabama.

Tim Parker graduated in 1966. He says his fondest memories of the business school are of some very talented professors like Minnie Miles and the late Jack Menning.

> *It was a transitional time for me in terms of learning how to study and how to do things on your own, and it took me several years. I was generally the 'Gentleman C Student,' but toward the last year or two I can remember how proud I was when I had a B average one semester. But it took me halfway through my junior year to learn how to study. It was the role models I saw—the good faculty members I was exposed to as well as good students.*
>
> *It took me a while to appreciate that, but I think that was the eye-opener. It was a lot bigger world than I had grown up seeing, and [I realized] there was a lot more to learn and that life is a voyage and you should never quit learning. I have been involved in ongoing adult education programs from that day forward. In fact I'm leaving next week for Turkey for a class reunion of a course I took at the Harvard Business School. We're going to be doing a lot of sightseeing, but I'm going to be in class from eight to noon for a whole week. Getting a college degree is not the end but just the beginning.*

I am an inveterate "career watcher" of former students. If I were able to list all of them (which I'm not), and rank order them according to the most impressive career, *Jon Rotenstreich* would be at the top. It all began in 1960 when, after six months of army service, he entered the University of Alabama "as immature as any eighteen-year-old freshman could be." Then he took his first finance course, remembered how he hated the army, and suddenly knew what he didn't want to do and what he did want. During our conversation he said, "Morris, no joke, I got the book for the [corporate] finance course, started reading it, and read it from page one to the end in three days! It hit a nerve with me. And up until that point I was going into the retail furniture business."

Jon credits his teacher Harry Johnson for "turning me on to finance. He shepherded me through, and he was the one who got me interested in going to the University of Chicago. I got a job with the bond department of the First National Bank of Chicago and went to the university in the evenings and the bank paid for it."

He remained at the bank for some eighteen months, saw more future elsewhere and accepted a job with Solomon Brothers in Atlanta, where he stayed until 1968 when he was transferred to New York. He became a Solomon partner in 1972 at the ripe old age of twenty-nine. The firm was sold in 1981; he remained on for another year, and then he went with IBM where he stayed from 1986 to 1991 when he joined Torchmark. In 1993 he started his own insurance company, which he took public on April 28, 1993. This brief summary does not really do justice to a remarkable career.

As the interview ended, Rotenstreich said: "The training I got at the University of Alabama was as good as any school could have been. My experience tells me that a lot of people with whom I competed went to better-known schools, but what I got at Alabama was a real foundation. It was like learning the three R's, which in my case were the accounting, marketing, business law, economics, and finance courses. I kept a lot of my books and still use them today. I had Judge Findley for business law, and he taught me something which has become my mantra—'whatever you do it must not be illegal, immoral, or against public policy.'"

The background of the interview with *Pat Saik* (Patti in the "old" days) is unusual. On March 1, 1994, as Richard and I were putting the finishing touches on this chapter, a young woman walked into my office. After a warm greeting, I asked if she had time for a short interview. Truthfully, I had wanted to have an interview with Pat Saik, but I did not have a recent address. (The moral of that story is, alums should keep in touch with us and update addresses.) She was on campus for only a few hours on business, but she agreed to the interview.

Pat was a 1969 graduate in marketing. We had become very good friends during her college career. She was a terrific student, president of the Marketing Club (a rare circumstance for a woman in the sixties), and was interested in a career in retailing. (I was faculty adviser of the Marketing Club and my major discipline focus was retailing. Pat says I was a mentor—I hope so.) I kept in close touch with her for years. I remember well that her first job was as a bridal consultant for G. Fox and Company in Hartford, Connecticut. I also remember that Pat was a true "child of the late sixties and early seventies." I thought to myself at the time that the position with G. Fox was not a good strategic fit for the Pat I knew. She said that retailing might have been a good option for her, but in an entrepreneurial setting where she could make her own decisions.

I remember when she came back to Law School and received a J.D. degree in 1974. She needed to feel she was doing something to contribute to the betterment of society.

> It was a tough time. Things were very much in turmoil. People were searching for something in their lives of which they could be proud. And of course there was a rebellion against the established authority. Law seemed to offer me a way to contribute. I was interested in civil rights law, employment discrimination, and when I returned to my home state, Louisiana, much of my early work dealt with such issues.
>
> In New Orleans I worked for a year with the United States Court of Appeals for the Fifth Circuit. I then went into private practice for two years, basically in labor law. Next I accepted a position with the U.S. Department of Labor in Nashville, handling mostly wage cases. In 1980 I was transferred to Washington, still with Labor in their Appellate Division, writing appellate briefs in appeals from regional offices around the country. I enjoyed the work a lot and stayed three years. Then the change in administration meant dramatic philosophical changes.

Pat said in 1983 she was "burnt out." She moved to Charleston where she began doing legal research and writing for other lawyers. That was a transition period for her, and after three years she wanted to move closer to her home territory. (Hammond, Louisiana—what good memories my wife and I have of the wonderful strawberries Pat used to bring us.) She now makes her home in Bay St. Louis, Mississippi, and is a contract attorney doing just about everything that takes place to prepare for a case.

Not surprisingly this interview grew into a sentimental visit with an old friend. I have merely hit the high spots. Pat is still seeking—she is still growing as a person. We talked a lot about how difficult it was "being a woman" in the sixties:

"I am not really much of an activist in the sense of joining and organizing. Certainly my sympathies and philosophy are in keeping with the women's movement. I appreciate the fact that you encouraged me, and you never said I couldn't do something because I was a woman. That was very unusual at the time."

I am so glad that Pat's work brought her to Alabama and to my office so she could be a part of our history.

Alma Sanders, who works for CNN, is a 1969 graduate. She leads a fast-paced, active life, and finds her career stimulating. She considers her father her real mentor. She explained:

> *He encouraged me in terms of how important a good education was. I never felt that being a woman would hold me back in any way.*
>
> *And I felt the same way at the University. When I went there I guess one of the most exciting things was that it never occurred to me that I was a woman in a man's world. It didn't feel that way. Obviously I stood out because there weren't that many women in my classes. But no one made me feel that I was at all out of place or that I was looked down on. No one discouraged me in any way about my choice of careers.*
>
> *I got into the communication business because I was an accounting major, and I accepted a staff accounting position, and the industry was interesting. I liked the diversity. Now, I am in administration and finance. Obviously, I don't crunch numbers like I used to.*

Eddie Terrell, Class of 1966, is the son of "Red" Terrell a 1927 graduate. He said he did a lot of growing up at Alabama. Following in the footsteps of his father who has been widely recognized for his expert tennis acumen, Terrell came to Alabama on a tennis scholarship. He admitted that much of his time was spent practicing tennis, and almost all of his other time was spent with school work. He had little time or interest for the "social part." In recalling people from his time at Alabama, he spoke fondly of Marcus Whitman and Clarence Spencer—in addition to his greatly admired coach, Jason Morton. Eddie Terrell started with First National Bank of Birmingham in 1971 and in 1993 was vice-president of business development. He commended his father for the many businesses in the area that wouldn't exist without "Red's" help: "I don't think a week goes by that I don't talk to somebody that he helped to start a business." In reflecting about his work at Alabama, Terrell said, "I really didn't have enough marketing. I didn't understand at the time how it would help me. And that is what I do! I've learned a lot about it since of course."

No history of the 1960 alumni would be complete without a statement from *Tommy Tillman* (Class of 1961) who is on the Board of Visitors and whose work with the Commerce Executives Society is legendary. When commenting on his commitment to C&BA, Tommy said, "I think that in some small measure it's something I need to do to pay back to the college the debt that I owe for the many ways in which C&BA, its faculty, and its grads have helped me in my business career."

Tom Moore *(right)* with Max Goldberg,
Class of 1925.

Tommy Tillman's modesty and fear of sounding as though he is bragging are so strong that he could not allow himself the opportunity to fully express how much he has done for his college. To keep faith with his wishes, we merely express our heartfelt thanks.

Faculty

John Bickley originally came to C&BA in 1940, but was drafted in 1942. Although he returned briefly after the war, his tenure at Alabama (after stops at the University of Washington, Ohio State, and Texas) really began in 1968. He remained until his retirement in 1986.

In reflecting on faculty colleagues who were important to him, he mentioned Marcus Whitman, Harry Bonham, and Jim Holladay. "Bert Morley kidded me incessantly about my friendship with Mary Louise whom I was dating [and later married]." Bickley also remembered that when he was drafted in 1942 he went off with Bert Bank. "He and I got on the Greyhound bus downtown with about thirty-five other guys and we went over to Fort McPherson in Atlanta for induction."

John Bickley came back to Alabama because

> there was a fund-raising campaign for what was called the Alabama Insurance Industry Chair of Insurance, but it really wasn't a chair—there wasn't enough money for that. But they offered it to me. [The salary] was just about what I was making at Texas, but I wanted to come back to Alabama so I accepted it.
>
> I came back because I just love this place. At that time this school really cared about teaching, and I have always thought teaching was the most important thing we do. I liked the atmosphere created by men like Marcus Whitman. Actually another reason I left Texas is that I was department chairman and they wouldn't let me out of it. I didn't want to be a chairman—I wanted to be a professor. When Marcus Whitman tried to make me chairman of the Finance Department at Alabama, I told him that [if he did] I'd go back to Texas.

Among Bickley's many accomplishments, founding the International Insurance Society and the Insurance Hall of Fame rank high; but his commitment to teaching and his devotion to his students take top priority.

Tom Moore (often called T. D.) joined the faculty of Commerce and Business Administration in 1965. Former dean Jack Fielden said that Professor Moore was extremely important to the college (perhaps an "unsung hero") and to him in particular.

In responding to that comment, Tom related the following:

> *In 1967 I started working with Jack Warner [CEO, Gulf States Paper Company] and other businessmen in the state on the formation of the Alabama Council on Economic Education. We selected a board of directors, mainly of CEOs of companies [that were] willing to support the council financially and were headquartered in Alabama. Jack Warner agreed to be its first chair. I [had been] contacted by a person in New York who convinced me that it would be a good idea to establish such a council. After I did a study on the status of economic education in the public schools in Alabama, I was convinced that there was a need for greater economic literacy among children in grades K through 12. I directed the council until Ed Caradine came on board about 1980 or 1981.*
>
> *In 1968, I think, I started working on the formation of the Commerce Executives Society. I knew we had a lot of alums out there, but we weren't getting good response—at the time we were only receiving three thousand dollars in private support, and that was all from the Alabama League of Savings Associations. I started looking around to see if any other business schools had their own alumni associations. I found one at the University of Texas that they called [and still do] Texas X's. With Dean Garner's blessings, I invited the director of the Texas program, Seymour Swartz, to visit us here for a day. Based on what we learned, we developed the concept for the Commerce Executives Society [CES].*

During Jack Fielden's second semester as dean, Moore (who, through his work with the Alabama Council of Economic Education, knew his way around the state of Alabama) was asked to be in charge of external affairs and serve as Fielden's "native guide." Frank Bromberg was the first national chairman of the CES and "rode herd" very strongly with Moore and Fielden.

According to Moore, "In the spring of 1973 we organized the Board of Visitors, which was drawn from the Board of Directors of the Alabama Council on Economic Education. Once again Jack Warner was the first chairman of the Board of Visitors. Next we started working on the Alabama Business Hall of Fame and had our first inductees in 1974. I got the idea from *Fortune* magazine, and we were the first state Business Hall of Fame in the country."

Recalling the development of C&BA's external relations, Moore said, "Munny Sokol was my life's blood as a mentor and friend. He just knew so much about making things work and how to deal with people. He understood relationships better than anyone I ever met." (*Note:* Sadly, Munny Sokol is in a nursing home; he is incapable of communicating and has been so for a number of years. He is greatly missed by all who knew him.)

Art Thompson, who arrived in July 1967, was among the last group of faculty members hired in the era of Dean Paul Garner.

When asked how he would like to be remembered at Alabama, Thompson's
furrowed brow indicated a thoughtful, but possibly unexpected, response would
be forthcoming.

Art Thompson took early retirement and, now, instead of teaching
twenty-year-old college students he teaches thirty- to fifty-year-old executives.
He is busy and happy with his new work. He still writes, is in his University office
often, and teaches one class a year for C&BA.

In 1966 *Mary Fish* gracefully entered our lives. Her warmth and charm have
been ever-present for twenty-eight years. She has always told good stories, and

Department of Economics faculty
members, 1969.

I sought anecdotes during our interview. A nice one relates to one of the great C&BA charmers, Howard Folts, Dean Garner's associate dean.

Jack Menning and Paul Garner.

> When we had the faculty lounge in "old" Bidgood, Ted Vallery, another young colleague in economics, and I met Howard there and told him that we both had a young man in class who was crazier than a loon. I don't think he was dangerous, but we were both young and wanted to "control" our classes. And he would all of a sudden raise his hand and say something totally off the wall, and it would disrupt class. Being young, we wanted to mold the class, so to speak. So Ted and I were both talking to Folts, and we told him about this crazy young man who belonged in Bryce [state hospital for the mentally insane]. He agreed and said that they had checked with his psychiatrist who felt that he was harmless and was best kept in the classroom. Then Howard looked at both of us and said, "We keep faculty in the classroom when they are crazy and should be in Bryce, don't we?"

She also remembered Murray Havens. When being interviewed by Dr. Havens, then head of economics, for a faculty position, she was very apprehensive because of the "image of the South." The time was just after the Selma-to-Montgomery civil rights march. "I asked Murray about how it would be here for me as I am a B'Hai, and I was also concerned about the racial issues. He said he really didn't think that would be too big a problem because he had marched at Selma, and he had waited for the dean to comment and the dean just said, 'I see you marched at Selma.'"

When asked what it was like being a female professor in the 1960s, Fish said, "I think Minnie [Miles] was the one who bore the brunt of that. I think this will indicate how progressive the school was. The first year I was here I became pregnant. I went to Murray and told him, and he said, 'Let us know what we can do to help you.' That was it. In a less progressive atmosphere I would have been asked to resign. I was probationary then. I didn't discuss it. No one knew it except Murray and T. D. Moore. We wore full and airy dresses, and I didn't show. No one discussed it." And she was back teaching in a week after the birth of her child.

Looking Back

Socially, technologically, and politically the nation and the world were entering a period of dramatic change, perhaps greater than at any prior time. It was a decade that saw the creation of the Peace Corps; Alan Shepard's suborbital Mercury capsule flight; George Wallace's "stand in the schoolhouse door"; the assassinations of John Kennedy, Martin Luther King, Malcolm X, Medgar Evers, and Robert F. Kennedy; the brutal killing of civil rights workers and of four innocent children in a Birmingham church; President Johnson's signing of the Civil Rights Act of 1964; the first heart transplant; man setting foot on the moon; Woodstock; the Beatles; and Charles Manson.

The University of Alabama itself experienced some rather significant events during this decade, not least of which was the 1963 enrollment of Vivian Malone and James Hood, the first black students to attend the University. Two years later Vivian Malone would graduate from C&BA. The University also enjoyed

a period of expansion and heightened self-esteem during Frank Rose's administration.

Likewise, the School of Commerce was building on its reputation under Dean Paul Garner's leadership and enjoying the fruits of an administration in Washington that was supportive of higher education. We seemed somehow isolated from the turmoil that was in evidence elsewhere, especially toward the end of the decade. But dramatic internal changes took place early in this decade. They may have gone unnoticed externally, but they caused shock waves in C&BA and the world of business education.

Faculty and Staff

C&BA attracted some extraordinary new faculty members in the 1960s. Many of them are or have been in important positions of leadership, including Barry Mason, Bill Gunther, and Tom Moore. Several great contributors to our development who came during the 1960s have passed away—W. Baker Flowers (accounting), John Moeller (business law), and Charles Thomas Moore (marketing). Our culture has indeed been strengthened by their presence. After serving C&BA with distinction, several colleagues from the 1960s have retired: Eric Baklanoff, Lee Cobb, Al Drake, Betty Loomis, Rae Mellichamp, Don Phillips, Frank Ryerson, Ed Smith, Art Thompson, and Ted Vallery. Others have moved on, accepting other responsibilities elsewhere: Bob Freeman, Allan Spritzer, and Bob Sweeney. How fortunate we are that the following long-term colleagues are still contributing, each in his or her own characteristic way: John Evans, Toppy Ezell, Mary Fish, Charles Leathers, John Mason, and Lonnie Strickland.

W. R. "Bill" Bennett

Few faculty members served the college with more dedication and in as many capacities as did Bill Bennett. The oral interview with Bill covered four decades, but the attention here is on his role in the 1960s.

Professor Bennett had come out of the 1950s as the "dean of salesmanship" and was a major contributor to C&BA programs in marketing, especially in preparing doctoral students in theory. As a part of his work in the sales area, he felt obliged to travel a great deal in the summers, working with various companies:

I worked for Goodyear, to give you an example, for three summers, and I was always going to meetings and the like in the summers. I decided that I would like to stay at home for a while, so when Dean Garner offered me the job of director of the Graduate Division, I gladly accepted.

I was Ned Anderson's successor. He had retired and then died before I took over. I was responsible for our graduate students, and at the same time, I tried to do whatever I could to serve the [Marketing] Department. I held the position from 1963 to 1971. During my tenure we were very centralized, but we moved back and forth over time from centralization to decentralization.

I was a department chair during Dr. Bennett's time in the graduate division, and I was also his colleague in marketing. I can state with complete confidence that no one could have been more dedicated nor more helpful than Bill. It was a real pleasure to work with him. In 1969 our designation was changed from School of Commerce and Business Administration to College. Bill Bennett saw no great significance in that action, as he sees the terms as interchangeable. But asking him to react to the designation brought up an interesting issue. "I felt that our graduate division should be designated 'Graduate School of Business' and Paul [Garner] felt the same way. So we started calling it the Graduate School of Business. I would never have done it if Paul hadn't gone along with it. Well, Eric Rogers [dean of the Graduate School] got real upset because Paul had not discussed it with him before we started using the designation."

John Bickley

Few colleagues relate to students like John Bickley. It seems appropriate to share with our readers a few of his comments in an interview for this history.

To my question, As you think back over your years here, what students do you remember most? Bickley replied:

It's a long, long list. Really, I stay in touch with a couple of hundred of them. I write to them. Yesterday Kirby Montgomery came down from New York. He had just gotten a new position with a brand new insurance company. I placed eleven of my students with the General Reinsurance Company, which is probably the finest insurance company in America. They stopped hiring our people because they said they had an "Alabama Mafia." Kirby was one of them. And there is Rick Napier. In Birmingham I think of Tom Curtin, and Jim Priester who's a lawyer. And there's Bob Daniels in Texas and Ari Deshe in Columbus, Ohio, [originally from Israel] who has started his own insurance company. I just got a letter from one of my students who is from Belgium who claims to be a "Bickley Boy."

Clearly, John's greatest joy in his retirement is keeping in touch with his beloved students and doing all he can to serve his insurance colleagues and the University of Alabama, especially C&BA.

June Montgomery

For the history of any institution, a major source of "inside" information is the secretarial staff, who really knew what was going on. If time had permitted,

I would have contacted every departmental secretary. Because that was clearly impossible, the best choice from this decade has to be June Montgomery.

Montgomery said she "came home" in the fall of 1960. After several years at Gulf States Paper using the skills she learned in the secretarial administration program in C&BA, she came back to the University in the summer of 1960 as Dean Garner's secretary.

Montgomery is now retired and enjoying herself. She "hangs out" most of the time in Perry County where her forebears lived in the early years of the nineteenth century. Although she clearly lives in the present, as we talked about the past, she reflected nostalgically on what a great honor it had been working for Dr. Garner. She said that she realizes that more and more as time passes.

Names were mentioned of old friends and coworkers—Gladys Poe, Judy Davis, Sara Christopher, Elizabeth Caldwell, and Mary Joe Mickelson. And of course we touched on the subject of old Bidgood Hall—the real one! I suspected as I hung up that June would never visit the new Bidgood, but would remember the building as it used to be. And that's okay too.

Barry Mason Revisits the Sixties

One of the truly great interviews for me was with Barry Mason. I had taught him when he was a master's student and worked closely with him while he was in our doctoral program. Reviewing his activities of the 1960s was akin to reliving one of my most enjoyable decades at Alabama.

Barry Mason as a Student

I asked first for a quick review of his early days at Alabama. "I was recruited by Harry Lipson who offered me the princely sum of fifteen hundred dollars from a Loveman's Scholarship. [Loveman's was a major department store in Birmingham with whom we had excellent relationships for many years.] That was a lot of money in the early 1960s. I earned my Master of Arts degree in marketing in 1964.

"During my master's program I worked with the Alabama Highway Project, continuing on for a Ph.D. at the encouragement of you and Tom Moore."

(*Note:* Charles Thomas Moore joined the C&BA faculty in 1962 and was the principal researcher, inspiration, and major funding source for a generation of graduate students. He was also a mentor for colleagues like me, and he taught us the value of and how to conduct contract research through his Highway Project, a federally funded economic impact study of the interstate highway system in Alabama. Tom had a background in transportation at Indiana University and he quickly responded to the opportunity, having brought the expertise, contacts, and the paradigms with him to Alabama.)

Mason continued:

> *After receiving my doctorate in 1967, I was convinced to remain at Alabama, work on the Highway Project, and get my research and writing underway. We began to develop and expand on the concept of economic and social impact. We did a lot of work on land use that spanned multiple years, generated a lot of money, a lot of good, scholarly publications, and support of graduate students. I*

Faculty and staff members from the marketing department, 1969.

was allowed to handle the day-to-day operations as a doctoral student on through the very early 1970s.

I am still waiting to grow up and go out and pursue another career. One of these days I will. It seems that every time I reach a certain plateau and I am getting bored and restless, some other wonderful opportunity comes along and every four or five years it seems that something new and different has arisen to challenge me.

Barry Mason Remembers Professors

When asked to think about professors who influenced him during his graduate work, Mason remembered the southern-gentleman-style of teaching and the respect for students exhibited by the late Marcus Whitman and Langston Hawley. He also remembered "the demanding style of Bill Bennett for

Management department faculty, 1969.

Finance department faculty, 1969.

whom you never did enough work or read enough. He would come in each class period and give you six more books to read and a lot of provocative questions to answer. I was terrified to let Dr. Bennett see me taking a break as he would ask why [I wasn't] busy. [Everyone] went to great extremes to avoid his seeing you on a break."

Mason talked about the expansiveness of Harry Lipson and his thought processes. He graciously said that I demonstrated a caring concern for students and a determination to take the rough edges off the way other people dealt with students.

C. T. Moore, Barry Mason's mentor, was described as "a hyperactive, always late, always get it done mentality. You stopped everything you were doing for Tom. Brilliant, creative, but very demanding without being aware of how demanding he was. He was in his own world and you had to adjust to that world. If you were going to be in his world, the benefits were quite enormous from a learning and growth perspective. And yet his way was basically to challenge, not to micromanage and leave. But he had great expectations and would outline in a very rough way what he wanted, and it was up to you as an individual to fill in the gaps."

Finally, Barry Mason reflected on Murray Havens who taught his own unique brand of economics. "You read a lot of books, but on his exam, you had to remember to give him Havens Economics and nothing else. While he

Business law department faculty, 1969.

encouraged you to read and consider alternative viewpoints, you'd better be prepared on an exam to give him Havens."

Barry Mason Reflects on Change: The Dynamics of the 1960s

Dean Mason described the era of his doctoral work as one in which Ph.D. students were basically caught in midstream. The new philosophical bases (following "the reports" mentioned in chapter 4) demanded more mathematical sophistication, greater awareness of the uses and applications of computers, and the necessity to be more heavily immersed in the behavioral sciences than might have been called for a few years earlier. "Not all faculty members could easily make the adjustment, so it was a period of rather wrenching change."

Probing for more insights into the dynamics of the 1960s, which on the surface seemed to be a time of relative peace in academe, I asked if, as a student, he had been aware of the changes taking place in business education:

Oh yes we were aware. We didn't know the antecedents of it, but we were having to read the material. In marketing, for example, John Howard's first marketing management book came out, and it was very sophisticated from a modeling perspective and we spent a lot of time looking at that. The decade of the 1960s saw articles appear with very new material. You will recall that Harry Lipson's article on formal reasoning and marketing strategy appeared in the Journal of Marketing *in about 1963. It was a very formative period in laying the foundations for a more rigorous program of study.*

Barry Mason Comments on "The Reports" and AACSB

Mason summarized how he viewed the impact of the reports.

They said cut out the intensely descriptive nature of material and look for more broadly based generalizations. To look for theory-based explanations for why things change as opposed to offering a descriptive treatise on how to market

Paul Garner—our first real internationalist.

Deans Garner and Mason at the time of the former dean's induction into the C&BA Faculty Hall of Fame.

The first research professors. Jean Gibbons, *seated*; Maurice Newman and Eric Baklanoff, *standing.*

bananas. We were seeing a whole new body of material developing in our various disciplines with the richness of theory and methodology that accompanied it.

So we saw an elimination of a lot of the narrow-based, descriptive, trade-focused courses; they were replaced by fewer but more conceptually and analytically rigorous courses with firm foundations for theory development, theory testing, and the modeling that would go along with the empirical testing of models. This is the natural evolution of any science, I think, which begins by description and classification initially, leading to the development of hypotheses and in turn to theories and repeated testing, and perhaps, even in the social sciences, some laws. We were moving from description and classification to the development of formal hypotheses for testing.

He said he believes the reports certainly influenced AACSB standards.

They influenced the reward structure for faculty, given that there was much more emphasis on research, which in turn led to a reduction in teaching loads so that faculty would have more time for research. It led to dramatic restructuring in the reward structure for faculty, so that the faculty who were caught in the middle of this paradigm shift, who did not have the skills to do the kind of writing that was necessary, suddenly, almost overnight, became second-class citizens. And everyone was chasing the young hot shots at the time.

As is true any time there is a paradigm shift, there was a whole generation of people left behind and a new group of "young Turks" who came in. It was, necessarily, a period of tension.

I haven't seen in recent years the kind of rampant shifts that we saw in the early 1960s. We see now refinements; much more stability in terms of the body of knowledge; new extensions, broadening of concepts, and new paradigms—not the radical shifts in the very foundations of skills, tools, and theories that drive a discipline.

Barry Mason Remembers Dean Paul Garner

Paul Garner was a product of the "old school" in many respects, perhaps like Lee Bidgood was. You still hear older faculty members [who were young then] talk about Paul and Ruth calling on them in their homes on a Sunday afternoon, unannounced. The horror was that you were there in your Bermuda shorts, unshaven, with your family equally unprepared, and the dean would "come-a-calling." [I remember a Sunday like that, and—in retrospect—it's a most pleasant memory.]

That was the residual of an earlier, much simpler era in our society. But Paul and Ruth were the quintessential southern gentleman and lady. And that was how you welcomed people to the community at that time. The young people who were coming in were not familiar with this social event and they were not particularly comfortable—their social mores were different, and less formal perhaps. No one resented this visit—it seemed a little "quaint."

Paul was to a large extent autocratic as were the other deans on campus. No formal evaluations of department heads or deans took place on a regular basis as is done today. Affirmative action had not been heard of. A dean decided whom he wanted to hire, and he did it on the spot.

There was no Faculty Forum. In the absence of a formal structure within which to register differing viewpoints, the dean could do as he pleased—a person of great power. Paul was basically running a very autocratic one-man show in the sense of power structure.

Dean Garner was twenty years ahead of his time in the international area. He was determined to bring the college into the forefront of internationalization. And yet, by and large, he did not hire faculty who shared his dream. Doug Lamont was hired and he converted Bill Bennett, but it has always puzzled me why he had such an ardent passion for international, and yet the faculty he hired were, by and large, very domestically focused.

Eric N. Baklanoff on International Studies

Eric N. Baklanoff, professor emeritus of economics, was the dean of the Office for International Studies and Programs (OISP) from 1968 to 1973.

OISP was organized in 1967 during the end of the Rose administration to give Alabama students a better appreciation of America's relations with the rest of the world. [The program] was charged with innovating and coordinating academic programs with an international dimension on the main Tuscaloosa campus, as well as at UAB and UAH.

The first dean for International Studies and Programs was the late Raymond McLain, who served in this capacity from OISP's inception until December 1968 when he was appointed dean of the College of Arts and Sciences. I succeeded Dr. McLain. . . . This five-year period [1968-73] saw rapid expansion of international initiatives that included study-abroad programs in Rome, the Yucatán, and the U.S. Summer Program at the University of Madrid; the M.A. in Latin American Studies whose enrollment reached fifteen students by 1972; and a Latin American publication series through the University of Alabama Press.

OISP also coordinated and supported the M.B.A./International Business Program and the interdisciplinary International Relations Major. To enhance faculty expertise in foreign relations, OISP created the International Opportunity Program for Faculty, which provided travel-research grants and encouraged

Baklanoff occupies a position of great historic value in a consideration of the international focus of the University and C&BA. In addition to those already mentioned as having been global in their perspective—Eric Baklanoff, Paul Garner, Bill Bennett, Doug Lamont—no history would be complete without including the names of John Evans, Mark Weaver, John Hill, Larry Foster, and Chad Hilton.

Tommy Tillman: Alumnus Extraordinaire

I can think of no better way to bring the decade of the sixties to a close than to dedicate the contents herein to one of my all-time favorite alumni, Tommy Tillman, Class of 1961.

His service to his college has been remarkable. He is Mister Commerce Executive Society and his contributions to the Board of Visitors are exceptional. Getting Tommy to talk freely during the interview was difficult. He was afraid he might sound boastful. When I thanked him for all he has done, he immediately changed the topic. He stressed "what the college has done for me and what it meant to me while I was there and in years since. It is from that sense of responsibility—repaying—whatever, that I have made the commitment to serve. The opportunity to serve on the Board of Visitors and to serve as Chairman of the Commerce Executives Society are commitments that I believe in a small way can help pay back to the college the debt I owe C&BA, its graduates, and faculty for the many opportunities that have been afforded me in my business career."

Well said, Tommy. You represent the 1960s student body with distinction.

Tommy Tillman, a man of
dedication and modesty.

Dr. W. R. Bennett working with secretary, Mrs. R. R. Fuller, 1969.

The University's president:

David Mathews (1969–80)[*]

[*]During a seventeen-month period when Mathews was on leave of absence, serving as Secretary of Health, Education, and Welfare in President Ford's cabinet, Richard Thigpen served as acting chief executive officer for the University.

The world is talking about:

While campaigning for the presidency at a Maryland shopping center, Alabama governor George Wallace is shot in an assassination attempt that leaves him partially paralyzed. (May 15, 1972)

The last U.S. troops leave South Vietnam, ending nearly ten years of American military presence. (March 29, 1973)

Pres. Richard M. Nixon resigns, and Vice-pres. Gerald R. Ford is sworn in as president. (August 9, 1974)

James (Jimmy) Earl Carter is elected president. (November 2, 1976)

Canada and the United States sign an agreement to construct a twenty-seven-hundred-mile pipeline to carry Alaskan natural gas across Canada to the continental United States. (September 20, 1977)

At Jonestown, Guyana, 911 people (including group leader Jim Jones) die by poison or gunfire when their leader convinces them that their lives are threatened. (1978)

Pope Paul VI dies on August 6. His successor, John Paul I, is elected August 26 and dies in his sleep on September 28. (1978)

The College of Cardinals elects fifty-eight-year-old Karol Cardinal Wojtyla, a Pole, Pope John Paul II; he is the first non-Italian pope since 1523. (October 16, 1978)

The University is talking about:

In the early 1970s "Quads"—free Sunday afternoon rock concerts—are one of several activities sponsored by the student-run Experimental College. In one school year the college offered free six-week courses in such disparate areas as folk, blues, and rock music; human ecology; psychic science; eugenics and euthanasia; motorcycle repair; and soccer.

Some programs begun at the University during Mathews's presidency reflect his interest in "closing the relevancy gap" between students and higher education; others are largely service oriented; still others fall into traditional academic categories. Between 1970 and 1976, New College, Weekend College, the External Degree Program, the School of Communication, the Graduate School of Library Service, the College of Community Health Sciences, and the Capstone College of Nursing are established. The School of

Mines and Energy Development opens; a School of Accountancy is formed within the College of Commerce and Business Administration; several institutes relating to law, higher education, and international programs are founded; and regional offices open in Mobile, Selma, Dothan, and Decatur.

Controversial speakers such as Abbie Hoffman of the Chicago Seven are banned from appearing on campus. The banning is a matter of considerable controversy in the spring of 1970.

On the evening of May 6, 1970, approximately one thousand University students hold a candlelight memorial march for the four Kent State students killed by National Guardsmen during an antiwar demonstration on that campus two days earlier.

Early on the morning of May 7, 1970, Dresler Hall, an intramural sports facility constructed after World War II, on the site where the Ferguson Center now stands, is destroyed by fire. (No one was ever indicted for arson, but local ACLU attorneys and journalists who investigated the matter stated publicly that the fire had been started by an agent provocateur and not, as many at first suspected, by University student dissidents.)

The infamous Mad Wednesday, May 13, 1970, is followed by high tensions on campus and the cancellation of final exams. Students go home for the summer after an emotional, high-conflict period in our history.

(continued on page 100)

<table><tr><td>

Chapter 6

</td><td>

Regrouping: The Seventies
The Garner Era Ends
The Fielden Era Begins

</td></tr></table>

Faculty "agents of change" in the C&BA culture:

Kenneth Austin (1978)
Trevor Bain (1974)
Kathleen Bindon (1979)
Barney Cargile (1979)
James F. Cashman (1975)
David Cheng (1974)
Ronald E. Dulek (1977)
Hazel F. "Toppy" Ezell (1979)
    (full-time faculty position)
Carl Ferguson (1975)
John H. Fielden (1971)
Jean D. Gibbons (1970)
Billy P. Helms (1973)
Donald L. Hooks (1971)
William H. Jean (1973)
Marvin J. Karson (1972)
Robert C. Kee (1979)
Badrig M. Kurkjian (1976)
Terrence Martell (1972)
T. H. Mattheis (1976)
Robert W. McLeod (1978)
Walter S. Misiolek (1975)
Maurice S. Newman (1977)
Charles Odewahn (1971)
Mickey M. Petty (1972)
David W. Phipps (1975)
Lena Prewitt (1970)

(continued on page 101)

In Their Own Words

Students

Owen Aronov, Class of 1974: "I grew up in a family real estate business, and I was always interested ultimately in becoming part of it. When I went to the University, I became even more energized to want to learn and excel in business in general. When I think about where I was when I entered the University and where I was after I got the wonderful foundation in general business principles, I'm just amazed. I was really motivated to be a success. The University has meant so much to me. I think particularly about the accessibility to professors like you [Morris Mayer]; that was so meaningful to me."

Tom Canterbury graduated from C&BA in 1976 (after taking several years off in the early 1970s). "Once I finally graduated, I never left." Tom says that he earned only one-fourth of his degree; the other three-fourths belong to his mother, to Gladys Poe (former registrar), and to Morris Mayer who nagged him so much from 1970 to 1975, that he finally came back to school. "As soon as I graduated I was recruited for a job as adviser in the college and eventually became the registrar and I've never had any real interest in leaving the college at all. It's just part of my life."

Ryan deGraffenreid, Class of 1972, credits the University of Alabama, and particularly the College of Commerce and Business Administration, with playing a significant role in the direction of his life. "The experiences there, the people that I met, the professors that I had the privilege of studying under all contributed toward my professional goals and then my political aspirations. It was a real privilege for me to have had the opportunity to attend the University and C&BA."

Mike Thompson, who graduated in 1977, found it difficult to remember specific names, but remembered his impressions of his days in C&BA. "The C&BA program was pretty tough. You had to concentrate and study in most

The University is talking about:

(continued from page 98)

Joab Thomas, dean of students in 1971, and Johnny Musso, who broke seven SEC records and fourteen University records as a running back for the Crimson Tide, are "drenched" into Jasons on Honors Day.

Alabama Business Hall of Fame is organized in 1973.

In 1973 Terry Points, a C&BA student from Birmingham, is the University's first African American Homecoming Queen.

The University showboat, the *Alabama Belle*, has a brief but lively career in 1974. Donated to the University by Gulf States Paper Corporation, the *Belle* travels the waterways of west and south Alabama during the summer. The tour ends when the *Belle* sinks under tow on the Warrior near Demopolis.

Jerry Pate, a C&BA student, wins the U.S. Amateur Championship in 1974 while a member of the University's golf team.

Denny Stadium is renamed Bryant-Denny in 1975.

In 1978 the Ferguson Center and the Law Center are completed.

Alabama football: the Tide defeats top-rated Penn State 14 to 7 in the 1979 Sugar Bowl and wins the national championship, the sixth for Coach Bryant.

College "hot buttons" during the seventies:

1972
- Dean Fielden renames departments in C&BA.

1973
- Modern numbering system is instituted.
- General business is renamed general management.
- A joint degree in business and law is instituted.
- Ph.D. requirements no longer include a secondary field in economics.

1974
- New Curriculum III, health care management, is implemented.

1975
- Fashion merchandising is added as Concentration VII in marketing and physical distribution.

1976
- Business law is redesignated as legal studies.
- Urban and regional planning adds program management to designation.
- Areas of concentration for the M.B.A. are expanded with the addition of legal studies, public utilities, applied econometrics, and economic forecast.

1977
- Master of Tax Accounting Degree is introduced.

1979
- M.B.A. students must declare area of specialization after completing thirty-three hours.

Participants in the Alabama Business Hall of Fame, September 1975. Richard Thigpen, Craig Smith, Ronald Reagan, Jack Warner, and John Fielden.

classes. I remember how tough accounting was on me as a general business major. Also I thought most of the students were pretty mindful of what they were doing. They seemed to be serious. It seemed to me that the classes continued to get smaller and smaller and the professors got better and better. As you got into upper-level classes, the professors took a lot more time with you. The classes were smaller and they seemed more intense."

Faculty

Ron Dulek was asked to address two specific issues: Why he came to Alabama and positive experiences he remembered during his years on the C&BA faculty. Ron's response was very straightforward:

> *I came to Alabama because I only had two legitimate job offers—one here and one at Ohio State. Neither Sally [my wife] nor I had ever lived in the South, but we wanted to try it. We decided to stay for three years after which we would move back to the Midwest. That was seventeen years ago.*
>
> *The other allure of Alabama was three people with whom I interviewed: Jack Fielden, Barry Mason, and Annette Shelby [who was teaching management communication]. Jack [a professor of management communication and the dean of C&BA] and Annette promised they would work with me; and Barry was simply impressive [as department head of management and marketing]. Barry taught me how to recruit—convince the person you really want him or her, but not so much that the person will ask for extra money.*
>
> *As for positive experiences, there were loads and loads. Working with Jack, Annette, Barry, Jim, and you, Morris; getting to know Lonnie Strickland and Art Thompson; and meeting and spending time with high-powered executives.*
>
> *I got lessons from Annette in what it means to be southern. I find the . . . South and Alabama fascinating. [They] are linked together in really interesting ways. My guess is that these ties strongly influence C&BA.*
>
> *Other positives: the students. I sincerely believe we have the best students in the nation. They combine courtesy and intelligence, a rare combination in this day and age. A recent positive experience is being permitted to do Commerce Executives talks throughout the state when Barry Mason cannot make it. I love meeting, seeing, and talking with former students, and I am amazed at the love our graduates hold for C&BA. That kind of love makes our jobs vitally important. Successful business people who graduated long ago will come up to me and tell me what a professor said twenty years ago. That's neat!*
>
> *Here's the most honest statement I can make—I can't think of a school where I would rather be.*

In describing the Fielden era, Ron Dulek used the words *vibrant, exciting, crazy.* "Fielden brought to the college instant change and concern about doing what he believed was right for our school, without concern with bureaucracy that causes things to move slowly. He always said he would do anything to make C&BA move ahead except one thing—his standard line that he taught me and that I live by is that 'curriculum belongs to the faculty.' And he would never touch that. It was his core principle."

Ron Dulek was indeed a major "agent of change" in C&BA's culture.

(continued from page 99)

Frank R. Rayburn (1974)
Robert A. Robicheaux (1977)
Patricia M. Rudolph (1976)
James A. Taylor (1978)
K. Mark Weaver (1976)
Darryl Webb (1971)
Richard Wiegand (1978)
Hsiu-Kwang Wu (1972)
Leonard Zumpano (1975)

(*Note:* The largest number of faculty to join C&BA in any single decade, this list includes only faculty members who remained with C&BA at least ten years.)

In the chapter on the sixties we heard from *Toppy Ezell* (B.S. 1967, M.B.A. 1969, Ph.D. 1974) as a student. We now take advantage of her unique status and let her talk as a faculty member. She traced her interest in teaching to being a grader for Frank Ryerson and Frank Foster (who passed away in 1993). She claimed that she chose her major for the Ph.D. because I convinced her that

> *marketing made the world go round. In the M.B.A. marketing class you were excited about marketing and it made marketing exciting to me.*
>
> *After I got my doctorate, everyone insisted that I interview with other schools. I did what I was told—I interviewed with one school and got an offer, but I simply did not want to leave—I wanted to stay in the business school.*
>
> *The year I got my [doctoral] degree the position of director of the M.B.A. Program came open and Dean Fielden hired me. I stayed in the dean's office from 1974 to 1979 doing things in addition to the M.B.A. like external funding. I was also teaching one course in marketing on an overload basis, usually at night. And then I joined the marketing department on a full-time basis.*
>
> *I have such good feelings about this place. You can't spend thirty-one years of your life at an institution and not have warm and fuzzy feelings about it. I greatly appreciate the opportunities that people gave me after I got my doctorate. You know most schools did not hire people who got degrees from that institution. I really did want to stay here for many personal reasons. I had two children I was raising by myself, and I had my parents here as well as my in-laws. I have no regrets in terms of what I have done with my career at Alabama. I am also pleased that my daughters both got Alabama degrees—Carla in art history and Deana in marketing.*

Lena Prewitt joined the C&BA faculty in 1970. She was born in Wilcox County, Alabama, and grew up in Perry County. She received a bachelor's degree from Stillman College and a master's and Ph.D. from Indiana University. She taught at Stillman and Texas Southern University in Houston for several years before working for the telephone company in Los Angeles. Before coming to Alabama, she taught at Florence State University (now University of North Alabama) for one year. For the next twenty-four years, Lena Prewitt served the University of Alabama. "I have never been patronized here and I have never regretted coming to Alabama's business school. All the deans I have worked with have been good for me as a person. I like people to leave me alone to do my work and Deans Garner, Fielden, Mitchell, and Mason have done that. It's the most important thing that has kept me at Alabama."

Looking Back

We came through the 1960s strengthened, but perhaps not completely prepared for the decade to follow. In C&BA our philosophical bases had gone through some extraordinary changes that were not clearly visible outside the family. The changes were essentially curriculum oriented and were part of a national process of adjusting to criticisms of U.S. business schools. A strong faculty assembled by Dean Paul Garner bought into the culture started by Lee Bidgood and further enhanced our reputation regionally, and even nationally in several areas.

Externally the stage was set for even more dramatic changes than we experienced in the tumultuous sixties. The unpopular Vietnam war racked our consciences, and our confidence in our institutions was shaken with the resignation of Pres. Richard Nixon. Regardless of political party affiliation or philosophical positions, the entire nation was shocked at the attempted assassination of Alabama's governor George Wallace during his campaign for the presidency. The Jonestown, Guyana, massacre was an apt but tragic end to the seventies.

At the central administration level of the University, the seventies were the era of Pres. David Mathews, whose tenure was either loved or hated. Few, however, can dispute that Mathews instituted some remarkable institutional advances. *Controversy* was the operative word throughout his administration. Students and faculty were restless—the spirit of the decade. Throughout the nation students demonstrated in opposition to the war and in protest of other issues. We were affected, though in comparison to other major universities in a minor way.

Lena Prewitt

The era of Paul Garner ended and the new regime began in the first year of the new decade with the arrival of John S. (Jack) Fielden in 1971. In 1970 Lena Prewitt and Jean Gibbons had joined the faculty. Their influence was felt for more than two decades, until their recent retirement. Gibbons, one of the world's foremost statisticians, married Jack Fielden.

A history of C&BA would not be complete without ensuring that future generations of students and faculty realize what a significant role was played by Lena Prewitt during the seventies, eighties, and nineties. Although a portion of her interview is presented in this chapter under the section In Their Own

Lena Prewitt, Emerita Professor of Management.

Words, a more in-depth look at this remarkable woman seems appropriate. She was one of the last professors hired by Dean Paul Garner.

I wanted to get Dr. Prewitt's perspective on being a black woman faculty member when she accepted Garner's invitation to join us. In typically Lena Prewitt manner she responded:

> At that time, as you know, the civil rights movement was in full swing. When Vivian Malone entered the University I was working at Stillman. I am a very private person. I was not going to march. I was not going to parade in the streets or burn my bra, even though I thought they were pretty good tactics. I sought a way I could contribute to the civil rights movement and help initiate social change in this country.
>
> By the time Dean Garner offered me a job at Alabama, I also had offers from Michigan State and Colorado State. I weighed those opportunities and discussed them with colleagues and family. I wondered how and where I could best serve. I finally decided that the best place for me to serve was the University of Alabama. I did not choose the University because I am a native Alabamian but because I thought this was the place I could make the greatest contribution to social change.
>
> I figured that Michigan State could easily find a black person to teach. I found that at Colorado State there was no trouble recruiting black professors. I thought, however, that Alabama would have difficulty attracting blacks. At that time, blacks who didn't know the South were very reluctant to come here. Even now when I travel outside of the state, people ask me why in the world am I at Alabama. How do you live there and why do you stay?

Dr. Prewitt acknowledged that when she was growing up in rural Alabama she felt black.

> I felt black and I was treated black, and I was a little apologetic for being black. But I went to Indiana University and no longer felt black. I got away from my blackness and from my feelings of inferiority and I got away from being apologetic. I learned to be comfortable with being black and very confident in who I am.
>
> I want you to know that I didn't come to the Commerce School because I was black. When I came, white universities were fighting for black professors, and I knew that. I was not going to come and sit by the window. I was not coming here to take care of black affairs. I was not coming if they were just making a place for me. If they wanted a management professor with all the rights and privileges and the responsibility, I would come. But I would not come to be black.
>
> I have never been patronized at the University, but that isn't to say that some people didn't intend to. You see if I had acted like the black model, I might have been patronized. But most of my colleagues here know who I am; I have confidence in that. I don't think I could have had a better career anywhere else—a different career maybe, but not a better one.

Lena enthusiastically credits all the deans she has worked with for making her tenure here such a good one. Deans Garner, Fielden, and Mason—they all understood her desire for independence. In thinking about the colleagues who meant a lot to her, she mentioned Don Phillips, Langston Hawley, Harold Janes, Bill Bennett, Horace Washburn, and of course Minnie Miles. She also thought fondly about the old faculty lounge in Bidgood where everyone came in and socialized. She was amused to think that when she first came into the room, the men had no idea what to do or say.

In thinking about students, she did not single out any one student. There had been, she said, so many special and exceptional students, so many number-one students. As a colleague of hers for almost a quarter of a century, I know she has been number one for many students whose lives she touched.

The Fielden Era

The remainder of this chapter focuses on the era of Jack Fielden, as seen from his perspective and from that of colleagues who were in a position to know the most. The first section is excerpted from a telephone interview with Fielden from his home in Pensacola.

Fielden on Fielden and the College

Nothing about Jack Fielden is routine. In reviewing his educational background, I became aware of that fact. In 1944, while attending the Wharton School, he enlisted in the Navy V-12 program (a college-degree program). He was sent to Supply Corps School at the Harvard Business School and, lacking a term at Wharton for his degree, was allowed to transfer Harvard credits to Wharton. He received his degree in 1945 in economics. He also got a certificate in lieu of an M.B.A. from Harvard Business School. It would have been possible to go back to Harvard, finish up and get the bona fide M.B.A., but illness precluded his doing that: "My time as a hero in the military amounted to catching tuberculosis and spending three years in navy hospitals. The navy retired me, presumably to die, but I didn't die. I got better. I figured I never could have a career in business. I thought that would be too demanding for someone with TB, so I started writing in the hospital, and I fell in love with English literature. The VA sent tutors to the hospital and I was able to get a background so I could go to Harvard and pursue English lit."

Harvard didn't work out, but Boston University let him into their master's program in English even before he got out of the hospital. He got his doctorate, spent a couple of years at Illinois, then went to Purdue where he received tenure. While at Purdue he heard that the *Harvard Business Review* was looking for an assistant editor, and with his joint backgrounds in business and English he got the job. He loved it.

In his first week on the job the editor gave him fourteen hundred pages of galley proofs; each page was eighteen inches long. What were the galleys? They were "the reports": the now-famous monumental studies of business education done by the Carnegie Foundation and the Ford Foundation. Fielden's job was to write a review, which was published in the *Harvard Business Review*. Fielden's wry sense of humor is apparent in his comment on the response to that review: "My article came out before the reports came out, so it was a sensation. The whole article was reprinted in the *New York Times*. Everybody lapped it up, and all of a sudden I was the celebrity, not the guys who wrote the reports. I got invited by the *Times* to write a yearly column of the state of business education. That really wasn't fair to the authors of the reports—Gorden and Howell, and Pierson—but that's the way the ball bounced. So I wrote other articles on

Jack Fielden.

business education and became accepted as an authority although, in fact, I didn't know anything!"

Fielden told a somewhat complicated story explaining how he became dean of Boston University (BU) at the age of thirty-eight, but suffice it to say he did it through influencing the right people and being in the right place at the right time. In addition, at the time everyone was throwing stones at business schools, and Fielden's Ph.D. in English made him more acceptable.

Fielden affirmed that he turned BU's business school around: "What an ego trip. We turned the place basically into a prep school for M.B.A.'s. We focused on math, economics, and psychology and very little on the functional field courses in business. We went for the three-two program, so that very bright students could go on, and their fourth year of the undergraduate program became the first year of the M.B.A. And it worked great. Then we started the evening M.B.A. program, and since Harvard did not have an evening M.B.A., we got terrific students."

When questioned about his involvement in external affairs, Fielden credited his Harvard experiences with giving him good tools and motivation for his forte, which was working with outside publics:

> *I learned a lot about fund-raising at Harvard, so when I came to BU, I [contacted] the presidents of Gillette and General Foods, and other big shots, and apparently I have a great ability to look pathetic, and they all wanted to help. They taught me long-range planning.*
>
> *I saw how executives behaved and was able to act like them and get along with them. . . . Businessmen are not like you and me. They are not crass, as some tend to think, but they are pretty tough. I'm a pretty good actor, and I learned how to get along with them, which essentially was keeping my big mouth shut about most things.*

It is no secret that Jack Fielden could not work with the president of Boston University, whom Fielden described as an Adolph Hitler. So he decided to get out. He interviewed at Minnesota and Alabama. In reflecting on that time, Jack remembered: "It's really weird. Minnesota was by far the stronger school at that time. I was always able to get along with 'business types,' but I was regarded with considerable suspicion by business faculties as you can imagine with my doctorate in English. Anyway, there was a man on the faculty who became my champion and was pushing my candidacy at Minnesota. Would you believe that he went on a skimobile trip with some Minnesota Viking football players and froze to death! So I accepted the challenges at Alabama."

Fielden realized that some colleagues at Alabama believed he was "off the wall," but he is convinced that he wanted only to move the college back into the mainstream. He said that if we had been a prestige school we could have gone our own way and done what we wanted to do. But Jack's objective, in his own words was "to catch up with the crowd." The recommended curriculum, following the reports, was adopted by AACSB and Jack felt C&BA had to conform.

Fielden on Organization

When Fielden arrived as dean of C&BA in the fall semester of 1971 (I was in England on sabbatical and Ed Smith was acting chairman of the Marketing Department in my absence), the first thing he did was appoint a reorganization committee. Jack pushed for the organization structure that was the trend nationally. We had a large number of departments (Fielden facetiously—maybe—says there were sixteen) and he initiated the four-area organization. "The structure I inherited consisted of a lot of chiefs and very few Indians. It was an awkward organization to work with. For example, in very small faculty groups [areas/departments], promotion and tenure [P&T] issues were serious. It was possible to move from associate to full professor in consecutive years. Not only would a small number of areas result in better promotion and tenure decisions, my span of control made much more sense."

Fielden on Faculty Governance

The Faculty Forum was formed, under the leadership of the late Baker Flowers, toward the end of Garner's tenure. Prior to that time, the faculty could not call itself into a meeting. Jack said that through the aegis of the Faculty Forum, the faculty started running the college. Jack believed in faculty governance, but his highest internal priority was to legitimate the forum, with the dean in charge.

Jack initiated the Faculty Executive Board (FEB) and the other standing committees (for example, Undergraduate Programs Committee, Promotion and Tenure Committee). A governance process was in place, and according to Fielden, "a lot of power was taken away from the department chairs, especially in P&T. Under the new governance structure the faculty was responsible, among other things, for the quality of the faculty, the Ph.D., the M.B.A. The faculty was responsible for electing representatives to the FEB, and then at a forum meeting, operating as a committee of the whole. No longer was the faculty on the outside throwing stones at the administration." (*Note:* The earlier eras of the college were characterized by an autocratic, centralized administration that, in its time, worked. The nature of the environment of the seventies unquestionably called for differing governance and organization structures.)

Fielden on External Activities

When Fielden arrived at C&BA, "the college" he said,

was in bad shape. The state was not putting any money in. The administration had not been singling out the business school for help. The funds went elsewhere. We had bad facilities, which hurt a lot. I remember I was promised by Mathews that our college was a number-one priority for a new building. When I questioned him about our position over the years, when other investments were being made, he responded that there were a lot of number-one priorities.

You can sit around and take your licking or you can get out and look for your own money. So we decided to . . . go outside and try to get the money. I told everybody that we were going to lose our accreditation. I had to do it. Mathews didn't like the "poor-mouthing." I went to Paul Garner and told him why I had to

Munny Sokol, adviser to deans.

do it, and that I would not blame him. He really was a hero and should be so recognized. I had learned about fund-raising from Harvard, which always poor-mouthed even with their enormous trust funds.

One fund-raising avenue that had been started under Garner with Tom Moore's leadership was the Commerce Executives Society. Fielden said:

Tom did it. When I arrived the society was very small, but it did exist. I did not have this concept at BU, and I thought what a great idea it is. We got some seed money from somewhere and put on a "grand opening" for the Commerce Executives, pretending that it hadn't existed before.

We had a big reception at Indian Hills Country Club, I think, and then trotted all the people over to Memorial [now Coleman] Coliseum and put on this slide show about all our problems and what we needed. Cards were passed out and we got five thousand dollars in annual pledges from a three-thousand-dollar cash outlay. You have to spend money to raise money—the cost of acquisition. [And] once you have them aboard, you've got to keep them happy.

We started the Commerce Executives Newspaper, which was an "all smiles" paper. I started editing it, Sam Himes did it for a short time, and then Betty Loomis did it for about twenty years. Betty used to come with a copy and I'd read it. Tom handled all the production and distribution.

In addition to understanding fund-raising and the mentality of business people, Fielden was savvy about the value of community leaders and how to utilize their influence. Tom introduced Jack to Munny Sokol, who came to Fielden's office one day and said, "Look, I'm sixty years old, and I don't know what to do with myself. I'm looking for something to do, but I don't know you from Adam and I'm not about to go to work for you as a flunky. If I help you, are you going to do what I tell you? You don't know a thing about the South, but you need to. I've lived here all my life."

Fielden knew a good thing when he heard it, and he quickly agreed to Munny's proposal. "We never had a cross word," Fielden said. "He took Tom and me to every nook and cranny in Alabama. We'd drag ourselves home at 11:30 at night and have a meeting at 8:00 in the morning. Munny was with us, and he gave us such good advice. What a wonderful man!" (*Note:* As noted in chapter 5, Munny Sokol is in a nursing home; he is incapable of communicating and has been so for a number of years. He is greatly missed by all who knew him.)

Another person commended by Fielden was Richard Gregory, who was a member of the University Development Office. Jack was complimentary about how easy he was to work with and how well he understood what C&BA was trying to do. Gregory passed away many years ago. It is good to remember this fine man in our history.

Tom Moore and Fielden got Jack Warner to head the Board of Visitors. The Alabama Business Hall of Fame, Fielden said, was Tom Moore's idea, although Fielden said he himself often gets the credit for it.

Bennett on Fielden and International Business

When Jack Fielden came, he made me associate dean. I handled everything Jack didn't want to do. You know, that's what the associate dean always does. It was really a mistake for me to get so involved, because I really didn't enjoy being associate dean. My graduate responsibilities were largely decentralized and were handled by the departments. [The change between centralization and decentralization of the graduate program occurred from time to time.]

Because I didn't like the associate dean's job, I told Jack that I wanted to get out of the position and teach international business. I had gotten very interested in the area when Doug Lamont was on our faculty in the sixties. When Doug left for Wisconsin the area really died. Jack's attitude was, What do you want to do that for? He really didn't know why anyone at Alabama would be interested in international business. He admitted that if it were Boston University, he'd understand.

Well, I asked for a sabbatical, and I went to Australia and New Zealand. When I got back, I started teaching international courses. During the year's leave, I audited all the international courses, like Baklanoff's and Evans's courses, and I tried to get myself where I understood what was going on. I started teaching the international courses and began building my relationship with the Department of Commerce in Birmingham in the international field. I then got acquainted, through the World Trade Association, with many people and started going to their meetings.

Bill Bennett put all his heart into developing an international focus at Alabama. He wanted to teach international business in a different way:

I wanted students to have actual contact with companies that were interested in overseas business and to learn about the opportunities for them in an overseas business. Dean Fielden didn't encourage me, but I knew a person in Birmingham who knew about the TEAM Program. It was a master's program that the Department of Commerce was interested in. So I had a bunch of students [my class] who traveled with companies. The program was a kind of consulting related to market research as to what the situation was in various countries for their particular product.

In 1978 I got a call from Montgomery. The development people wanted to talk with us. They wanted me to do some research for them in the Latin American markets. We did it and followed with several more things for them. The University had been talking about having an international trade center, and Mark Weaver had the contact with the Small Business Administration. He had been talking with them and found out they were interested in establishing a regional international trade center in the Southeast. So he talked to them about Alabama. And with my TEAM program and various visits, we got our first grant for the International Trade Center. Mark didn't want to be the director, so I took it on.

Bill is enthusiastic with the progress the center has made under the leadership of Nisa Miranda.

Bennett's international commitments and contributions were recognized with the naming of the W. R. Bennett International Trade Center upon his retirement in 1983. His broad-based University contributions were recognized when he was awarded the Algernon Sidney Sullivan Award and received an honorary doctorate from Alabama after he retired.

Art Thompson Remembers Fielden

Art Thompson, along with Barry Mason, was one of the first faculty members to work closely with Jack Fielden. Art saw their roles as second lieutenants with Bill Bennett (senior associate dean) serving as a kind of mentor in the early days of Fielden's tenure. As Thompson recalled,

> *Bill was always the senior, wise man who knew the ropes. I saw Barry and me as maybe the young Turks who were perhaps more Jack's agents of change. My title was director of academic planning, which was just a name we made up because Jack didn't want to go to [Central Administration] and have a whole flock of associate or assistant deans. I think Barry was called director of research.*
>
> *I stayed in the job a year. The time frame was never discussed, but I got very frustrated and learned that I really didn't want to do what I was doing, and I wasn't very good at it. I thought that I might want to be a dean one day or a chairman, and what I learned very, very quickly was that I didn't really want to do any of that and wasn't happy doing it because I felt like I was never getting my work done. I was always in some meeting or going to hear this or that around and about the campus, or talking to this person or that person, and didn't ever feel like I had time to do anything. I also think that Jack's way of managing and my way of doing things clashed, which is not to say that either one of us was wrong, but they did not mix. Everyone does things his own way, and Jack, properly I think, ran things more through the department chairmen and through Dr. Bennett. So I asked myself, what was there for Art to do? Art didn't like being a staff assistant who thinks of ideas and tosses out trial balloons.*
>
> *I did learn something very important. It was a wonderful experience to see how a new dean comes into a new situation and begins to reshape the college. Jack would do business in his office, but he would not manage by walking around, understanding what was happening, feeling the tempo out there. That's more my style. I would be up and down the halls and around and about sort of talking to people and sort of hearing what was going on and trying to capture the mood, and he would not, as best I could see, do any of that. He would ask me what the mood was. And he'd ask Barry, but I tended to know more than Barry because he didn't have the strong lines of communication with people in other departments that I did.*

The history of our college would be incomplete without Art Thompson's perspective of those days "in the dean's office." He is a person who respects people even if he disagrees with their ideas or process.

Barry Mason Remembers Fielden

Two colleagues who were closest to the new regime were Art Thompson and Barry Mason. Art and Barry are very different people, and certainly Bill Bennett differs from the two. It makes for good oral history, I believe, to look at the same phenomenon from differing perspectives. The Jack Fielden era cries out for such interpretations.

In recalling those days, Barry Mason began by saying:

> *When Jack came, he felt that the college was living in the early fifties in methods of teaching, in programs, in curricula. He believed he had to jump-start the faculty into a much more modern era. Remember, Jack had come from Boston University, a private school and he also worked with the* Harvard Business Review *as associate editor. He brought the private school perspective in terms of fund-raising. He picked up the Commerce Executives Society, and initiated the Board of Visitors and the Alabama Business Hall of Fame. Jack led the reorganization of the college in a very dramatic way.*
>
> *He reduced the number of departments to four, which is exactly what we have today. He hired a lot of young people. He also went after some senior scholars, like H. K. Wu, to bring in overnight academic credibility. He also led an effort to refine our curriculum. I think he did a good job. Much of what he put in place at the beginning of the seventies is still visible today, which is testimony to the wisdom of what he saw and what he was able to put in place. He was very smooth, very sophisticated, and a worldly kind of individual.*

The seventies came in like a lion and went out in the same manner. As Mason reflected on the Fielden era and particularly on the difficulties Jack faced toward the end of his tenure, he commented:

> *The whole world fell apart at that time. . . . It was the period of the faculty senate revolution led by Bob Barfield [professor and later dean of engineering, now retired]. Virtually every dean on campus was fired or resigned. Most department heads, too. Jack was once again caught up in a paradigm shift. Such ferment indicated that the faculty, in maturing, was asserting its right as never before to self-governance and assuming a very active voice in issues that affected their interests.*
>
> *There were department heads in Arts and Sciences and elsewhere who had been in their positions as long as twenty-five years, and many faculty members felt that these individuals were well beyond their prime and should not have still been in those roles. At that time there were no mechanisms for review, in other words no way to remove them from office. So the senate, in conjunction with others, set out to change that.*

The name of a reporter for the *Tuscaloosa News*, Jack Wheat, is part of our history. Getting caught up in the feelings of disillusionment with Pres. David Mathews, Wheat became the voice of campus discontent. Mason remembered: "So the faculty, aided by Wheat, managed to knock out the president and the vice-presidents, all the deans, and a lot of the department heads. The results were that we saw the development of governance and accountability structures that are here today. So again, part of Fielden's problems were part of the maturation movement sweeping the campus at that time. What happened to Jack would have happened to anyone who was dean at that time."

Mason philosophized for a moment when he said:

Without question, Barry Mason understands the pressures of "deaning." Few
among us can speak with the depth of perception of the seventies that he can.

Ron Dulek Remembers Fielden

Although he joined the faculty toward the end of Fielden's deanship, Ron
Dulek probably knew Jack Fielden as well as anyone on the faculty (with the
notable exception of Jean Gibbons who married Jack). I decided to present
Dulek's "memory piece" as an actual Q&A. It seemed to be the best approach.

> **Morris Mayer:** How would you describe Jack Fielden and the Fielden
> era?
>
> **Ron Dulek:** First of all, you've got to realize I cannot be unbiased
> where Jack is concerned.
>
> **MM:** Everyone with whom I've talked is biased about something.
>
> **RD:** The era was vibrant, exciting, crazy. Jack had the concepts
> twenty years ago that corporations talk about today. He talked
> about the things Tom Peters talks about—about being capable of
> instantly changing and having to. That's what Fielden brought to
> the college and he brought it in the seventies. He was concerned
> about doing what's right for the college and was unconcerned
> about the bureaucracy that causes those things to move slowly.
>
> **MM:** How did he avoid bureaucracy?
>
> **RD:** I don't think he did. I think he took it on. But there's one thing
> that's really important that I learned from him despite that
> constant desire to change and to lead in a corporate mode. He
> would always say he would do anything he could do to make the
> school move ahead except for one thing. His standard line that
> he taught me, that I live by, is "The curriculum belongs to the
> faculty." And he would never touch that. It was his core
> principle. I think that's what gives an institution integrity. The
> faculty will never compromise themselves on the curriculum. It's
> a belief that permeates the college, and I'm sure that is a tribute
> to Jack.
>
> **MM:** Part of the culture?
>
> **RD:** A very important part of the culture that we don't often
> acknowledge.
>
> **MM:** What was Jack's feeling about research in the school?

RD: He believed in it in a number of different ways. He believed it was necessary because "it is the academic game." If you want to play in that game, then you've got to do it. He believed also that research involved being a teacher of teachers; that if you want to be a doctoral-granting institution, then part of your job is to teach other people about the field.

MM: Was he saying that we all have to serve as role models?

RD: Yes. For the next generation and for other professors—peers. And on a national scale, not a state or regional scale. He viewed the Ph.D. as a national degree; that if you get a doctorate you should be capable of being placed anywhere in the nation, and therefore you must compete on national norms.

MM: Can you separate Jack from the Fielden era as you describe each one?

RD: I think not. It's a matter of leadership. Every year is a reflection of who the dean is. If Jack were vibrant and alive, so was his era. He said often you have to have eight or ten balls in the air at the same time.

MM: How did he feel about "biting the bullet" and doing things that were distasteful?

RD: I don't think he liked it, but he was willing to do it. He viewed it as part of his job, and he accepted that. He felt it's part of being a leader.

MM: What's Jack going to be remembered for?

RD: The easy answer is that he will be remembered for setting up the fund-raising mechanism that we are now benefiting from. But he also set up the structure for the college that we still have today. Few people give Jack credit for that. But if you ask me, the most important contribution Jack made is that he sowed the seeds that led us to being nationally competitive. In fact, as I look at where we are now, where we were in the late seventies, and what I hear of times before that, I can see a kind of continuum. Lee Bidgood and Paul Garner seem to have set out to make us a regional leader, [a

Joseph Warren Hawkins Jr., one hundred thousandth graduate from the College of Commerce, 1979.

position] we had achieved in the late sixties and early seventies. Jack said, "Let's raise the stakes. We need to be nationally competitive." I remember he used to joke that we needed to have a business school of which our football team could be proud. Jack laid the groundwork for us to achieve national prominence. What's interesting from the perspective of the 1990s is that we have achieved what Jack desired.

Thus we bring down the curtain on the seventies and the major part of the Fielden era.

The world is talking about:

The U.S. Olympic committee votes to boycott the Summer Olympics in Moscow. (April 22, 1980)

Sandra Day O'Connor becomes the first woman to sit on the U.S. Supreme Court. (1981)

Minutes after Ronald Reagan is inaugurated as president, the fifty-two Americans held hostage are released after 444 days of captivity. (January 20, 1981)

President Reagan is shot in the chest by would-be assassin John W. Hinkley Jr. (March 30, 1981)

The American public becomes aware of an apparently new disease—Acquired Immune Deficiency Syndrome (AIDS). (1982)

In one of the most significant antitrust cases in history, the Justice Department orders American Telephone and Telegraph Company (AT&T), one of the world's largest corporations, to divest itself of the twenty-two Bell System companies that provide most local telephone service in the United States. (January 8, 1982)

The first artificial heart transplant is accomplished at the University of Utah Medical Center. (December 2, 1982)

When the space shuttle *Challenger* is launched from Cape Canaveral, Florida, Sally Ride becomes the first U.S. woman to travel in space. (June 18, 1983)

Two hundred forty-one U.S. marines and sailors, members of the multinational peacekeeping force in Lebanon, are killed when a TNT-laden suicide terrorist blows himself up in marine headquarters at Beirut International Airport. (October 25, 1983)

Former vice-president Walter Mondale wins the Democratic presidential nomination, and in a historic move on July 12, 1984, he chooses a woman, Rep. Geraldine Ferraro (D-NY), as candidate for vice-president.

Ronald Reagan is reelected president in the greatest Republican landslide in history, carrying forty-nine states against Walter Mondale. (November 6, 1984)

What will become known as the Iran-Contra affair begins. One day before the 1986 congressional elections, it is reported that the United States had sent spare parts and ammunition to Iran. Over the next months it is revealed that additional arms sales had been made to Iran and profits diverted to a fund for Nicaraguan contras.

Moments after liftoff, the space shuttle *Challenger* explodes, killing six astronauts and Christa McAuliffe, a New Hampshire teacher. (January 23, 1986)

The Tower Commission Report finds President Reagan confused and uninformed in Iran-Contra hearings. (February 27, 1987)

Federal grand juries in Miami and Tampa return indictments against Gen. Manuel Noriega, the effective ruler of Panama, charging that he had protected and otherwise assisted the Modellin drug cartel. (February 4, 1988)

George Bush, vice-president under Ronald Reagan, is elected the forty-first president of the United States. (November 8, 1988)

The largest oil spill in U.S. history occurs when the Exxon *Valdez* strikes Bligh Reef in Alaska's Prince William Sound. The spill, estimated at 240,000 barrels, extended forty-five miles. (March 24, 1989)

Former National Security Council staff member Oliver North becomes the first person convicted in a jury trial in connection with the Iran-Contra scandal. (May 4, 1989)

Legislation passed by Congress to rescue the foundering S&L industry is signed into law by President Bush. (August 9, 1989)

U.S. troops invade Panama, overthrowing the government of Manuel Noriega, who eludes capture, takes refuge in the Vatican mission, and then surrenders to the United States on January 3, 1990.

Operation Desert Shield troops leave for Saudi Arabia to defend that country following the invasion of its neighbor Kuwait by Iraq. (August 7, 1990)

The U.S. Senate approves the nomination of Clarence Thomas to serve as an associate justice of the Supreme Court. Approval comes after an investigation of alleged sexual harassment leveled against him by Anita Hill, a law professor at the University of Oklahoma. (1991)

R. H. Macy and Company, owner of 251 retail stores in the United States, files for bankruptcy. (January 27, 1992)

Trans World Airlines (TWA) becomes the latest major U.S. air carrier to file for bankruptcy. (January 31, 1992)

Rioting, looting, and arson sweep south central Los Angeles in late April and early May after an all-white jury acquits four policemen on all but one count in the beating of a black man, Rodney King. (1992)

(continued on page 116)

Chapter 7 Preparing for the Millennium: The Eighties and Nineties
The Era of Deans Fielden, Smith (acting), Mitchell, Petersen, and Mason

(continued on page 117)

In Their Own Words

In remembering his college years, 1977 to 1981, *Marcus L. Bruchis* focused on what being a student in C&BA meant to him. Most important to Bruchis was that his Alabama experience taught him to be independent:

> *It may sound corny, but my time in the Commerce School taught me to be independent—to think for myself, and that has been very important to me in my career. And speaking of career reminds me of the services of the Placement Center [now called the Career Center]. Certainly the people in placement, like Mary Barlow, did a great deal for me, but a lot of the job seeking falls on the student. You've got to be aggressive; it's not going to just happen.*
>
> *I [really] wanted an interview with Xerox, but my name was not drawn in the lottery. [The lottery was the interview system in place at the time.] The day of the interview I just sat in the Placement Office for a long time after the company representative had completed his interview schedule, and as he was leaving I went up to him and requested an interview. He granted me the time, and my first job was with Xerox.*
>
> *At this time I am vice-president of leasing for Aronov Realty Company in Montgomery. As I look back, the two most valuable courses I had were retail management and GBA 490. My career in leasing retail space was enhanced as I knew how the retailer thinks and behaves. GBA 490 gave me a genuine appreciation of competition and running a business. I learned a little about real entrepreneurship.*
>
> *One of the best things that happened to me was being awarded the Elton B. Stephens Scholarship in Selling. All of my jobs have been sales or sales related, and having that accomplishment on my record was a real plus for me. It differentiated me and said that the faculty [believed] I would have a bright sales career.*

And he has!

The following excerpts are from an unusual interview; unusual because both of the former students with whom I talked are employed by University Housing and work together in the marketing function.

The world is talking about:

(continued from page 114)

Gov. Bill Clinton of Arkansas defeats incumbent George Bush to become president of the United States. (November 3, 1992)

A United Nations-sanctioned military force, led by American troops, arrives in Somalia to ensure the delivery of food to starving people in the war-torn nation. (December 9, 1992)

President Clinton appoints his wife, Hillary Rodham Clinton, as head of the Task Force on National Health Care Reform. (January 25, 1993)

Four federal agents are killed during an unsuccessful raid on the compound of a religious cult near Waco, Texas. The confrontation between the Branch Davidians and law enforcement officials

ends tragically in April when the cult's compound burns to the ground, killing seventy-two cult members. (February 28, 1993)

Republican governor Guy Hunt of Alabama is convicted of a felony, diverting money from an inaugural fund to his personal use. (April 22, 1993)

O. J. Simpson is accused of murdering his former wife and her friend. (1994)

The University is talking about:

Following a year of public controversy, during which the faculty delivered a "no confidence" vote in the administration, Mathews resigns effective July 1, 1980.

The sesquicentennial anniversary of the university is celebrated in 1981.

Paul "Bear" Bryant becomes the winningest football coach in history in November 1981.

Coach Bryant retires and the Student Recreation Center is completed in 1983.

Pres. Joab Thomas is named in the top ten university presidents of a comprehensive institution.

Construction begins on the Paul W. Bryant Conference Center and Bryant-Denny Stadium is expanded in 1986.

The indoor practice field, the second largest building on campus is completed in 1986. (Coleman Coliseum is the largest building.)

The Frank Moody Music Building opens in January 1988.

The University wins the NCAA gymnastics championship in 1988.

The Alston Building is completed in 1992.

Alabama football: the Crimson Tide wins its twelfth national championship in 1992.

The Student Government Association (SGA) is abolished in 1993.

The Bruno Business Library and the Sloan Y. Bashinsky Sr. Computer Center open in 1994.

College "hot buttons" during the Eighties and Nineties:

1980
- UA becomes one of the first universities to establish a School of Accountancy.
- Curriculum IV, computer science, is established.

1984
- Five-year Master of Accountancy Degree is offered.

1987
- Manderson Graduate School of Business is named.
- Executive Master of Business Administration (E.M.B.A.) is established.

1988
- Industrial management is changed to management science.
- New concentrations in Management Program are added: human resources management, general management (formerly a program by itself), entrepreneurship and small company management.

1989
- Culverhouse School of Accountancy is named.
- Hess Institute for Retailing Development is established.
- Broad knowledge requirement for Ph.D. is eliminated.

1990
- Upper and lower divisions are established in C&BA.
- Prelaw curriculum is dropped.

1991
- Graduate program in transportation is dropped.

1993
- M.B.A. program at forty-eight hours commences (announced in 1991).

1994
- Health care management (previously a separate curriculum) is now under management and marketing.

Over the past decade *Gena Hawkins Johnson* (M.B.A. 1982) and *Shirley Maksoud Darr* (B.S. 1982, master's in marketing 1983) have not only worked together but also taught for the Management and Marketing Department on an adjunct basis.

Johnson was particularly enthusiastic about the strong friendships that developed during her graduate work at Alabama.

> *My first year in the M.B.A. program was the first lock-step program, so that meant that we all had classes together and the twenty-five members of the class became exceptionally close friends. As a matter of fact, we had our tenth reunion in May of 1992 at the same house at the beach that we rented in May of 1982 following graduation. And every single person came between Thursday and Sunday. It was just wonderful. I am godmother of one of my classmate's children and another classmate is godfather of my child. We all stay in touch much more than just at Christmas time. We are all still very close.*

Darr took a different tack, as directed by the interviewer.

> *I came to the University not really knowing what I wanted to major in. I had a lot of different interests. I entered as an "undeclared" C&BA major mainly because my older brothers had done that. The faculty and classes that I had in Commerce convinced me that I was in the right home. Once I took my first marketing course, I was just enthralled. I thought, "Oh, this is wonderful," because it really combined a lot of things I was interested in.*
>
> *I could really relate to all of my marketing classes. I worked for Housing as an undergraduate student and loved it. When I was able to work in marketing for Housing, I was able to combine the things I liked best. The classes I had and the teachers I had, gave me an excellent background and base to apply in the nonprofit setting. The Commerce School gave me an education—and a career.*

In a telephone interview from his home in Connecticut, *Wiley Mullins*, Class of 1980, said:

> *When it was time to make a decision about where to go to college, I was faced with a lot of choices. Would it be a small, liberal arts school like Tuskegee Institute or a major state university like Alabama? I opted to come to the University of Alabama, and I have never been disappointed.*
>
> *Alabama, and especially the business school, is a wonderful place—a wonderful place to get tested and to stretch your mind and feel like you're on the cusp of things. I think when you walk down the aisle at the Coliseum on graduation day, you really have confidence that you can make it—that you can deal with whatever comes your way. It was a great beginning for me!*
>
> *I benefited from being thrown in with such varied people with many different points of view. I was challenged, and I also challenged others. I really benefited, but I sincerely feel that a lot of people benefited from what I had to offer.*

Wiley is currently devoting his energies to marketing his own line of soul food, called Wiley's.

The following three individuals represent those who are poised for the approaching millennium. *Kelly Nunnelly Litford* received her B.S. in accounting

Faculty that carry on the C&BA culture:
(continued from page 115)

Myung J. Kim (1989)
George F. Klersey Jr. (1989)
Vicki Knoblauch (1991)
Thomas A. Lee (1991)
James Ligon (1990)
James T. Lindley (1982)
Alan Lord (1989)
Gene A. Marsh (1981)
David M. Miller (1983)
H. H. Mitchell (1981)
John Mittenthal (1994)
Robert Morgan (1991)
William H. Motes (1981)
Frank H. Page Jr. (1991)
Paul Pecorino (1994)
Russell J. Petersen (1986)
Walter A. Robbins (1982)
Michael L. Roberts (1987)
William D. Samson (1984)
Harris Schlesinger (1987)
Charles Schmidt (1984)
Edward J. Schnee (1982)
Clyde J. Scott (1981)
Anson Seers (1980)
R. Shane Sharp (1991)
Larry E. Stanfel (1988)
Jay U. Sterling (1984)
Mary Stone (1981)
Paul D. Thistle (1982)
Sharon L. Topping (1983)
Charles Turner (1984)
Jerry Weaver (1980)
Deborah Wheless (1980)
William H. Woodall (1988)
Liming Zhao (1991)

in 1992; *Chapel Hill* is a 1993 graduate of the M.B.A. Program; and *Kristy Ellis*, after receiving a bachelor's and a master's in marketing, expects to receive her Ph.D during C&BA's seventy-fifth anniversary year.

Kelly Litford was glad to talk about her alma mater:

> *My parents went to Alabama, and my dad was a graduate of C&BA, as was my sister (Kim, Class of 1993). My brother, Todd, is in Commerce now.*
>
> *My accounting classes definitely prepared me for what I have been doing as a public accountant. They certainly prepared you technically, and they also alerted you to the different professional aspects of the job. Not just accounting, but for the business world in general. When I was serving as a Commerce Associate [outstanding students who serve as hosts for the college] I got to meet business people from all over the state and that was a wonderful opportunity. I run into some of those people today.*
>
> *I was the editor of the* Commerce Courier *for a couple of years, and believe me, those additional writing skills that I got from being editor and the organizational skills really help with any career. In my career, communication skills are so important.*

Litford commended Dr. Klersey's auditing class and Gene Marsh's CPA Law Review class. Her enthusiasm for her education and her position are contagious.

Chapel Hill believed his M.B.A. enhanced his speaking abilities and his personal communication skills. He made a number of contacts who will benefit him down the road. He is with Stern, Agee, and Leach, and at the time of the interview was in training in the Atlanta office of the Birmingham-based firm to be a stockbroker. "I am working in research right now. In the M.B.A. program we did quite a bit of fundamental analysis and work as far as evaluating different firms. I naturally gained a lot in that area."

In recalling his coursework, Hill said his first-year accounting course was valuable to him, especially in the work he is currently doing. He was also complimentary about some of his marketing courses, and he particularly liked courses in which he met executives in top management positions.

Bill Bolen—the University's most honored student of 1991; a marketing major who worked with Dow Chemical and then attended Harvard Business School.

He commented in closing, "Teach your students interaction. [The faculty] were always available anytime we had problems or questions, and we weren't afraid to come talk to them. They were always very helpful." We try.

Kristy Ellis's three-degree commitment to our college makes her an ideal choice as the final alumni interviewee.

Edward Smith, long-time contributor to C&BA.

> *I attended the University as an undergraduate from the fall of 1985 until the spring of 1989. Then I entered the master's program in the fall of 1990 when I also started the doctoral program in marketing. My career goal is to get a tenure-track position teaching marketing.*
>
> *Why did I opt to remain here rather than take a job after receiving a bachelor's degree? I have always loved school, and that's what I found I am good at. None of the job offers interested me, and some very influential people in my life inspired me to stay on. I just felt like that was the right thing to do. My interest in going for the Ph.D. and remaining at Alabama developed during my master's work. I was at a really wonderful university, and I didn't feel I could do any better anywhere else.*
>
> *The faculty, their attitude, and the way they treated me as a student was the real attraction. The reputation of Alabama's doctoral faculty is increasingly being regarded as a national contender. The wonderful new facilities have really put Alabama's business school on the map! When I get my doctorate [in 1994], I'll be very proud to have it from Alabama.*
>
> *Dean Barry Mason, in addition to you [Morris Mayer] and Sharon Beatty, had great influence on my decision. Dean Mason said the only reason I should leave is if I could find some place better. And he said, "I don't think you can." I trusted his opinion because I know that he is somebody who is nationally known and very well regarded. When you say "Barry Mason," people listen.*

Each year the graduate faculty of marketing selects one doctoral student to represent Alabama at a national American Marketing Association Doctoral

Consortium. In 1992 Kristy Ellis was our choice. Students from all the prestigious institutions attend the consortium, and Ellis said,

> *I felt good. I really did. I fit in fine, and I am convinced that I had as good an education as anyone there. I was a little intimidated by Harvard and MIT at first [because of their images], but as I look back and know what I do now, I am certain that our Ph.D. program is as good as any if not better. I know that, and I am proud. Our Visiting Speakers Program is better than any in the country. Dr. Beatty has created a remarkable advantage here. I had heard all of the top educators mentioned at the Consortium.*

These young people are typical of their cohorts. With such fine representatives of the 1980s and 1990s, our future seems secure.

Looking Back

After six decades of remarkable organizational stability at both the University and the college levels, the years of the eighties encompassed a decade of somewhat more leadership changes. In central administration, Howard Gundy was acting president for a year following David Mathews's departure. Gundy stepped aside for Joab Thomas, who served for seven years and left to assume the top administrative position at Penn State University, after a one-year leave of absence from Alabama. Roger Sayers moved from academic vice-president to the presidency in 1988, a position he holds in 1994. His tenure has been one of exciting faculty expansion and physical growth for C&BA.

The roster of deans of C&BA in the 1980s and 1990s include:

Jack Fielden, who returned to full-time teaching in 1980;

Edward Smith, who, dedicated to serving as he always was when called on, was acting dean while a search committee under my chairmanship recommended to President Thomas, Dr. Kenneth Uhl of Illinois for the deanship.

H. H. (Bill) Mitchell, who accepted a five-year appointment as dean upon the recommendation of the revived search committee; the committee acted quickly after the untimely death of Dr. Uhl during the Christmas break 1980, just before he and his wife were to arrive in Tuscaloosa;

Russell Petersen, who served two years at UA and has continued to serve in administrative posts at other universities;

Barry Mason, who in our seventy-fifth anniversary year is in his sixth year as dean.

The eighties were the Reagan-Bush years. As we get further from those years the things I remember best are the advent of AIDS, Iran-Contra, Oliver North, the Exxon *Valdez* oil spill, the S&L bailout, and Desert Storm. The picture in my mind's eye of that decade is not bright. Thus far in the nineties we think of Pres. Bill Clinton and Hillary Rodham Clinton, Somalia, Bosnia, Haiti, more AIDS, the tragedy in Waco, former governor Guy Hunt and Gov. Jim Folsom, and the O. J. Simpson "media event." A brighter decade in the making? I'll let the reader (and the future) decide.

As for the University, the environment was for the most part quite "bullish." Coach Bryant became the winningest football coach in history, but the decade also saw his retirement and death. The University was 150 years old, and we celebrated. The Moody Music Building and the Bryant Conference Center opened, and Bryant-Denny Stadium was expanded—all in the eighties. And the nineties? Thus far, the operative phrase in this decade has been Building for the Future. The college is ready for the millennium with the completion of the magnificent business campus, which includes Alston Hall, the renovation of Bidgood Hall, and the dedication of the Angelo Bruno Business Library and the Sloan Y. Bashinsky Computer Center. But the 1990s are not just an era of pride in our physical facilities; we also celebrate our culture and values, which have nurtured us for seventy-five years, and the leadership illustrated by our faculty, student body, alumni, and administration, which have got us where we are.

Focus on Faculty, Centers, and Institutes

As I look at the names of "new" colleagues listed in the beginning of this chapter, I am struck by how critically important this group is in our college. To generalize is difficult, but some descriptors do come to mind when I look at the list: young (certainly from my vantage point); research and publication oriented; outstanding teachers; effective administrators (currently or potentially); holders of named professorships; and diverse in educational backgrounds, focus, and disciplines. The strength of this group of colleagues is the best evidence I can present that the College of Commerce and Business Administration is strongly positioned to welcome the millennium that rapidly approaches.

Dean Barry Mason sees institutes as a natural growth of and adjunct to a commitment to work with the private sector as well as to support and accelerate economic development. Business schools must have a way to stay in touch, a way to be supportive, and also a way to lead. Deciding which section would be best for addressing institutes (or centers) presented transitional and organizational choices. To handle these entities chronologically (that is, to discuss each one within the decade of its inception) had a certain logic. But it did not fit my concept of how this history should be approached. (The inception of the Bureau of Business Research was discussed in chapter 2 because it was such an important element of the Bidgood philosophy.) They might have been addressed in the decade within which each director arrived; I could justify that approach just as logically as I could justify chronology. The rationale for addressing them in this section is that their missions are not tied to any time period or for that matter to any particular colleague, although the director does set the tone and affect priorities of the institute. Reviewing them in the present as a part of the faculty focus of this section made sense to me. I hope the readers agree.

Barry Mason Reflects

Dean Mason's response to the question, What are you proudest of as dean? provided an excellent commentary on the C&BA faculty:

> *The thing that I am the proudest of is the genuine commitment to and feeling of excitement about good teaching at all levels, especially undergraduate teaching. The enormous amount of time, effort, energy, and innovation that has come from the faculty is not externally directed. I am delighted with the things John Formby has done in principles of economics where the D and F rate is down in the 30 percent range from 60 percent to 70 percent. I am so pleased with what Rob Ingram has done in basic accounting. These two key scholars with national reputations voluntarily took it upon themselves to fundamentally restructure how principles courses are taught. And in so doing to say loud and clear to young colleagues that it's not enough to be a good scholar, you must also be a superb teacher.*
>
> *I am proud of the fact that the faculty are working together as peers with mutual respect where departments are largely administrative conveniences and not barriers to cross disciplinary teaching and research.*

John Formby and Rob Ingram

In reflecting on the accomplishments of the faculty, Dean Mason referred to John Formby and Rob Ingram, two of the most respected faculty members in the college. During the interviewing phase of this history project, I interviewed these two men and asked them to tell me why they came to Alabama and if it had been a good choice.

"I haven't regretted coming here once," Formby said.

> *I came here as a department head [which I had been for two years before coming here], but I knew I wasn't going to stay a department head. It was not part of my deal, I just knew that I got into the administrative stuff far too young. I never really wanted it to become my principal focus. I came in 1983; Dean Mitchell hired me. I'm not quite sure what the remainder of my career will be. When I came here I thought I'd probably stay ten years and be gone. But I may be here for the rest of my time. I don't know what tomorrow holds, but my research has simply taken off like a rocket since I gave up administration. It's been delightful to spend my time as I'm doing now. I started out in this business to be a teacher. Since I gave up the job of associate dean, I have basically been doing my teaching and research.*

Rob Ingram, who came to Alabama in 1985, said he was asked to apply for the Ernst & Whinney (now Ernst & Young) professorship, which he did. "Thus," he explained,

> *I had economic incentives to come to Alabama. . . . I was on the faculty at the University of Iowa. My family and I saw Alabama as an opportunity to leave the Iowa winters and return to a more favorable climate. I am from Alabama, and*

the move afforded the opportunity to be closer to family. Additionally, I saw an opportunity to make a contribution to a developing research program by working with other faculty and graduate students. Nevertheless, my motives for coming to Alabama were largely personal.

My most positive experiences have been in assisting in the development of a quality educational program in accounting and, more generally, in C&BA. Much progress has been made in creating an educational environment for students that is at the forefront of accounting education nationally. Teaching is important at Alabama, and faculty are encouraged to be innovative and pursue teaching excellence. At the same time considerable flexibility exists to pursue research interests that complement educational efforts and are relevant to real-world problems.

It is interesting that Ingram, like Formby, gave up his administrative job, as director of the School of Accountancy, to return to full-time teaching and research.

Carl Ferguson and CBER

Bill Gunther, current director of CBER (Center for Business and Economic Research) agreed that the perspective of Carl Ferguson, who joined the staff in 1975 and was director for twelve years, would have greater historical value than his own. Ferguson began the interview by justifying this conclusion:

One of the most interesting facts historically . . . is that the Bureau [Bureau of Business Research, later CBER] was one of the founding members of the Association of University Business and Economic Research (AUBER). Our Bureau and AUBER were key players in the development of what became the Department of Commerce Bureau of Economic Analysis in Washington. Dr. Chapman, the Bureau's first director, was recognized as a very, very important force at the national level back in those days.

Henry Moore and Ed Rutledge—major players in CBER's history.

The Bureau played a very important role in the development of regional economic analysis and, in turn, strengthened the quality of economic analysis carried out at the national level. During those early periods, the Bureaus like today's CBER, were very, very important forces in the U.S. higher education system.

I asked Ferguson if the change in name from Bureau of Business Research to CBER was significant? He said he suspected that people with specific training in economics really felt compelled to inject their name and the notion of economic analysis into the title: "so bureaus of business research became centers for business and economic research, suggesting that somehow the economic research was much more important or 'higher class.'"

Carolyn Sawyer, an analyst with CBER in the 1970s.

Left to right: Annette Watters, Deborah Hamilton, and Carl Ferguson —CBER in the eighties.

Reflecting on prior directors of CBER, he named H. H. Chapman, C. N. Moore, Henry Moore, and Ed Rutledge. He described Rutledge as a kind of "caretaker director" and was not sure what his exact title was. Rutledge was in the dean's office for a time, and Ferguson was named associate director of CBER. According to Ferguson,

> *Ed was a very important person in the transition of the Center. Henry Moore was very close to important people in state government and he really made a legitimate effort to quantify and bring as much empirical strength and credibility to state analysis as was being done anywhere in the country at the state level. After Henry retired, the Center was a poor stepchild. It bounced around from person to person, and it went for a time I think without a director.*
>
> *During much of that period Ed was a doctoral student in statistics, and when he became ABD [having completed his doctoral work All-But-Dissertation] he began to work in the Center full time. Jack Fielden, I think, placed Ed in the caretaker mode. Because he had worked with Henry Moore, Ed had pretty good contacts in Montgomery, and he used them. When I got to the Center, Ed was picking up the pieces and was involving CBER in a variety of ways with state government. For a number of reasons the Center's credibility was in question, and Ed was trying to restore that credibility. This was about the time I came—1975.*
>
> *I was hired as an assistant professor of marketing. As a graduate student at Missouri I had worked in their Center like Ed Rutledge did here.*

Ferguson commented favorably on the staff of CBER. "I was fortunate that we had a staff that was really quite committed to doing some good work for the state. The approach was to do good projects that we thought really ought to be done, show them to the State people, and ask for a show of interest." Apparently it worked.

He saw the center in his day as the lead agency for economic and demographic research in the state and, to the extent that it was appropriate, in the region. Ferguson felt CBER was a clear and direct avenue to federal data that could be used by business for economic analysis to analyze regional markets.

Ferguson stated his philosophy of the service function of CBER: "As a matter of policy, we would do work for the faculty of any type if it had any relationship to what our fundamental mission was. One of the first things we did was something as simple as manuscript typing. I immediately said that we will do any manuscript typing that anyone wants us to do. We had the first word processors on campus." Ferguson was proud of the fact that because of its exemplary service CBER became so important during his twelve years that the center's budget grew through major increases from central administration.

He has been back to full-time teaching since 1988, and I would say he has the same enthusiasm about that activity as he did as CBER director. He is a flexible, versatile man to whom the University owes much.

Lonnie Strickland and the Management Institute

Many faculty members (including me) remember fondly the Management Institute. Lonnie Strickland said it started in 1972 with a contract to do management training, requested by the federal department of Health, Education, and Welfare (HEW). At the outset he and a graduate student ran it.

Strickland was very open about how at first the training sessions were held in uncomfortable rooms at Martha Parham West (College of Continuing Studies). The attendees were quick to complain about the physical facilities, so he moved the four-week programs to North River Yacht Club—quite a change in ambience.

Strickland found out what others were doing in management training and learned how to do it better. Eventually the programs were packaged and mobile. The staff grew and HEW demanded more and more workshops. The most delightful vacation locations were selected for the workshops (for example, the Broadmore and the Breckenridge, in Colorado, and the Phoenix Biltmore) and the attendees were treated like royalty. Staff members, for example, would get a photo of each participant, memorize their names, and as they checked in, call them by name. Impressive.

Photographs were taken during the program, showing participants, faculty, and staff in various settings, and a slide show was shown at the end of the workshop. A dinner dance was held on Thursday evenings to keep participants from leaving before Fridays. Attendees would present testimonials before University officials, and Strickland likened these events to old-time tent revivals. At the concluding ceremony, Strickland, always the dramatic actor, would convince everyone there that "I love you people." He claimed that at one session, the acting president, Howard Gundy, was in attendance. As emotions peaked, he stood up and yelled, "Can't we do one more week?" The

Jimmy Harrison (CEO Harco) and Ronald Bruno (CEO Brunos), speakers at the 1989 Alabama Reunion Retailing Day.

word was out in HEW that you hadn't lived until you had attended an Alabama Management Institute Workshop.

Chuck Odewahn took over Strickland's role, and the institute had several more years of tremendous success. Many C&BA faculty, as well as other Alabama professors, participated as teachers in the programs. We got to see the best this country has to offer in lodging, made extra money, and felt that we were making a significant impact on some fine people. The image of Alabama soared.

As with all "products," the institute had a life cycle. When it was over, we all knew it would never be the same again.

Bob Robicheaux and the Hess Institute

The following excerpts are from an unidentified newspaper article (probably the *Tuscaloosa News* or the *Birmingham Post*) in November 1984:

> The Hess Institute was established at the UA College of Commerce and Business Administration with a gift from Parisian of Birmingham to support the retailing industry through teaching, research, and service.
>
> Parisian has given $20,000 as the first in a series of contributions totaling $100,000 to fund the Institute.
>
> Current retailing programs at UA, such as the annual Retailing Day which brings national retailing executives to campus for a day-long workshop with faculty and students, and a variety of new programs will be operated through the Hess Institute.
>
> Plans include an executive development program for middle and top managers, a Parisian Lecture Series featuring nationally known retailing executives and academicians, faculty development and research programs, career counseling and placement assistance for students, and retailing conferences.
>
> The Institute is named for Parisian president Donald E. Hess, his father, Emil C. Hess, and other family members.
>
> Morris L. Mayer has been named Director of the Institute according to H. H. Mitchell, dean of the college of C&BA.

Bob Robicheaux, the current director of the Institute said:

Speakers at 1991 Retailing Day *(left to right)*: Clyde Anderson, CEO Books-a-Million; Frank Bromberg, President Brombergs; Jim Wilson, CEO Jim Wilson Associates; and Richard Yielding, CEO Yieldings.

changed over time. Prior to the sixties most faculty members had degrees from outside the South; in the sixties and early seventies we hired many from southern schools. In the seventies and eighties a broader geographic base emerged. Robicheaux was cautious, but said, "Because job opportunities at the time were good, we think it means that Alabama was competing more favorably at the national level for 'big time' schools' products." My own suspicion is that in the earlier days southern schools had not "got into the doctoral production business" to the same extent as the universities in some other sections of the country had.

"Another thing that struck me," said Robicheaux, "was the productivity of our faculty compared to other divisions on campus. Our credit-hour production and utilization of our facilities were just astronomical. Everything was off the chart of what was standard. We were over capacity. In terms of enrollment, during the study period we were bursting at the seams."

And how did we fare in the self-study? "We came out with flying colors." Thanks, Bob.

Given the structure of our faculty and where people are in their careers, together with the dynamic, evolving field of retail marketing, I think the Hess Institute can expand and support more research. Research by doctoral students and faculty. I think the institute can be broader, but certainly not in any way to diminish the importance of the retailing focus. I think we can address vendor relations, distribution, information systems, legal issues, slotting allowances, diversions, international transfer arrangements—things that directly impact what happens at the retail level of the channel.

So, if I might say what I would like to see as a possibility for the Hess Institute, it is to provide a focal point for broadly defined retail and marketing distribution type research projects. Such research will directly or indirectly affect the way retailing is done and will also affect the consumer experience at retail. I'd like to see Retailing Day expanded, perhaps into a Retailing Week, maybe going back to more of an Executive-in-Residence format. I'd like to see more food retailers involved.

David Glass (CEO Wal-Mart), speaker, 1990 Retailing Day.

Trevor Bain and the Manpower Institute

The Manpower Institute was instituted in 1972 in the early days of Jack Fielden's deanship. A major grant proposal was submitted to the Department of Labor about winter 1973 by Chuck Odewahn and Allan Spritzer. It was not funded, and Fielden felt that without someone with credibility and background at the institute, the chances of getting funds were slim. For two years Alabama was unable to raise any grant money. Good people and good papers were not enough. We needed a name. Trevor Bain had experience in successful grantsmanship with the Department of Labor, which made him attractive to Dean Fielden. Another factor was the retirement of Langston Hawley. His position needed to be filled, and Bain's interests coincided with Hawley's. So Trevor Bain joined the C&BA faculty in August 1974.

In 1975 Fielden asked Bain to be the research director of the institute. Al Spritzer's interests had begun to center on administration, and he was serving as assistant dean for Student Affairs. Chuck Odewahn was moving in other directions, and long-time management professor Harold Janes was not interested in the institute. Shortly thereafter Bain was made director of the institute. (*Note:* The late Harold Janes was a master teacher and a joy as a colleague. His retirement, followed by a long illness and death, was a blow to me. I still miss him. Alan Spritzer left Alabama to become dean of the business school at East Tennessee, and Chuck Odewahn became involved with the graduate program and the Management Institute here at the University.)

During our interview, Trevor Bain recalled the early history of the institute:

> *In 1972 there were a large number of [prominent] industrial relations and manpower institutes at well-known universities like Michigan State, Cornell, UCLA, Berkeley, Princeton, and Illinois. Al [Spritzer], who was very instrumental in getting [the Manpower Institute] off the ground, in a sense tried to clone what had been going on successfully at Big Ten and other major universities.*
>
> *Fielden was supportive of the institute concept, and that was the major reason I was hired. Before I came, Al took some of his own research and some of the research of his students, and he put out a series of working papers. Getting these circulated around served as a PR effort and helped get the institute known among colleagues. By the time I got here, they were selling the working papers, with the money being kept in CBER because the center reproduced the papers, and selling the papers covered their costs.*

Bain commented on how the papers were marketed: "There are a number of bibliographic services that list research institutes. Every major library, think tank, and research group in the country has access to the major ones. We are listed, and anyone interested can find us very easily."

Myron Fotler was the first person hired to join the institute as research director. He had done a lot of research in the area, but he was not hired for grantsmanship. (Fotler is now at the University of Alabama at Birmingham after serving a time in C&BA.) When Bain became director of the institute, he called Bill Fulmer who was teaching at Harvard and whose work was primarily in industrial relations. Bain said he thought Fulmer, who had a doctorate in industrial relations from Wharton, came largely because of an opening in the policy area and because he was originally from Alabama. Bain also got Bill Malonney, a Ph.D. from Michigan, to join him.

> *We were beginning to build a really strong—nationally strong—group of people in human resources management and industrial relations. And we got the grant [a little over half a million dollars] in the next round, which was four years after the last round, which we missed. I got hired at the upswing of the public funding business. So I started to contact public officials in the states in the South and the federal government and attend their meetings, and I did some surveys for them. I delivered some reports and started to appear on the programs. We ran some one-day conferences here.*
>
> *The grant made it possible to carry out the objective of the institute, which was to encourage faculty research in manpower, industrial relations, and human resources. There was also a large training component.*

In 1994 Trevor Bain celebrated his twentieth anniversary as a member of C&BA's faculty, and he looked back with pleasure at the support he received and the value of the institute. We are in a very different funding era, and the activities have changed, but the positive contributions of the institute continue to please Trevor Bain.

Paavo Hanninen and the SBDC

The Small Business Development Center (SBDC) is a service arm of the college. It works to improve the economic quality of life in West Alabama through the development of new small businesses and the expansion of existing businesses. Assisting two hundred to three hundred new or existing businesses each year, the SBDC provides entrepreneurs with education and training opportunities that cover a wide range of business topics. Specifically, the center assists new or existing firms in devising business plans and assessing new markets, answers basic start-up questions, and addresses miscellaneous other small business needs. Counseling, work training, and information transfer form the core of SBDC activities.

The center is located within the college in order to maximize the benefits of the college's extensive business resources. Faculty, students, library holdings, and other units of the college, such as CBER, support SBDC in its mission.

A special emphasis of the center continues to be procurement assistance, which takes the form of computer-generated bid notifications forwarded to clients, bid package preparation, bonding, pricing, and quality assurance.

Paavo Hanninen has had full management responsibility for the center since his appointment in March 1984. He came to the University with an M.B.A. from the University of Mississippi; he had also worked for that institution's SBDC. The University's center is part of the state's SBDC, a consortium of eleven universities throughout the state that is partially funded by the U.S. Small Business Administration. After ten years, Paavo Hanninen is a visible and respected colleague in the university, the college, and the state.

Dave Miller (Productivity Center) and Nisa Miranda (William R. Bennett International Trade Center).

Dave Miller and the Alabama Productivity Center

The Alabama Productivity Center is a vehicle for improving the productivity of manufacturing and service firms throughout the state of Alabama. A primary activity of the center is coordinating applied research projects in which University faculty and students work jointly with a company's management and labor to resolve specific production, marketing, or other operational problems. These projects have simultaneously a research and educational focus—and a real-world impact. Other activities of the productivity center include education and development in the area of office automation and basic research in productivity analysis and improvement technology.

Dave Miller is the director of the Alabama Productivity Center. A feature story in the April 26, 1987, *Birmingham News* clearly depicted the center's activities at that time. Selected companies and specific tasks mentioned in the article serve to illustrate what the center is about.

- Alabama Die Casting: Quality control systems design

- Alabama Metals Industries: Improved materials handling system, automation of press area, scheduling

- Alabama Power Company/General Garage: Artificial intelligence, sandpaper study and paint tool improvements, warehouse design, tool room study

- Alabama Power Company/Material Services: Work simplification

- Container Services International: Front-lift truck vs. side-lift truck

- OMNI International: Inventory systems analysis and plant layout

- West Alabama Rehabilitation Center: Market study

Dave Miller was quoted during the article: "The purpose of the University's involvement is not just to save money for companies; it's to provide an opportunity for our faculty and students to get immersed in real-world research area." Miller clearly expressed his philosophy and the goals for the center.

In the same article, one of Miller's students, Bart Singleton of Monroeville, commented on his involvement with the center: "Having the opportunity to work around people this knowledgeable in the industrial management field has been the major benefit of working at the Productivity Center. What makes it fun is that each project is an individual challenge."

Joseph (Rae) Mellichamp and the Artificial Intelligence Lab

A special section on research in the student newspaper, the *Crimson White*, April 11, 1984, featured a picture of a smiling Rae Mellichamp and the following headline: "Computers thinking like humans could be important decision-maker in nation's missile defense system." Thus began UA's Artificial Intelligence Lab.

The article reported that Professors Mellichamp (management science) and James Hill (engineering mechanics) received a research grant of $189,000 from the U.S. Army Ballistic Missile Defense Systems Command based in Huntsville, Alabama. Students would be chosen to work with the professors in the research. Alabama was chosen because of its unique capabilities in developing the kinds of mathematical models that are required. Mellichamp was quoted as saying that computers have to be programmed to think like people: "We have to feed all the information that a human would use in making a decision into the computer and program it to analyze that information to make the right decision." Mellichamp stressed that, "Artificial Intelligence Systems are not fail-safe, but they can be as effective as humans, who are not fail-safe either." Rae Mellichamp retired in 1994 after commendable service to his college and University.

In the preceding section on the Alabama Productivity Center, artificial intelligence is listed as a task under Alabama Power Company/General Garage. The Artificial Intelligence Center and the Productivity Center cooperated to the benefit of all parties.

William R. Bennett Alabama International Trade Center (AITC)

The trade center was, of course, mentioned during the discussion of Bill Bennett's career (see chapters 5 and 6). The following states the mission of the center: A nonprofit organization dedicated to the development of international business, the AITC actively seeks opportunities to assist firms and public agencies in successfully concluding international business agreements and projects. The center's director is Nisa Miranda. Fittingly, the full name of the AITC honors W. R. Bennett, whose commitment and dedication to the center's mission is renowned.

Center for Economic Education

Recently retired professor T. D. Moore is discussed in some detail in chapter 5. In addition to his other accomplishments, Professor Moore initiated the Center for Economic Education. The center's mission is to provide an interdisciplinary approach to the development of teacher education programs,

Left to right: Pres. Joab Thomas, Hugh Culverhouse, and Rob Ingram conferring on Mr. Culverhouse an honorary professor of accounting.

curricular materials and media, experimental teaching programs, economic education libraries, and information dissemination services.

The S. Paul Garner Center for Current Accounting Issues

The Culverhouse School of Accountancy established the center in 1988. It has been successful in fostering and enhancing accounting research and education by acting as a focal point for scholarly activities and providing a vehicle for faculty efforts to address accounting issues. The center also provides financial support for faculty research, administers professional development programs, and develops and manages seminars and workshops. The Research Workshop Series, which was established to facilitate interaction between faculty and professional accountants, brings nationally recognized accounting researchers to campus to meet with faculty and graduate students.

The center is funded by contributions from the accounting firms of Arthur Andersen, Coopers & Lybrand, Deloitte & Touche, Ernst & Young, KPMG Peat Marwick, and Price Waterhouse. Accounting firms also provide grants to support faculty and doctoral students through the center.

The center is named for S. Paul Garner, dean emeritus of the College of Commerce and Business Administration. Dean Garner's contributions to and impact on the college have been well documented throughout this account of C&BA's first seventy-five years. His remarkable knowledge of our past has, in fact, been a primary source for the authors. But his accomplishments are by no means all in the past. As recently as 1993 Paul Garner was named one of the Accounting Educators of the Year and honored at the annual meeting of the American Accounting Association. The center ensures that future generations of accounting students will recognize the name S. Paul Garner, internationally known and beloved educator.

Focus on the Administration

Jack Fielden's era, though clearly extending into the 1980s, is discussed in chapter 6. This section focuses on Deans H. H. "Bill" Mitchell and Russell

Petersen. Because this chapter embraces the 1990s, the reader might expect to find a detailed account of Barry Mason's impact as dean. Dean Mason is not, however, "history"—he is the present and the nineties belong to him. In addition, he has been a major source of the oral portion of the history. His philosophical comments, perspectives about all phases of the college, and singular insights offer a well-defined picture of the man and the administrator. His views of the future are clearly reported in the epilogue, and anything the authors might say would be redundant. His accomplishments speak for themselves.

But a "word picture" of Dean Mason, compiled with the help of Ron Dulek, is too tempting a possibility to pass up. Presented below, therefore, in no particular order are some of Barry Mason's attributes as perceived by colleagues:

> "Builder" of the new commerce campus (with the assistance of Edd Mansfield, Marilee Brown, and Bonnie Barnett)
> Charismatic to all his publics
> A leader who understands what leadership is (he must never look tired or disheveled)
> A natural and deliberate leader
> Tireless worker
> Committed
> Kind and understanding, yet demanding
> Gentle man
> Humanitarian capitalist and entrepreneur
> Understands symbolism
> Has respect for faculty

H. H. "Bill" Mitchell

No interview was more delightful than the one with Bill Mitchell at his home in September 1993. I asked him to start his story in 1935 when he came to Alabama as a student. Bill Mitchell would be valuable in this history even if he had not been dean. His relationship with our college goes back almost sixty years.

He began with recollections of his early years. "When I came to the Commerce School, Lee Bidgood was dean. I was just scared to death of him. His colleagues weren't afraid of him, but students were. I had the dean for two courses, but I didn't know him well. My favorite of all my teachers was Marcus Whitman. He was my mentor in a way. I was a general business major, but I was interested in transportation so I took those courses."

In remembering other teachers, he said he had only one course with Miriam Locke, but she was memorable in freshman English. And he recalled Larry Nations, a marketing professor, with whom he had American literature. This, of course, was at the time Dean Bidgood had his own English in the college (see chapter 2). Mitchell said he learned his economics from Dr. McDougall, and he had social security with Bert Morley. He studied statistics with Dr. Chapman, and algebra with John Gill, who later became head of the statistics department.

Bill Mitchell said he was lost in algebra and was certain he was going to fail it. "I had an NYA [National Youth Administration, similar to work study today] job and I couldn't fail algebra. I worked thirty hours and made fifteen dollars. Tuition was twenty-five dollars a quarter. Would you believe that? Anyway I made a C in algebra. The only other C I made was under Harry Bonham in principles of marketing. I liked him as a teacher, but he gave these pop quizzes all the time."

Mitchell got his master's degree at Alabama after World War II and, at the suggestion of Lang Hawley and Ned Anderson, his doctorate at North Carolina. He taught at Auburn for about five years, then was department head at Mississippi State for a short time. He went to VPI (Virginia Polytechnic Institute) as a department chair with the promise of a deanship when the school was formed, and in 1961 he became dean. He stayed at Virginia Tech as dean for twenty-two years.

This brings Dean Mitchell full circle. Virginia Tech had a mandatory retirement policy, and Mitchell was not ready to stop "deaning." When Ken Uhl died before he could assume his position here, our search committee got wind of the fact that Mitchell was leaving VPI and was entertaining the idea of going to the University of Alabama at Huntsville. (As a matter of fact, Dean Mitchell had offers from Memphis State and Louisiana Tech, as well as Huntsville.) As chairman of the search committee I was authorized to call Bill Mitchell and see if he might be persuaded to talk to us. He said he was always interested in talking to Alabama.

"I came as dean in 1981," Mitchell said during our interview, "and served until 1986, and they were the best years I ever had." When I asked him why, he said,

> Well I guess Roger Sayers [at that time, academic vice-president] put it into perspective, because when he hired me he said that neither one of us was taking any risk. The worst scenario was that I'd only be dean for maybe three years. Anytime I wanted to quit, I could. When you don't have to work, it's beautiful. It turned out I stayed five years. I was able to do things that I could not have done had I been worried about my status. We had always wanted to come back to Alabama to retire; all our children were back in Alabama.

Recalling his five years at C&BA, Mitchell noted that he was proud of the people we hired the first year he was here and that the Productivity Center was started while he was dean. He continued:

> Lonnie Strickland says that I put in the Executive M.B.A. (E.M.B.A.), but I didn't. The only thing I did was when Lonnie came to me and said we ought to have one I said okay, you go out and raise some money to get us started. So he raised fifty thousand dollars and gives me credit for it.
>
> Ed Smith was my associate dean, and he was the one who kept me out of trouble. He pointed out the pot holes and the danger spots. He was one of the most loyal employees an institution can have.

Thus we conclude what might be called "Mitchell on Mitchell." How fortunate we are that he and Audrey chose Tuscaloosa for their retirement.

Dean H.H. (Bill) Mitchell with students—
"managing by walking around."

What a valuable source of information we have with Dean Garner and Ruth, as well as the Mitchells, nearby. Now we get a bit more insight about Bill Mitchell and his era from others.

A. J. "LONNIE" STRICKLAND ON MITCHELL

The difference between Fielden and Mitchell, Strickland said, was that "Jack was a conflict manager who met one-on-one with his chairpeople. Mitchell was more of a consensus builder. I feel that Bill and I had an excellent working relationship. He came in as dean at a time when we needed a calming influence. His success was assured—he had nothing to lose."

Strickland was working on the E.M.B.A. program (he was director of the M.B.A.), and he remembers a "typical Mitchell sense of humor" incident. "I was invited by the Tuscaloosa Exchange Club to talk about the E.M.B.A., and Bill introduced me. 'Lonnie has written more books than I have read. If I want to meet with Lonnie, I have to make an appointment to see him in the Atlanta Airport.'"

Remembering the efforts to get the E.M.B.A. off the ground, Strickland reflected on the position Dean Mitchell took. "A faculty can analyze an issue to death," Mitchell said, "and at some point you have to go on faith. I am going to ask the faculty to do that—to go on faith with the E.M.B.A." He thought Strickland needed a title, and he came up with coordinator, which Bill Mitchell said no one understood. He used humor and patience and very gentle pushing to get things done. He navigated rocky roads with success. He budgeted his time so he could walk around and see how people were doing. His management style has been described as "managing by walking around" (see chapter 6 for Art Thompson's comment about his years with Mitchell at VPI).

Strickland continued, "Bill felt that a dean should be Dean of the Faculty and needed to be seen with the faculty. He never spoke negatively of any faculty member, so he gathered lots of information. He was a pluralist who believed in diversity. He labeled me as an entrepreneur, and he ran interference for our program [the E.M.B.A.] for which I am extremely grateful."

Lonnie Strickland knew and respected Bill Mitchell. His insights are a welcome addition to this history.

BARRY MASON ON MITCHELL

In commenting on the five years of the Mitchell era, Mason reemphasized the fact that toward the end of the Fielden era, the campus was experiencing a time of great unrest (see chapter 6 for more detail):

The unrest was driven by the search by the faculty for much more involvement in governance. The Faculty Senate took the leadership in putting those processes in place, and that "cleaned out everybody." Central Administration was looking for a period of consolidation, reflection, healing of wounds—peace and calm. And Bill brought that. During his tenure very little went on in terms of fund-raising, external relations, public relations, and many of the things that had been put in place were not capitalized on or accelerated. Bill's charge was to "hold it together," go into a holding pattern, get everybody feeling good about one another.

Russ Petersen.

Russell Petersen

Although Russ Petersen's tenure as dean was only two years, several colleagues worked closely with him, and their perceptions assist in putting together a fairly clear picture of the man and his impact on the college. John Formby served as Russ's associate dean; Ron Dulek was deeply involved in working with Petersen on the strategic plan; and Barry Mason was his senior department chair.

JOHN FORMBY ON PETERSEN

"I'd describe Russ," said Formby,

as a very hard-working guy who had ambitions to make the college more consistent with national standards, because he believed we were lacking there. I think his approach was to try to create some standardized policies and procedures. I think more than anything else, that was his biggest impact on the college.

Basically his strategic plan is the one that we're using now. His policies and procedures are still in place, with some modifications. To accomplish what he wanted to do, he had to overcome a lot of resistance and obstacles.

Several other things should be mentioned. Russ initiated the faculty summer research program; cycled teaching policy; and the Faculty Scholars Program.

John Formby—innovative teacher and researcher.

The Faculty Scholars Program involved incoming freshmen who were competitively awarded a fellowship for four years—assuming they performed satisfactorily—during which time the student worked with a faculty mentor on teaching research or service activities. Darren Bayne of Headland, Alabama, was my Faculty Scholar for four years, and I can think of no other student-faculty relationship that has been more rewarding. Gene Marsh and Sharon Beatty served as the first two chairs of the advisory committee.

Formby continued:

I think one of the most important policies Russ initiated—and quite frankly, I didn't like this policy; I thought it was a bad idea, but I think it has turned out to be a very good idea. . . . Russ, sort of rode roughshod over everyone to initiate the policy dealing with the allocation of merit salary increases. For the first time we had a written policy that said here's how we are going to reward teaching, research, and service. Basically, he said it was 50 percent reward for teaching and 50 percent for research. Service was expected, but the department heads could take up to 20 percent of their merit money and allocate it to truly distinguished service. Any funds that remained were allocated on the basis of a 50–50 split between teaching and research. I think it serves the college well today.

John Formby perceived Petersen's tenure as short but productive, which his foregoing remarks clearly support. Formby added, "Russ was often a very small voice in a lot of noise."

RON DULEK ON RUSS PETERSEN

Dulek discussed Petersen by comparing him to Fielden:

> *Russ brought to the school the same thing that Jack brought fifteen years earlier—the understanding of what national standards were and what you have to do to be competitive. Jack really worked the community. He got the right contacts, he listened, and he had the power structure on his side. Fielden also knew he didn't understand and thus was frightened by the southern mentality, but he learned to understand it.*
>
> *But Russ had never been a dean before; certainly Jack had. He was a person who was making a transition from being a department head to a dean, and I don't think he understood that he had to be a public figure. A dean has to deal with several publics—the faculty, administration, alums, community, and of course students. It's a very difficult job.*
>
> *Russ brought us the gift of how we should be structured. He didn't stay long enough to implement many of his ideas. Russ set up the strategic plan and Larry Foster and I wrote a lot of it. We clarified what Russ was saying.*

BARRY MASON ON RUSS PETERSEN

Dean Mason commented frankly on Russ Petersen's impact on C&BA:

> *I liked Russ. We got along well. I respected him and we never had a cross word. He put the first long-range plan in place, and we have continued to build on it and refine it each year. He never really had a long-range computer plan, but I think some of his thinking certainly influenced what we did beginning in 1988. Nothing that Russ did programmatically has been undone. Nothing that he valued by way of scanning the future has proved to be wrong. You can't fault a man who helped accelerate the push toward quality and growth.*
>
> *He was much more concerned with efficiency than effectiveness. Being so passionately committed to getting things done, sometimes he really didn't understand the key players. He really didn't understand their perspective and he did not understand the centers of influence in the college. But he left a legacy that I think will stand the test of time, much like Jack Fielden did.*

Vivian Malone Jones, Class of 1965

On April 15, 1994, Vivian Malone Jones, the first black graduate of the University of Alabama and C&BA, was honored during ceremonies celebrating C&BA's seventy-fifth anniversary. Below are excerpts from Dean Barry Mason's introduction of Vivian Jones:

> We thank you so much for joining us for one of the continuing highlights in the seventy-fifth anniversary year of the college. Vivian Malone Jones, the first African American graduate of the University of Alabama, received her bachelor's degree in general management in 1965. In reflecting on this historic day in the life of the college, my thoughts, as I am sure yours, go back to the farsightedness of our University leaders in the 1960s, the courage of the students who at that time blazed the way for others to follow.

Ms. Jones is the director of the Office of Environmental Justice for Region IV, Environmental Protection Agency, in Atlanta. She is no stranger to civil rights. A native of Monroeville, Alabama, she was thrust into national prominence by becoming the first black graduate of the University.

Her active professional and personal life have been remarkably successful and full. She has one more goal: She would like to teach in a historically black college to further inspire young African Americans.

After Dean Mason introduced the president of the Capstone Business League, who welcomed Ms. Jones, Pres. Roger Sayers was called on for comments. He and Dean Mason later unveiled the portrait of Vivian Malone Jones, which hangs side by side with the portrait of Catherine Miles, the first female doctoral graduate of the University of Alabama who is also a business graduate.

During Vivian Jones's remarks she recognized Dr. Minnie Miles, who was in the audience, and thanked her for being a mentor and role model. She went on to say, "I chose to attend the University because I felt at that time it offered the best available education in the state. I did not expect the obstacles that I encountered, believe it or not. But I was willing to accept those challenges [in order to be able] to enter and graduate from the University. With the help of many of my friends and associates, I was able to [accomplish those goals]."

It was an afternoon to remember.

Catherine Miles

One of the most significant events of C&BA's seventy-fifth anniversary celebration was the ceremony recognizing Catherine Miles as the first woman to receive a Ph.D. at the University of Alabama and the first person to receive that degree in business. Miles was the honored speaker on April 7, 1994, in Alston Hall. Her portrait hangs next to Vivian Malone Jones, the first African American student to receive a degree from Alabama. The recognition of both Dr. Miles and Ms. Jones was particularly appropriate in 1994, the Centennial

Vivian Malone Jones with Minnie Miles in front of Ms. Jones's portrait, 1994.

Year of Women on Campus.

Ricky Melancon interviewed Miles by telephone from her home in south Florida. In recalling her years at Alabama, she said she enrolled in 1936 under her maiden name, Ellis. She was not in business at that time:

> I started in Home Economics because that seemed to be the trend for women at that time. Also I worked for a year in Dean Agnes Ellen Harris's office [dean of Home Economics]. Then in 1937 I married E. L. McGinty. To make sure I could add to our family income, I went the "traditional" way, that is I went to a business college to learn shorthand, typing, and a little bit of record keeping. After completing the course, I took a job. I didn't like stenographic work, but I was fascinated with accounting. I guess that's why I went into the School of Business later because I wanted to go into CPA work.

Miles's husband went into the military; they had two children; then Mr. McGinty died. She came back to Reform, Alabama, to live with her parents, who were willing to look after her two children so she could return to the University of Alabama in 1946. Both of her parents had been to college and their seven daughters grew up with the understanding that they would go to college. Four of them, including Catherine, got degrees from Alabama.

When Miles returned to the University, she majored in accounting. She also met her second husband, who was a returning GI, at the University. The fact that there were few women in business, especially in accounting, did not seem to concern her. She was doing what she wanted to do, and she was an outstanding student. Gender simply was not an issue with her nor with the faculty and other students. (I was a fellow student of hers at the time and attest that she set the pace in her classes and was well respected.)

Gender was, however, a factor in the marketplace. After being told by all the interviewers for CPA firms that they didn't hire women, she decided to further her education and maybe her chances for a job, and get a master's. When the master's did not help, she decided to go into higher education and work toward a Ph.D. She was concerned about getting three degrees from the same institution, but "looking back on it," she said, "I have no objection whatsoever to having done that; it was so much better for me and for my daughters, because my parents could still look after them during the week and I would go home on weekends. The education I got at the University of Alabama was as good as I could have gotten anywhere."

Catherine Miles had a wonderful career in higher education as a professor and administrator. Alabama and the college honored themselves by recognizing this remarkable woman.

The Early Nineties

It is impossible to reflect on the nineties with anything like historical objectivity. History is being written as we live it. Some time must pass before we can evaluate the nineties as we have earlier decades. We are too much a part of it to really see it.

Walt Misiolek.

So we merely present a short potpourri of prideful things that have been a part of the early years of the nineties. The ordering does not suggest importance, merely the authors' preference.

Outstanding College Leadership

Dean Barry Mason has put together an excellent management team to carry out the goals and objectives of C&BA. Senior associate dean Walt Misiolek is Barry's right-hand man, and together they lead an able group of administrators. Until his retirement in 1992, associate dean for undergraduate programs Al Drake served the college with dedication. Chuck Odewahn, in his usual spirit of cooperation, reluctantly accepted Dean Mason's invitation to serve as associate dean until Chuck felt comfortable that the staff could carry out the functions of the office without him. Odewahn returned to full-time teaching in the fall semester of 1994. Dave Heggem, director of Student Services, and Tom Canterbury, registrar, constitute the administrative staff of the student-oriented

David Heggem presents the Gladys Poe award to Christy McAdams.

Graduating seniors at annual picnic.

(Top) Alston Hall with Bruno Library in background. *(Bottom)* Bashinsky Computer Center.

operations. Outstanding advisers and counselors complete the professional staff.

Other important players in Mason's team are Bill Gunther and the other CBER staff; Tony Linn in external relations, who assumed Tom Moore's responsibilities upon Tom's retirement; Zeb Hargett, development; and Marilee Brown, who keeps everyone honest in her control position. The valued secretarial staff are exceptionally efficient.

The real work of the college—the captains in the trenches as it were—is directed by a strong group of department chairs: Tom Howard, director of the Culverhouse School of Accountancy; Billy Helms, economics, finance, and legal studies; Hutton Barron, management science and statistics; and Ron Dulek, management and marketing. These individuals, along with others, serve as the Administrative Policy Committee (APC), the dean's operating committee.

Recent College Recognitions

In an article ranking business schools nationwide for quality and value, *Business Week* considered applicants' scores on the GMAT to assure a "core level of quality" among the business schools, and then compared each school's tuition to the starting salaries of its graduates to see which offered the most value.

C&BA's M.B.A. program was cited by *Business Week* as one of twenty quality business schools nationwide that offers consumers "the most bang for the buck." In addition, the M.B.A. program was featured in McGraw-Hill's publication *Best Business Schools in the Nation*. Calling us "Alabama's best M.B.A. school," the McGraw-Hill publication noted that Alabama has been steadily increasing the quality of its students.

According to Princeton *Review*'s "Student Access Guide to the Best Business Schools, 1994 Edition," we offer one of the lowest-cost, most-sought-after M.B.A. degrees in the country. C&BA students surveyed commented that the standards are high and the program is insightful and targeted toward today's business needs. The authors also noted that Alabama is among only a dozen or so schools where students are satisfied with the way the school is run.

Bob Allen, director of the M.B.A. program in C&BA's Manderson Graduate School of Business, noted that "while many M.B.A. programs across the country have had trouble keeping their enrollment up, ours is up 30 percent this year [1993]." Allen also said that our M.B.A. is adopting a new, more rigorous curriculum that was implemented in 1994: "We still have a strong emphasis on the basic core courses, but we have integrated themes of leadership, professionalism, team building, and management communication into the curriculum."

A well-respected publication, the *Gourman Report,* rating programs in American and international universities, rated our undergraduate program as "very good" with a score of 4.04 on a 5.0 scale, placing us 52d in the nation. (UAB ranked 80th and Auburn 122d.)

C&BA's undergraduate accounting program was ranked twelfth in the nation and its graduate program sixteenth according to a 1992 survey of accounting faculty published in *Public Accounting Report.* In addition, the international accounting journal *Abacus* reported that two C&BA faculty members here have been ranked among the top accounting researchers in the world. Thomas Lee, Culverhouse Professor of Accounting, was listed as the third most productive accounting scholar in the world for the twenty-year period from 1968 to 1988. Robert Ingram, Ernst & Young Professor of Accounting and former director of the school, was listed as the thirty-seventh most productive scholar for the same period.

The Capital Campaign

In May 1992, the University of Alabama kicked off the largest capital campaign in its history. Led by C&BA's $25 million "lead" gifts, the campuswide campaign had an auspicious beginning. As part of the $165 million Campaign for Alabama, $27.5 million was earmarked for the Commerce School—evidence of the University's commitment to achieving a new standard of excellence in business education.

Dreams of a new state-of-the-art business library and computer center became reality in January 1994 when doors to the $8.5 million Angelo Bruno Business Library and the Sloan Y. Bashinsky Sr. Computer Center were "opened for business." Gifts of $4 million from Mr. Bruno and $3 million from Mr. Bashinsky, both non-alums from Birmingham, set the stage for more than $17 million in new and renovated facilities for the college as part of the capital campaign effort. Others making significant contributions to the new Bruno Library and Bashinsky Computer Center include the Charles Anderson family (Florence), Dr. and Mrs. William

Dean Barry Mason speaking at the dedication of the Bruno Library and Bashinsky Computer Center.

The Bruno family at the dedication.

The Bashinsky family at the dedication.

R. Bennett, Emeritus Professor of Marketing (Tuscaloosa), and Compass Bank.

While the library and computer center were being built, Bidgood Hall, cornerstone of the Commerce School, underwent a much-needed $9 million renovation and expansion. Aided by a gift of $1.5 million from C&BA alumnus John Richard Miller and his wife, Virginia (UA 1941), Bidgood Hall was transformed into a world-class teaching facility with the latest in audio and visual technology. Yet this historic campus landmark retained the charm of yesteryear that has distinguished it as "the Commerce School" since 1928.

Other major benefactors contributing to the renovation and expansion of Bidgood Hall include Asa H. Bean (Tuscaloosa), Mr. and Mrs. John Brilbeck (Tuscaloosa), the family of Carl T. and Elizabeth Jones (Huntsville), Susan Hulsey (Birmingham), John Russell Thomas (Alexander City), and William M. Schuler (Birmingham). Corporate gifts from Arthur Andersen and Andersen Consulting; Nippon Life Insurance Company (Japan); Stern, Agee and Leach (Birmingham); Duncan-Williams (Memphis); and First National Bank of Jasper and its affiliated banks throughout the state were instrumental in making the renovation and expansion of Bidgood Hall possible.

In addition to brick-and-mortar funds, the capital campaign placed strong emphasis on identifying means to support student scholarships and to promote faculty excellence in teaching and research. This $10 million campaign priority goal was completed exactly one day before the national campaign kick-off when Hugh F. Culverhouse of Tampa, Florida, announced that he would contribute $10 million in endowment support for the college, the largest gift in the history of the University. Culverhouse had previously given more than $3 million to the college's accounting program, which is named in his honor. The announcement of Hugh Culverhouse's death on August 25, 1994, was sad news not only to family and friends but also to the many people who have benefited directly and indirectly from his benevolence.

Culverhouse's gift, coupled with the gifts from Angelo Bruno and Sloan Bashinsky, prompted C&BA campaign chairman Lewis Manderson to suggest to his steering committee that they raise the campaign goal from $27.5 million to $40 million—which they did on May 27, 1992, the day the Campaign for Alabama officially began. Manderson, incidentally, matched his previous gift of $1 million with an additional pledge of $1 million for the M.B.A. program named in his honor.

(Top) John Bickley and Barry Mason. *(Middle)* Paul and Ruth Garner, and Andy Penz. *(Bottom)* Alice Kingery and Helen Ryerson.

Ollie Delchamps and Frank Bromberg.

The success of the capital campaign is due solely to the efforts of the many loyal friends, faculty, and alumni of the Commerce School. Led by the enthusiasm of Dean Barry Mason, whose vision and tireless efforts have given meaning to the campaign, contributions for priority needs at the college have been met time and time again. Associates and family of Durr-Fillauer Medical contributed more than $750,000 to establish a chair in business ethics. AmSouth Bank gave $600,000 to establish the William A. Powell Eminent Scholars Chair in Banking and Finance. An anonymous friend in Birmingham has pledged $1 million to support the Department of Management and Marketing.

Other major contributors include the late William Tandy Barrett (Tuscaloosa), Harry Brock (Birmingham), Mr. and Mrs. James Harrison (Tuscaloosa), Raymond Hughes (Enterprise), Tom E. McMillian (Brewton), Minnie Miles (Tuscaloosa), Paul Garner (Tuscaloosa), Mr. and Mrs. James D. Nabors (Alexander City), the late Stephen J. Ross (New York), the late Ehney Camp (Birmingham), the late A. C. and Cecile Craig (Tuscaloosa), and Mr. and Mrs. Kem Wilson Jr. (Memphis). Others too numerous to name have also contributed generously. Corporate endowments and gifts to the college include Parisian's, Alabama Power, Daehan Kyoyuk (Korea), State Farm Insurance, and SouthTrust Bank.

At the time this part of our history is being written, the campaign is not yet halfway over. Our college has received more than $37 million in gifts and pledges toward its $40 million goal. The impact is already being felt with teaching and administrative facilities second to none in the United States. Growing endowments have resulted in an increased number of scholarships for students with special financial needs as well as those with high academic standing. Additional academic support allows the college to attract nationally recognized teachers to the campus

Mayme Bonham.

Morris Mayer and Paul Garner.

and to provide program support that will ensure excellence in the classroom and for research.

I can think of no better place to close this history of our first seventy-five years. Clearly we are prepared to welcome the new century thanks to the remarkable support of our friends and the leadership of those who work for us all in remarkable ways. As former student, emeritus faculty member, and devoted alumnus, I am proud to have been a small part of our history.

Epilogue

The following commentary is adapted from an article by C&BA dean J. Barry Mason in the spring 1994 issue of *Focus*.

Contemplating the Future

Higher education is in the midst of a challenging era. Business schools are struggling to redefine business education. In May 1992 the Strategic Issues Committee of the American Association of Collegiate Schools of Business (AACSB) issued a report entitled "Crisis and Survival." Critical challenges noted included budget cutbacks in many states, need for quality improvement processes, better integration of teaching and research missions, and the need for organizational structures that respond more effectively to the current environment. Many of these issues were echoed in a December 27, 1993, editorial in the *Birmingham Post-Herald*. The authors observed that the issues business schools are facing will remain with us through the nineties. The pressures for change are the greatest since the Pierson, and Gordon and Howell reports in the late 1950s that reshaped business schools, transforming business education from a series of disciplines founded largely on descriptive research to disciplines firmly grounded in the foundations of economics, mathematics, and the behavioral sciences with an explicit priority on analytically and conceptually rigorous research.

Our curricula, our methods of teaching, and our perspective on what students need to know are again under scrutiny. As with most things, there is some merit in the criticisms we hear. But the danger is that in our rush to respond to the pressures for change we may do great damage to the academy and not realize it until it is too late.

Lyman Porter and Lawrence McKibbin began the current debate about the future of business schools in 1988 with their report entitled *Management Education and Development: Drift or Thrust into the Twenty-first Century*. The authors charged that b-school curricula are characterized by (1) a lack of general education breadth, (2) an inadequate focus on the external environment and the international arena, (3) a lack of adaptation to the new information/service society, (4) a failure to integrate adequately across functional areas of business, and (5) the underdevelopment of people skills.

The AACSB responded to the call for change by issuing new accreditation guidelines that are mission driven. As such, they allow curricula to be tailored to the needs of individual colleges as opposed to the cookie cutter approach that previously characterized accreditation. Colleges now have the flexibility to develop programs uniquely appropriate to their mission in meeting the needs of their constituencies.

Students at computers in a multimedia classroom in the Bashinsky Computer Center, 1994.

Given that some of the criticisms and pressures for change are valid, how do we respond affirmatively to them while protecting the integrity of the classroom?

Clearly, it seems that we will have to look more carefully at what we can afford to do in a resource-constrained environment. And we will need to examine the kind of education we need to offer our students over the next decade. The world of business and industry has changed dramatically over the past several decades, and business education has not kept up with all the changes. Russ Ackoff, a widely known operations research professor, has stated that our methods of teaching and course content are most appropriate for a pre–World War II corporate world. This will not do.

Globalization, information technology, changes in management structures, and the electronic superhighway especially appear to be the driving forces that must guide our thinking as we reassess our undergraduate curricula, our professional master's degree programs, and our research-based programs of doctoral study. These four issues, often acting interactively with the ones identified by the AACSB, are in the process of transforming higher education.

Clearly, land, labor, and capital no longer are the key ingredients for corporate success. Rather, the way in which knowledge is created and disseminated will be the driving force that will shape higher education in the twenty-first century. The changes that occur will be swift and complex, and they will require the faculty to continually master new subject matter and new ways of communicating it to students. Students will need to hone their critical thinking skills and become more adept in oral and written communication, more technologically literate, and facile in the application of leadership skills.

Globalization

Global competition has accelerated in recent years. Faculty members will increasingly need to travel to various nations around the world to share information and ideas with their counterparts. Our students must also become more knowledgeable about the cultures of other nations. They must know about their history and geography, their management styles, and their ways of doing business. Our students must also become fluent in one or more languages other than English. Ideally, they will spend some time in another country on an internship or as part of a program of academic study.

Recently, we evaluated the merits of a request to provide delayed video academic instruction in Germany. Our expectations are that the diversity in our classes and in our faculty profile, as a result of such efforts, will accelerate. Faculty members, in the last three years, have spent sabbaticals or have been on externally funded research leaves to Australia, Colombia, Japan, China, Scotland, Taiwan, and other nations. We have also had visiting instructors for a semester or longer from countries such as Australia, Japan, Scotland, and Belgium. The college receives advice and counsel from a strong International Business Advisory Board, including executives from Taiwan, Japan, Belgium, Italy, Bangkok, and elsewhere.

Information Technology

Accelerating changes in information technology are helping the college respond to the challenges and opportunities that are a part of today's global world. The college offered its first interactive course in fall 1993 between the Huntsville, Birmingham, and Tuscaloosa campuses of the University. We are likely to see additional interactive instruction in the near future as universities wrestle with the realities of constrained budgets and the need to provide specialized instruction to large and diverse audiences. Alston Hall, Bidgood Hall, the Bashinsky Computer Center, and the Bruno Business Library were built in anticipation of the use of fiber optics as a link to networks with worldwide connectivity to databases and other sources of electronically stored and disseminated information. Our students already have the capacity to search the card catalogs of many of the world's greatest libraries from a personal computer terminal. They also have access to huge electronic databases and can conduct computer-based searches of massive amounts of information worldwide.

Additionally, the faculty in most of the new classrooms can instantly switch between such instructional aids as laser disks, slides, CD-ROMs, and videos, as well as a variety of PC-based software applications for use in multimedia exercises. Instructors control sound, lighting, and computer and video technology from the lectern by using a menu-driven touch screen.

The faculty are also on a LAN (local area network) for electronic mail. They have worldwide access to colleagues via the Internet. Indeed, the volume of data flowing via this technology will soon exceed the volume of information transferred by telephone calls. Before the close of the nineties the University will renovate a dormitory for C&BA students in the proximity of the Bruno Business Library. Each room in the dorm will have a personal computer and will be networked into the Bruno Business Library and the Bashinsky Computer Center. Learning will no longer be confined to the classroom, the library, or study halls. Students will have access to academic resources from their home or dormitory on an as-needed basis.

Executive M.B.A. students currently are electronically linked to the campus for purposes of information-sharing with faculty members. All students can communicate with the faculty via electronic mail. Computer technology and electronic gateways to information have advanced to the point that interactive teaming, access to richer resources, and the flexibility of twenty-four-hour, seven-day-a-week programs of study and instruction are a reality. These technologies will allow us to respond to the need for lifelong teaming in a technologically dynamic world and to respond to the needs of nontraditional audiences who need access to programs of instruction but cannot come to campus to receive it.

Changes in Management Structure

The era of distributed computing is upon us. Distributed computing means the redistribution of power and the elimination of the traditional management hierarchy. Individuals no longer have to go up, over, around, or down the organization. They simply tap into bases for the information they need. The University clerical staff, for example, increasingly will have access to the same data as deans, vice-presidents, and the president. Students are already able to complete much of their registration electronically. Student and personnel records are available electronically to individuals with the need to view them. Soon, purchase orders will be electronically sent and received. As with the private sector, the University will begin to see the elimination of middle-management positions that have the primary job responsibility for developing and disseminating information. Decision making in student admissions, classroom scheduling, and budgeting will be more streamlined and less cumbersome.

The traditional departmental structure may also become obsolete. Organizational structures will be more flexible as teams are formed to address various issues and then dissolved when their need no longer exists. The University, colleges, and departments will be restructured almost routinely. Organizational change has been around for many years. The difference is the need for a continuously reconfigured organization . . . to make the college more responsive to the needs of employers, students, government officials, and others with whom we interact on a daily basis.

The Electronic Highway

The emergence of an information-age economy based on intangible knowledge and communication is a fourth massive challenge that will redefine what we teach and how we teach it. We are already grappling with the issues of how to integrate telecommunications subject matter into the curriculum, a vitally important subject in an economy based on communication and intellectual capital. Lifelong teaming is increasingly a reality. A massive challenge is how to configure technology in such a way as to help students understand how knowledge is created, sorted, stored, and shipped electronically. In 1994 *Fortune* magazine reported that for the first time investments in computers and telecommunications equipment have exceeded capital spending for industrial, construction, and other "old economy" equipment. Libraries as we know them are likely to be things of the past as universities find ways to substitute information technology for investments in physical assets. Satellite uplink and downlink technology, the fiber-optic highway, and advances in compressed video technology will make worldwide instruction available from a single site. The University, for example, already offers instruction in Japanese to more than fifty-five high schools in Alabama and elsewhere. Similarly, the University's integrated science program is being offered via satellite technology. The College of Commerce and Business Administration for several years has offered graduate credit courses on a delayed video basis.

The college, thanks to a major gift as part of the capital campaign, has developed two studio classrooms to allow us to remain on the cutting edge of alternative methods of subject matter delivery via various telecommunication technologies. We are currently seeking funds for a satellite uplink. Within the college, new staff positions, such as software specialists, database managers, and network supervisors, are being created to support the new instructional technology.

Redefining Curricula and Course Content

As we respond to the challenges facing us, what we teach and how we teach it will change dramatically. Curricula and course content must be redefined in response to pressures for change. Employers today especially value critical analysis, problem identification, and the ability to communicate effectively— skills traditionally honed in liberal arts courses. Number crunching will no longer suffice. As faculty, we must focus on communication, problem framing, and creativity, not cookbook skills-oriented practices. The world is changing too fast for us to teach students everything they need to know. We must teach them instead how to learn what they need to continue to grow.

Our students must become more skilled in group presentations, small group dynamics, problem identification, and technology applications. These skills cannot be developed in a lecture format. Classes must become more interactive, and class sizes must be limited to manageable numbers. Lectures will not become obsolete, but they must be more flexible in terms of breakout sessions, videotaping of student presentations, and other formats. Experiential learning, judgment, and reasoning must be emphasized in the applications of the new technology.

Memorization and objective tests will not suffice in the new environment. Our exams must require the use of such real-world skills as judgment, problem solving, and how to obtain and use knowledge. Above all, the faculty must believe in the value of education and that teaching skills must be honed and refined over time. A "take it or leave it" attitude toward students cannot be tolerated. William Graves, editor of *National Geographic Magazine,* illustrated this point in a story about why the world-famous violinist Jascha Heifetz left the glamour of performing to become a teacher. According to Graves, Heifetz explained that "my old violin professor in Russia told me that if I worked hard enough someday I would be good enough to teach."

The new methods of instruction and course content will demand more time and effort from the faculty. New curricula and materials must be developed. Textbook-based lectures must be supplemented by cases, class projects, and writing assignments. Above all, we must strive to bring flexibility to the development of teaching materials, curricula, and teaching approaches appropriate for the demands being placed upon the college.

As with most institutions in society today, we are facing externally imposed pressures for change. It will be up to us whether we provide direction for change or whether change will be imposed on us. We have an opportunity as a faculty to return to the basics of education—which is what attracted us to this profession in the first place. A rapidly emerging global perspective, sophisticated technology that is in the reach of all of us, a changing student body, and new management paradigms appropriate for the twenty-first century all must be acknowledged and addressed. Together we can usher in a new era for the college that will provide exciting new opportunities and challenges in fulfilling our traditional trilateral missions of teaching, research, and service.

Appendix A

Alabama Business Hall of Fame Inductees

ARONOV, AARON MORRIS (1919–1991). Nationally Known Real Estate Developer; One of Alabama's Most Distinguished Citizens. Inducted: October 13, 1992.

AYERS, HARRY MELL (1885–1964). Publisher; Civic Leader; Southern Spokesman. Inducted: September 14, 1976.

BARNETT, JOHN BIGHAM (1874–1952). Lawyer; Banker; Civic Leader. Inducted: October 14, 1980.

BASHINSKY, SLOAN Y. (1919–). Leading Executive; Philanthropist. Inducted: October 7, 1993.

BEDSOLE, JOSEPH LINYER (1881–1975). Merchant; Businessman; Humanitarian. Inducted: September 14, 1976.

BELLINGRATH, WILLIAM ALBERT (1868–1937). Pioneer in the Coca–Cola Bottling Industry; Civic Leader; Philanthropist. Inducted: October 16, 1986.

BIDGOOD, LEE (1884–1963). Educator; Scholar; Counselor. Inducted: November 22, 1977.

BLOUNT, WILLIAM HOUSTON (1922–). Outstanding Corporate Executive; Active Participant in Myriad Phases of Community Life. Inducted: October 7, 1993.

BLOUNT, WINTON MALCOLM "RED," JR. (1921–). Internationally Known Builder and Entrepreneur; Statesman; Patron of the Arts; Philanthropist. Inducted: March 6, 1989 (for 1988).

BROCK, GLEN PORTER, SR. (1896–1987). Railroad Executive; Civic Leader; Humanitarian. Inducted: October 14, 1982.

BROCK, HARRY B., JR. (1926–). Innovative Banker; Influential Professional and Civic Leader. Inducted: October 7, 1993.

BRUNO, ANGELO J. (1924–1991). Outstanding Food Chain Executive; Philanthropist. Inducted: October 13, 1992.

BRUNO, JOSEPH S. "JOE" (1912–). Entrepreneurial Food and Drug Chain Store Executive; Humanitarian. Inducted: October 5, 1989.

CARVER, GEORGE WASHINGTON (c. 1861–1943). Agricultural Researcher; Educator; Humanitarian. Inducted: October 14, 1980.

CLEMENTS, WOODROW WILSON "FOOTS" (1914–). Outstanding Marketer; Corporate Executive; Leader in the Soft Drink Industry; Exemplary Citizen. Inducted: March 6, 1989 (for 1988).

COFFEE, GENERAL JOHN (1772–1833). Frontiersman; Soldier; Promoter; Planter. Inducted: October 16, 1986.

COMER, BRAXTON BRAGG (1848–1927). Founder of Avondale Mills; Governor of Alabama; Textile Pioneer; Benefactor of Education. Inducted: October 8, 1974.

COMER, JAMES MCDONALD (1877–1963). Textile Industrialist; Civic Leader; Humanitarian. Inducted: November 3, 1981.

CRAWFORD, GEORGE GORDON (1869–1936). Iron Master; Civic Leader; Humanitarian. Inducted: October 14, 1980.

CULLMANN, JOHANN GOTTFRIED (1823–1895). Latter–day Pioneer; Town Builder; Advocate of Democracy. Inducted: October 22, 1987.

CULVERHOUSE, HUGH FRANKLIN, SR. (1919–1994). Tax Lawyer; Land Developer; Professional Football Team Owner; Philanthropist. Inducted: November 7, 1991.

CUNNINGHAM, EMORY 0. (1922–). Distinguished Publishing Company Executive; Advocate of Educational and Economic Growth in the South; Exemplary Citizen. Inducted: October 7, 1993.

DANIEL, ROBERT HUGH (1906–1983). Pioneer in the Alabama Construction Industry; Dedicated Citizen. Inducted: October 18, 1984.

DAVIS, TINE WAYNE, SR. (1914–1980). Grocery Chain Executive; Philanthropist. Inducted: October 14, 1982.

DEBARDELEBEN, HENRY FAIRCHILD (1840–1910). Dynamic Industrial Pioneer; "The King of the Southern Iron World. " Inducted: October 22, 1987.

DELCHAMPS, ALFRED FREDERICK (1895–1978). Entrepreneur in the Retail Food Industry; Leader in Educational, Civic, and Religious Activities. Inducted: November 18, 1984.

DRUMMOND, HERMAN EDWARD (1905–1956). Miner; Innovative Businessman; Dreamer. Inducted: October 16, 1990.

GARNER, SAMUEL PAUL (1910–). World–Renowned Business Educator and Scholar; The University of Alabama's "Ambassador to the World"; Dedicated Citizen. Inducted: October 13, 1992.

GASTON, ARTHUR GEORGE (1892–). Businessman; Community Developer; Humanitarian. Inducted: November 3, 1981.

GILMER, BEN SCREWS (1905–). Corporate Executive; Humanitarian. Inducted: October 18, 1984.

GWALTNEY, EUGENE CLEVELAND (1918–). Innovative Textile Executive; Dedicated Citizen. Inducted: November 7, 1991.

HAMILTON, CHARLES ANGLIN (1876–1942). Manufacturer; Entrepreneur; Community Leader. Inducted: October 23, 1979.

HAND, JOHN ANTHON (1901–1989). Banker; Civic Leader; Humanitarian. Inducted: October 23, 1979.

HARBERT, JOHN MURDOCK, III (1921–). Entrepreneur; Internationally Known Construction Company Executive; Philanthropist. Inducted: October 7, 1993.

HARDING, WILLIAM P. G. (1864–1930). Alabama's First Central Banker; Distinguished Citizen. Inducted: October 16, 1986.

HAUGHTON, DANIEL JEREMIAH (1911–1987). Leader in the Aerospace Industry and in Civic Affairs; Philanthropist. Inducted: March 6, 1989 (for 1988).

HENDERSON, CHARLES (1860–1937). Statesman; Industrialist; Philanthropist. Inducted: September 23, 1975.

HENDERSON, FOX, SR. (1853–1918). Financier; Entrepreneur; Patriarch. Inducted: November 1, 1983.

HESS, EMIL CARL (1918–). Innovative Retailer; Philanthropist. Inducted: October 22, 1985.

HULSEY, WILLIAM HANSELL (1901–1985). Investment Executive; Real Estate Developer; Civic Leader; Philanthropist. Inducted: October 16, 1990.

JELKS, WILLIAM DORSEY (1855–1931). Newspaper Editor and Publisher; Alabama's "Business Governor"; Insurance Executive. Inducted: March 6, 1989 (for 1988).

JEMISON, JOHN SNOW, JR. (1908–1988). Entrepreneur; Investment Banker; Civic Leader. Inducted: October 16, 1990.

JEMISON, ROBERT, JR. (1802–1871). Statesman; Planter; Businessman. Inducted: November 3, 1981.

JEMISON, ROBERT, JR. (1878–1974). Builder; Civic Leader; "Mr. Birmingham." Inducted: October 17, 1978.

JOHNSON, CRAWFORD TOY (1873–1942). Businessman; Civic Leader; Humanitarian. Inducted: November 22, 1977.

JONES, CARL TANNAHILL (1908–1967). Engineer; Civic Leader; "Mr. Huntsville." Inducted: November 1, 1983.

KILBY, THOMAS ERBY (1865–1943). Business Leader; Humanitarian; Alabama's First "Modern" Governor. Inducted: October 22, 1987.

LANIER, GEORGE HUGULEY (1880–1948). Pioneer Textile Industrialist; Civic Leader; Humanitarian. Inducted: October 22, 1985.

LEE, ARTHUR HENRY (1893–1977). Entrepreneur; Civic Leader; Philanthropist. Inducted: October 14, 1982.

MALONE, WALLACE DAVIS, SR. (1896–1968). Banker; Conservationist; World Traveler. Inducted: September 23, 1975.

MARTIN, THOMAS WESLEY (1881–1964). Leader of Alabama Power Company; Nationally Recognized Utility Executive and Attorney; Historian; Humanitarian; Founder of Southern Research Institute. Inducted: October 8, 1974.

MAY, BEN E. (1889–1972). Business Leader; Humanitarian; Patron of Medical Research. Inducted: September 23, 1975.

McGOWIN, JAMES GREELEY (1871–1934). Lumberman; Patriarch; Leader. Inducted: October 17, 1978.

McKINLEY, JOHN KEY (1920–). Corporate Executive; Chemical Engineer; Patron of the Arts. Inducted: October 14, 1982.

McMILLAN, ED LEIGH (1888–1977). Lawyer; Lumber Executive; Historian. Inducted: October 17, 1978.

McRAE, JOHN FINLEY (1896–1982). Banker; Civic Leader. Inducted: November 1, 1983.

McWANE, WILLIAM (1898–1978). Leader in the Forge and Foundry Industry. Inducted: October 5, 1989.

MILLER, THOMAS R. (1843–1914). Pioneer Lumberman; Entrepreneur; Businessman. Inducted: November 22, 1977.

MITCHELL, SIDNEY ZOLLICOFFER (1862–1944). Pioneer Hydroelectric Power Developer; Financier; Visionary. Inducted: October 22, 1985.

MOODY, FRANK MAXWELL (1877–1941). Banker; Civic Leader; Humanitarian. Inducted: September 14, 1976.

MOODY, FRANK MCCORKLE (1915–1993). Outstanding Leader in Alabama Banking; Model Citizen; Philanthropist. Inducted: October 13, 1992.

MOORER, THOMAS J. (1912–). Admiral, U. S. Navy (retired); Corporate Executive. Inducted: October 12, 1982.

MOXLEY, STEPHEN DEWEY (1898–1967). Industrialist; Engineer; Inventor; Civic Leader. Inducted: October 18, 1984.

NOBLE, SAMUEL (1834–1888). Ironmaster; Founder of Anniston, Alabama. Inducted: October 16, 1990.

NOOJIN, BALPHA LONNIE (1885–1950). Athlete; Educator; Businessman; Politician. Inducted: October 23, 1979.

O'NEAL, EDWARD ASBURY, IV (1905–1977). Chemical Industrialist; International Businessman; Corporate Executive. Inducted: October 18, 1984.

OSBORN, PRIME F., III (1915–1986). Lawyer; Railroad Executive; Civic Leader. Inducted: November 1, 1983.

OUTLAW, GEORGE CABELL, SR. (1886–1964). Lawyer; Businessman; Civic Leader. Inducted: October 12, 1981.

PERSONS, JOHN CECIL (1888–1974). Citizen; Soldier; Lawyer; Banker. Inducted: September 14, 1976.

PHIFER, J. REESE (1916–). Entrepreneur; Humanitarian. Inducted: November 7, 1991.

PIZITZ, LOUIS (1868–1959). Merchant; Humanitarian; Friend. Inducted: September 23, 1975.

PLUMMER, FRANK A. (1912–1987). One of Alabama's Premier Bankers; Dedicated Citizen. Inducted: October 5, 1989.

PRATT, DANIEL (1799–1873). Pioneer Industrialist; Architect; Civic Leader. Inducted: October 17, 1978.

RADCLIFF, ROBERT HERNDON, JR. (1917–). Outstanding Business Executive and Civic Leader. Inducted: October 5, 1989.

RAST, THOMAS E. (1920–). Outstanding Real Estate Executive; Champion of Higher Education; Dedicated Citizen. Inducted: October 7, 1993.

ROBERTS, EDWARD AUBERT (1898–1964). From Cargo Checker to President of Waterman Steamship Corporation; Founder of Southern Industries; Guiding Spirit of Modern Mobile's Civic Development. Inducted: October 8, 1974.

RUSHTON, JAMES FRANKLIN (1876–1927). Businessman; Civic Leader; Philanthropist. Inducted: September 23, 1975.

RUSHTON, WILLIAM JAMES (1900–1987). Insurance Executive; Soldier; Civic Leader; Humanitarian. Inducted: October 14, 1980.

RUSSELL, BENJAMIN (1876–1941). Founder of Russell Manufacturing Company; Public Servant and Civic Benefactor; Organizer of the First Alabama State Chamber of Commerce. Inducted: October 8, 1974.

RUSSELL, THOMAS DAMERON (1903–1982). Businessman; Philanthropist; Textile Industry Leader. Inducted: October 23, 1979.

SAMFORD, FRANK PARK (1893–1973). Guided Liberty National Life Insurance from a Small Fraternal Benefit Society to One of the Twenty Largest Stock Life Insurance Companies in the United States; Public Benefactor; Samford University Bears His Name. Inducted: October 8, 1974.

SAMFORD, FRANK PARK, JR. (1921–1986). Outstanding Executive in the Insurance Industry; Productive Citizen. Inducted: October 22, 1987.

SELLERS, WILLIAM D., JR. (1913–1990). Distinguished Transportation Executive; Benefactor of Higher Education and Community Services. Inducted: November 7, 1991.

SHELTON, BARRETT CLINTON, SR. (1902–1984). Exemplary Citizen and Community Builder; Outstanding Newspaper Editor and Publisher. Inducted: October 22, 1985.

SHOOK, PASCHAL GREEN (1872–1966). Industrialist; Civic Leader; Humanitarian. Inducted: October 17, 1978.

SMITH, JAMES CRAIG (1905–1977). Textile Manufacturer and Industrial Spokesman; Civic Leader; Educational Benefactor. Inducted: November 22, 1977.

SPAIN, FRANK EDWARD (1891–1986). Entrepreneur; Lawyer; Civic Leader; Philanthropist. Inducted: October 14, 1980.

SPRAGINS, MARION BEIRNE (1892–1973). Banker; Industrial Developer; Civic Leader. Inducted: November 22, 1977.

STERNE, MERVYN HAYDEN (1892–1973). Investment Strategist; Civic Leader; Humanitarian. Inducted: September 23, 1975.

STOCKHAM, HERBERT CLARK (1888–1958). Captain of Industry; Civic and Religious Leader. Inducted: October 16, 1986.

THOMPSON, HALL W. (1923–). Distinguished Business Executive and Community Leader. Inducted: October 13, 1992.

WARNER, JONATHAN WESTERVELT (1917–). Industrialist; Art Collector. Inducted: November 1, 1983.

WARNER, MILDRED WESTERVELT (1893–1974). Led Gulf States Paper for over Twenty Years; The Only Woman President of a Major Integrated Paper Company; Philanthropist; Gracious Lady, Daughter, Wife, and Mother. Inducted: October 8, 1974.

WEIL, ISIDOR (1856–1946). International Cotton Buyer and Exporter; Civic Leader; Patriarch. Inducted: November 3, 1981.

WESTERVELT, HERBERT EUGENE (1858–1938). Pioneer Paperman; World Traveler; Inventor. Inducted: October 23, 1979.

Appendix B

C&BA Faculty Hall of Fame

These individuals served their college with distinction and are honored by their colleagues for careers dedicated to excellence. May they always be remembered as those who made significant contributions to generations of students and colleagues.

1989 SAMUEL PAUL GARNER (1910–)
Dean Emeritus
Professor Emeritus of Accounting

1989 MARCUS WHITMAN (1902–1988)
Chairman Emeritus of Programs in Finance
Professor Emeritus of Finance

1990 JOSEPH E. LANE JR. (1922–1989)
Professor Emeritus of Accounting

1990 MINNIE C. MILES (1910–)
Professor Emeritus of Management

1991 LEE BIDGOOD (1884–1963)
Dean Emeritus

1991 WILLIAM R. BENNETT (1918–)
Professor Emeritus of Marketing

1992 CHESTER H. KNIGHT (1895–1949)
Professor and Chairman of Accounting

1992 JOHN S. BICKLEY (1917–)
Professor Emeritus of Insurance

1993 HARRY D. BONHAM (1900–1967)
Dean Emeritus of Administration
Professor and Chairman Emeritus of Marketing

1993 CHARLES R. SCOTT JR. (1914–)
Professor Emeritus of Management

1994 HERMAN H. CHAPMAN (1894–)
Professor and Chairman of Accounting and Statistics
Director Bureau of Business Research

1994 A. J. PENZ (1906–)
Chairman and Professor Emeritus of Accounting

Appendix C

Austin Cup: Outstanding Undergraduate

NAME	YEAR	HOMETOWN
W. Paul Thomas	1934	[unknown]
Russell K. Branscom	1935	[unknown]
William E. Wade	1936	[unknown]
Marx Leva	1937	[unknown]
Glenn V. Gibson	1938	Tuscaloosa, Alabama
Edmund P. Sliz	1939	Easthampton, Massachusetts
George M. Murray	1940	Bessemer, Alabama
G. Allen	1941	Dixon Springs, Tennessee
George Bloodworth	1942	Gadsden, Alabama
Edward Bryan Hale	1943	Pineapple, Alabama
Vernon W. Cole	1944	Fort Payne, Alabama
Allan L. Korn	1945	Margaretville, New York
Libby Anderson	1946	Birmingham, Alabama
Herschell E. Morrison	1947	Cullman, Alabama
Fred Blair First	1948	Birmingham, Alabama
James W. Battles	1949	Hollywood, Florida
George E. Kizziah	1950	Birmingham, Alabama
Norra Dean Dickey	1951	Anniston, Alabama
E. Bryant Ivey	1952	Talladega, Alabama
James K. Owens	1953	Gordo, Alabama
Fred A. Brett	1954	Tuscaloosa, Alabama
James R. Lawrence	1955	Pickensville, Alabama
John F. Yeager Jr.	1956	Marion, Alabama
Eldridge J. Samples	1957	Ozark, Alabama
Murray D. Wood	1958	Birmingham, Alabama
Denana Floyd	1959	Atlanta, Georgia
Jeanette Peery	1960	Florence, Alabama
B. T. Tillman Jr.	1961	Greenville, Alabama
Anna C. Cook	1962	Pushmataha, Alabama
Glenn J. Ahrenholz	1963	Tuscaloosa, Alabama
Sally L. Wahlsten	1964	Pittsburgh, Pennsylvania
Janis Rogers	1965	Nashville, Tennessee
Chester F. White	1966	Montgomery, Alabama
Hazel F. Ezell	1967	Tuscaloosa, Alabama
Sara Anne Long	1968	Mobile, Alabama
Patricia E. Saik	1969	Hammond, Louisiana
W. Henry Agee	1970	Pine Hill, Alabama
Doster L. McMullen	1971	Tuscaloosa, Alabama
Stephen L. Norris	1972	Arlington, Virginia
Deborah K. Hartman	1973	Mt. Vernon, Indiana

Lana English   1974   Luverne, Alabama
Patricia E. Black   1975   Geneva, Alabama
Leroy Tanker   1976   Birmingham, Alabama
Carol R. Grant   1977   Birmingham, Alabama
Randy L. Prince   1978   Birmingham, Alabama
Bronwyn L. Smith   1979   Birmingham, Alabama
Ronald A. Levitt   1980   Birmingham, Alabama
Kenneth A. Grodner
          (co–winner)   1981   Mountainbrook, Alabama
Martha E. Waters
          (co–winner)   1981   Birmingham, Alabama
Lucille Reymann   1982   Birmingham, Alabama
Carlos N. Kennedy   1983   Tuscaloosa, Alabama
Carin Lupuloff   1984   Omaha, Nebraska
J. Paul Compton Jr.   1985   Georgiana, Alabama
Cary William Baxley   1986   Sylacauga, Alabama
Shere Ellen McBryde   1987   Bessemer, Alabama
Winston Howard Gillum Jr.   1988   Sylacauga, Alabama
Anita 0. Scott   1989   Tuscaloosa, Alabama
Jerry Finney
          (co–winner)   1990   Gastonia, North Carolina
Robert Sigler
          (co–winner)   1990   Tuscaloosa, Alabama
William H. Bolen Jr.   1991   Statesboro, Georgia
Shannon D. Sylvis   1992   Hendersonville, Tennessee
Kamal S. Hosein   1993   Florala, Alabama
Stephen W. Linville   1994   Huntsville, Alabama

Appendix D
Board of Visitors

Members Emeriti

Charles C. Anderson
Aaron Aronov
M. Palmer Bedsole
Harold B. Blach Jr.
Winton M. Blount III
W. R. Bond
James J. Britton
Ben B. Brown
Dwight Carlisle
Charles H. Chapman Jr.
Donald Comer Jr.
James S. Crow
Tine W. Davis
Marvin R. Engel
Michael S. Gaffney
Gene C. Gwaltney
John A. Hand
Holman Head
Dan L. Hendley
Jimmy Hinton
Dexter D. Hulsart
Lewis F. Jeffers
Fred G. Koenig Jr.
Ernest F. Ladd Jr.
Edward L. Lowder

Robert Mangum
Frank Mason
A. Bruce Matthews
William H. Mitchell Jr.
Frank M. Moody
Robert Morrow
Harry M. Rhett Jr.
Leonard H. Roberts
William J. Rushton III
Frank P. Samford Jr.
John S. P. Samford
John H. Schuler
William D. Sellers Jr.
J. Craig Smith
Charles A. Snyder
Morris Sokol
James B. Sommerall
William M. Spencer III
Ellis Taylor
Ronald Thomas
E. Bruce Trickey
Mary George Waite
Marvin L. Warner
Robert H. Woodrow

Current Members

Charles E. "Eddie" Adair
N. Q. Adams
Clyde B. Anderson
Owen W. Aronov
W. E. "Ed" Babin
James B. "Jim" Boone Jr.
Young J. Boozer
John M. Brilbeck
Frank Bromberg Jr.
David G. Bronner
Ronald "Ron" G. Bruno
Jack R. "J. R." Brunson
James "Jim" L. Busby
Karen Jones Campbell
R. Eugene "Gene" Cartledge

Woodrow W. "Foots" Clements
J. Weldon Cole
David J. Cooper
John R. Cooper
Hugh F. Culverhouse, Esq.
T. Wayne Davis Jr.
Oliver "Ollie" H. Delchamps Jr.
James "Jimmy" H. Dill
Samuel "Sam" A. DiPiazza Jr.
Elbert A. "Larry" Drummond
Marshall Durbin
William E. "Billy" Ezell III
Joseph "Joe" M. Farley
Sam P. Faucett III
Robert "Bob" L. Fitts

Morris W. "Buster" Frank
Wayne H. Gillis
Glenn J. Griffin
Dwight Harrigan
Elmer Harris
James "Jimmy" I. Harrison Jr.
Taylor H. Henry
James "Jim" S. Holbrook Jr.
Richard "Rick" D. Horsley
G. Thomas "Tom" Hough
W. Carl Jernigan
Carl E. Jones Jr.
D. Paul Jones Jr.
Donald "D. R." Ray Jordan
Peter L. Lowe
John A. Lyon Jr.
Wallace D. Malone Jr.
Lewis M. Manderson Jr.
Marvin L. Mann.
Leroy McAbee
Sid L. McDonald
J. Robert " Bob" McGehee
Thomas "Tom" E. McMillan Jr.
J. Richard Miller III
John R. Miller
Harris V. Morrissette
James "Jim" D. Nabors
Larry E. Newman
Frank A. Nix
L. Dean O' Farrel
Arthur R. Outlaw
Goldie Paine
Timothy M. "Tim" Parker Jr.
Beverly C. Phifer

William A. Powell Jr.
Alvin "Al" L. Reeser
Van L. Richey
Richard "Ricky" H. Robinson
Jim Rogers
Jon W. Rotenstreich
Alma Gates Sanders
Helen B. Sevier
Barrett C. Shelton Jr.
William "Bill" H. Stender Jr.
Fred T. Stimpson III
G. Robin Swift Jr.
Howard M. Tepper
John R. Thomas
Michael "Mike" D. Thompson
E. Gene Thrasher
Benajah T. "Tommy" Tillman Jr.
R. Neal Travis
William "Bill" T. Ventress Jr.
Jack W. Warner
W. Edgar Welden
William "Billy" A. Williamson Jr.
Kemmons "Kem" Wilson Jr.
Murray D. Wood

OFFICERS:

Chairman:
    Ronald G. Bruno
Vice Chairman:
    James I. Harrison Jr.
Secretary/Treasurer:
    James D. Nabors

Appendix E

C&BA Faculty (1919 to 1993)

The following faculty list records full–time faculty members who taught in C&BA during the past seventy–five years and is drawn from material found in the University catalogs. The precise dates of initial employment and subsequent promotion have been difficult to determine in some cases due to incomplete information. Some faculty members from other divisions of the University who taught special C&BA courses in their disciplines are included in the list.

ADAMS, Benjamin Michael, B.S. (Northeast Louisiana), M.S. (Arkansas), Ph.D. (Southwestern Louisiana). Assistant Professor of Statistics, 1989.

ADAMSON, Wendell Mavity, A.B., M.A. (Indiana). Instructor of Statistics and Statistician, Bureau of Business Research 1931; Assistant Professor, 1939; Associate Professor of Business Statistics and Statistician, Bureau of Business Research, 1946.

ALBRIGHT, Thomas L., B.F.A. (North Carolina—Greensboro), M.B.A. (California State—Stanislaus), Ph.D. (Tennessee), C.P.A. (California). Assistant Professor of Accounting, 1990.

ALLAWAY, Arthur W., B.B.A., M.B.A., Ph.D. (Texas). Assistant Professor of Marketing, 1982; Associate Professor, 1988.

ALYEA, Paul E., M.S., Ph.D. (Illinois). Instructor of Economics, 1934; Assistant Professor, 1935; Associate Professor, 1939; Professor of Finance, 1945; Professor Emeritus, 1964.

AMIDON, Jeanette Marie, M.A. (College of Puget Sound). Instructor of Statistics and Business Analyst, Bureau of Business Research, 1941.

ANDERSON, Edward Hutchings, M.S. (Florida), Ph.D. (North Carolina). Associate Professor of Economics, 1939; Professor of Management, 1946; Director of Graduate Division, School of C&BA, 1948.

ARCE, Daniel G., B.A. (Olivet College), M.A. (Western Michigan), Ph.D. (Illinois). Assistant Professor of Economics, 1991.

ASHBY, Wilson T., M.A., Ed.D. (Oklahoma). Associate Professor of Secretarial Administration, 1956; Professor and Head of Secretarial Administration, 1961.

AUSMUS, Ora May, B.B.A. (Texas Tech), M.A. (Alabama). Instructor of Business Statistics, 1946; Instructor Emeritus, 1976.

AUSTIN, Edward Knox, M.S. (Columbia). Associate Professor of Commerce, 1935; Associate Professor of Marketing, 1945; Associate Professor Emeritus, 1972.

AUSTIN, Kenneth R., M.S., Ph.D. (Kentucky), C.P.A. (Ohio). Assistant Professor of Accounting, 1978; Associate Professor, 1985.

BAILEY, Earl L., B.S., M.S. (Oklahoma). Assistant Professor of Business Statistics, 1955.

BAIN, Trevor, B.A. (City College of New York), M.I.L.R. (Cornell), Ph.D. (California—Berkeley). Professor of Manpower and Industrial Relations and Director, Manpower and Industrial Relations Institute (now Human Resources Institute), 1974; John R. Miller Professor of Human Resources Management, 1983.

BAKLANOFF, Eric N., M.A., Ph.D. (Ohio State). Professor of Economics and Dean for International Programs, 1969; Board of Visitors Research Professor of Economics, 1974; Professor Emeritus, 1992.

BARRETT, Arnold L., M.A., Ph.D. (Virginia). Associate Professor of Economics, 1957.

BARRETT, Bruce E., B.S. (College of Charleston), M.S., Ph.D. (Clemson). Assistant Professor of Statistics, 1989.

BARRON, F. Hutton, B.S. (Davidson College), Sc.M. (Brown), Ph.D. (Pennsylvania). Professor of Management Science and Head, Department of Management Science and Statistics, 1983.

BARTON, J. Cullen, M.A. (LSU). Instructor of Commerce, 1938.

BEARDEN, William O., Ph.D. (South Carolina). Assistant Professor of Marketing, 1976.

BEATTY, Sharon E., B.S.B.A. (Central Florida), M.B.A. (Colorado), Ph.D. (Oregon). Assistant Professor of Marketing, 1986; Associate Professor, 1988.

BENNETT, William R., B.A. (Birmingham–Southern), M.B.A. (Louisiana State), Ph.D. (Illinois). Assistant Professor of Marketing, 1950; Associate Professor, 1953; Professor, 1957; Director, Graduate Division, C&BA, 1963; Director, International Trade Center, 1979; Professor Emeritus, 1983.

BENNINGER, Lawrence J., M.A., Ph.D. (Missouri). Associate Professor of Accounting, 1955.

BICKLEY, John Strock, A.B., M.B.A., Ph.D. (Wisconsin). Instructor of Economics, 1940; Assistant Professor of Finance, 1947; Alabama Insurance Industry Professor of Finance, 1968; Frank P. Samford Chair of Insurance Professor, 1975; Professor Emeritus, 1986.

BIDGOOD, Lee, M.A. (Virginia), LL.D. (Alabama), D.C.S. Hon. C. (New York University). Professor of Economics, 1913; Dean, School of C&BA, 1919; Professor and Dean Emeritus, 1954.

BINDON, Kathleen, B.A. (San Jose State), M.B.A., Ph.D. (Pennsylvania State), C.P.A. (Florida). Instructor of Accounting, 1979; Assistant Professor, 1981; Associate Professor, 1987.

BIRD, Ronald E., Ph.D. (North Carolina). Assistant Professor of Economics, 1975; Associate Professor, 1979.

BLOOD, Forrest Clifford, M.A. (Nebraska). Instructor of Economics, 1939.

BLOOD, Hermine Heye, M.A. (Iowa). Instructor of Secretarial Studies, 1939.

BOND, Elden A., M.A. (Columbia). Assistant Professor of Psychology, 1939. Taught special business psychology courses in C&BA.

BONER, Russell, M.A. (Illinois). Instructor of Economics, 1937.

BONFIELD, Edward, M.A. (Alabama), Ph.D. (Illinois). Lecturer in Marketing, 1970; Assistant Professor, 1972.

BONHAM, Harry Dwight, B.S. in B. and P. Adm. (Missouri), M.A. (Chicago). Instructor of Accounting, 1923; Assistant Professor of Business Administration, 1924; Associate Professor of Economics, 1927; Professor of Marketing, 1945; Acting Dean of Administration, 1957; Professor Emeritus, 1966.

BOYA, Unal O., M.S. (Middle East Tech—Ankara, Turkey), Ph.D. (North Carolina). Instructor of Marketing, 1981; Assistant Professor of Marketing, 1982.

BRETT, Frederic A., M.S. (Alabama), Ph.D. (Alabama). Temporary Instructor of Accounting, 1956; Instructor of Accounting, 1957; Assistant Professor, 1958; Associate Professor of Management, 1961; Professor, 1963.

BROOKS, C. C., A.B. (Iowa State Teachers College), M.A. (Columbia). Assistant Professor of Economics, 1926.

BROOKS, Robert, B.S. (Florida State), Ph.D. (Florida). Assistant Professor of Finance, 1989.

BROWDER, Olin L., Jr., A.B., LL.B. (Illinois), S.J.D. (Michigan). Instructor of Business Law, 1939; Assistant Professor, 1940.

BRYSON, Jay H., B.A., Ph.D. (North Carolina). Assistant Professor of Economics, 1989.

BUBLITZ, Bruce, M.A.S., Ph.D. (Illinois). Instructor of Accounting, 1980; Assistant Professor, 1981.

BURKETT, Morris Anderson, B.S., LL.B. (Alabama). Instructor of Economics, 1941.

BUTTERFIELD. M. A. (Oklahoma), Ph.D. (Illinois), Assistant Professor of Commercial Spanish, 1938; Associate Professor, 1944.

CAMPBELL, Claude A., M.A. (Peabody), Ph.D. (Vanderbilt). Instructor of Economics, 1930.

CAMPBELL, Donald Lee, M.A., Ed.D. (North Dakota). Associate Professor of Office Administration, 1968.

CAMPBELL, Harry M., M.A. (SMU). Instructor in Business English, 1941.

CARGILE, Barney R., B.S., M.A.S. (Illinois), Ph.D. (Missouri), C.P.A. (Illinois). Assistant Professor of Accounting, 1979; Associate Professor, 1985.

CARNEVALE, Carol M., M.B.A. (Toledo). Assistant Professor of Management, 1987.

CARROLL, Carolyn A., B.A. (Illinois State), M.S. (Southern Illinois), Ph.D. (Illinois State). Assistant Professor of Finance, 1984.

CASHMAN, James F., B.S., M.A., Ph.D. (Illinois). Assistant Professor of Organizational Behavior, 1975; Associate Professor, 1978; Professor, 1984.

CHAKRABORTI, Subhabrata, B.Sc. (Calcutta), M.A., Ph.D. (SUNY—Buffalo). Assistant Professor of Statistics, 1984; Associate Professor, 1989.

CHAPMAN, Herman Hollis, A.B. (University of Michigan), Ph.D. (Columbia). Assistant Professor and Head of Accounting, 1921; Associate Professor, 1922; Associate Professor of Accounting and Head of Business Statistics, 1924; Professor of Statistics and Accounting, 1927; Director, Bureau of Business Research, 1930; Professor Emeritus, 1959.

CHAPPEL, Henry W. Jr., M.A., Ph.D. (Yale). Assistant Professor of Economics, 1979.

CHARLTON, Jesse M. Jr., M.B.A. (LSU). Instructor of Commerce, 1938.

CHARNETSKI, Johnnie R., M.B.A., Ph.D. (Texas). Associate Professor of Management Science, 1982.

CHENG, David C., B.A. (National Taiwan), M.A., M.Ph., Ph.D. (Yale). Assistant Professor of Economics, 1974; Associate Professor, 1976; Professor, 1982; Acting Head, Department of Economics, Finance, and Legal Studies, 1987.

CHERRY, George M. Jr., B.S. (USMA), M.B.A. (LSU—New Orleans), C.P.A. (Louisiana). Assistant Professor of Accounting and Information Systems, 1971.

CHILTON, Arthur B., LL.B. (University of Alabama). Professor of Law, 1920. Taught early commercial law courses for C&BA.

CHISHOLM, John W. Jr., M.A. (LSU). Instructor in Commerce, 1939; Instructor of Economic History, 1940.

CHUNG, Jain, M.A. (Miami, Ohio), Ph.D. (VPI). Assistant Professor of Statistics, 1985.

CLYMER, Louise, M.A. (Iowa). Instructor in Secretarial Studies, 1942.

COBB, A. Lee, M.A. (Florida), D.B.A. (Indiana). Associate Professor of Business Statistics, 1964; Professor, 1965.

COLEY, Marion, M.B.A., LL.B. (Alabama). Lecturer in Business Law and Economics, 1956; Acting Assistant Dean, C&BA, 1957; Associate Professor of Business Law, 1958; Acting Head of Business Law, 1965.

COLLINS, Robert George, M.A. (Miami University.). Instructor in Marketing, 1952.

COLLINS, Sydney Albert, M.A. (South Dakota). Instructor in Secretarial Studies, 1937.

CONERLY, Michael D., B.S. (Lamar University), M.S., Ph.D. (SMU). Assistant Professor of Statistics, 1982; Associate Professor, 1988.

CONSTANTIN, James A., M.B.A., Ph.D.
(Texas). Assistant Professor of Finance,
1947; Associate Professor and Research
Assistant, Bureau of Business Research, 1951.

CORLEY, Donald, B.S. (Auburn), J.D.
(Cumberland). Assistant Professor of
Business Law, 1969.

CORRIHER, J. D., M.B.A. (Indiana), Ph.D.
(Alabama). Instructor in Economics, 1956;
Instructor in Accounting and Information
Systems, 1975; Assistant Professor, 1976;
Assistant Professor Emeritus, 1987.

COVER, James P., B.S.M.E. (Virginia Tech),
Ph.D. (Virginia). Assistant Professor of
Economics, 1982; Associate Professor, 1988.

CRAMER, Dale L., M.A., Ph.D. (LSU).
Associate Professor of Economics, 1958;
Professor, 1963; Head, 1968; Acting Head of
Department of Economics, Finance, and
Legal Studies, 1981; Professor Emeritus,
1988.

CROWN, Deborah, B.S. (North Central
College), M.S. (Colorado—Denver), Ph.D.
(Colorado). Assistant Professor of
Management, 1990.

CURTIS, William R., M.A. (North
Carolina), Ph.D. (Illinois). Instructor in
Economics, 1935; Assistant Professor, 1937.

DANIEL, Norman, M.S. (Tennessee), Ph.D.
(Indiana). Lecturer in Finance, 1964;
Assistant Professor, 1965.

DAUGHERTY, Carroll R., M.A., Ph.D.
(Pennsylvania). Professor of Economics and
Director, Bureau of Personnel and
Placement, 1928.

DAVIES, Jonathan J., M.A. (Florida),
D.B.A. (LSU), C.P.A. (Louisiana). Assistant
Professor of Accounting and Information
Systems, 1975; Associate Professor of
Accountancy, 1978.

DAVIS, D. Larry, Ph.D. (Utah). Assistant
Professor of Economics, 1972.

DAVIS, Earl, B.S. in B.A., LL.B. (Boston
University), M.B.A. (New York University),
Ph.D. (Alabama). Temporary Instructor in
Business Law, 1959; Associate Professor,
1962.

DAVIS, John, M.A. (Southern Methodist).
Instructor in Economics, 1956.

DAVIS, Margaret M., M.A. (Alabama).
Instructor in Commercial Spanish, 1931.

DENSMORE, Max L., M.B.A. (Western
Michigan), Ph.D. (Michigan State).
Associate Professor of Marketing,
Communications, and Logistics, 1972.

DICKINSON, Edmund C., A.B., J.D.
(Michigan). Professor of Law; Instructor in
Commercial Law beginning in 1920.

DODSON, Norman E., M.A. (Alabama).
Instructor in Business Statistics, 1946.

DOWNS, Thomas, B.S. (Florida State),
M.S., Ph.D. (Purdue). Associate Professor of
Finance, 1989.

DRAKE, Albert E., M.S. (Kentucky), Ph.D.
(Illinois). Professor of Quantitative Methods,
1966; Associate Dean for Undergraduate
Programs, 1989.

D'SOUZA, Giles, B.A. (University of
Karachi—Pakistan), M.B.A. (Catholic
University of Leuven—Belgium), Ph.D.
(Texas—Dallas). Assistant Professor of
Marketing, 1990.

DUGAN, Michael T., B.S. (University of
New Orleans), M.Acc., D.B.A. (Tennessee),
C.P.A. (Louisiana). Assistant Professor of
Accounting, 1985; Associate Professor, 1988.

DULEK, Ronald E., B.A. (St. Mary's
College), M.A., Ph.D. (Purdue). Assistant
Professor of Written Business
Communication, 1977; Associate Professor,
1981; Professor, 1985; Head, Department of
Management and Marketing, 1988.

DURAND, Richard M., Ph.D. (Florida).
Assistant Professor of Marketing, 1976;
Associate Professor, 1978.

DURHAM, Lawrence B., Ph.D. (Delaware).
Assistant Professor of Organizational
Behavior and Director of University
Planning, 1974.

DYKEMA, Frank Edward, M.A., Ph.D. (Michigan). Instructor in Commerce, 1939; Assistant Professor of Economic History, 1940; Associate Professor of Economics, 1947; Professor, 1951; Professor Emeritus, 1967.

EASTWOOD, Richard Lyman, Assistant Professor of Economics, 1946.

ELDER, Harold W., B.A. (Hendrix College), M.B.A. (Arkansas), Ph.D. (VPI). Instructor in Economics, 1981; Associate Professor, 1988.

EPLEY, Donald R., M.A. (Wichita State), Ph.D. (Missouri). Assistant Professor of Economics, 1972.

EVANS, John S., B.A., M.A. (University of Texas), Ph.D. (Wisconsin). Lecturer in Economics, 1968; Assistant Professor, 1970; Associate Professor, 1973; Professor, 1981.

EZELL, Hazel F., B.A., M.B.A., Ph.D. (Alabama). Temporary Instructor in Office Administration, 1969; Administrative Assistant to the Dean for the M.B.A. Program, 1974; Assistant Professor of Marketing, 1979; Associate Professor, 1983.

FERGUSON, Carl, B.S. (Southwest Missouri College), M.B.A., Ph.D. (Missouri—Columbia). Assistant Professor of Marketing, 1975; Acting Director and Director of the Center for Business and Economic Research, 1977; Associate Professor, 1978; Professor, 1985.

FERRELL, M. Elizabeth, B.A. (College of St. Benedict), M.B.A., Ph.D. (Texas Tech). Assistant Professor of Marketing, 1989.

FIDLER, Alice, M.A. (Alabama). Instructor in Business English, 1937.

FIELDEN, John S., B.S. (Wharton School of Finance and Commerce), M.A., Ph.D. (Boston). Professor of General Business Administration and Dean, College of C&BA, 1971; University Professor of Written Business Communication, 1979.

FINDLEY, Herbert Lyman, A.B., LL.B. (Alabama). Lecturer in Business Law, 1932; Professor and Head of Business Law, 1946; Professor Emeritus, 1965.

FISH, Mary, B.B.A. (Minnesota), M.B.A. (Texas Technological College), Ph.D. (Oklahoma). Assistant Professor of Economics, 1966; Associate Professor, 1967; Professor, 1969.

FLEWELLEN, William C. Jr., M.S. (Alabama), Ph.D. (Columbia). Assistant Professor of Accounting, 1946; Assistant to the Dean, 1947; Associate Professor, 1953; Assistant Dean, 1955; Professor, 1957.

FLOWERS, W. Baker, M.S. (Alabama), Ph.D. (Texas), C.P.A. (Texas). Professor of Accounting, 1963.

FOLTS, Howard A., M.B.A. (Alabama). Instructor in Economics, 1948; Instructor in Marketing, 1953; Assistant Professor, 1955; Assistant Dean, 1959.

FORD, Robert A., M.B.A. (Texas). Instructor in Finance, 1955; Assistant Professor of Finance, 1956.

FORD, Tim, B.S. (Auburn), LL.B. (Alabama). Lecturer in Business Law, 1963; Assistant Professor, 1964.

FORMBY, John P., B.A. (Colorado College), Ph.D. (Colorado). Professor of Economics and Head, Department of Economics, Finance, and Legal Studies, 1982; Senior Associate Dean for Academic Affairs, 1987; Hayes Distinguished Professor of Economics, 1989.

FOSTER, Franklin J., A.B. (Drury), M.B.A. (Pennsylvania). Instructor in Economics, 1937; Instructor in Economic Geography, 1940; Assistant Professor of Marketing, 1946; Assistant Professor Emeritus, 1973.

FOSTER, Lawrence, B.S. (Oklahoma), M.B.A. (Harvard), Ph.D. (Texas). Miller Professor of Business Administration, 1984; Acting Director, World Business Program, 1984.

FOTTLER, Myron D., Ph.D. (Columbia). Associate Professor of Health Care Management, 1976; Professor, 1979.

FOUTS, Harold E., A.B., B.S. (Missouri). Instructor in Business Administration, 1922.

FREEMAN, Robert J., M.B.A., Ph.D. (Arkansas), C.P.A. (Alabama). Assistant Professor of Accounting, 1965; Associate Professor, 1969; Professor, 1973.

FULMER, William E., M.A., Ph.D. (Pennsylvania). Associate Professor of Human Resource Management, 1978; Director of the M.B.A. Program, and Interim Director of Graduate Studies, 1979; Professor, 1982.

FUTHEY, Bruce, M.A. (Iowa), C.P.A. (Louisiana). Instructor in Accounting, 1938; Assistant Professor, 1946; Associate Professor, 1946.

GALLALEE, John M., M.E. (Virginia). Professor of Mechanical Engineering, 1912; taught Industrial Organization and Management, 1923.

GAMBRELL, Joe Lowry, M.S. (Alabama). Instructor in Commerce, 1939.

GARBER, Lucille, M.B.A. (Northwestern). Instructor in Economics, 1945.

GARNER, Samuel Paul, M.A. (Duke), Ph.D. (Texas), D.Ec. (Pusan), C.P.A. (Texas, Alabama). Associate Professor of Accounting, 1939; Professor, 1943; Head, Department of Accounting, 1949; Dean, 1954; Dean and Professor Emeritus, 1971.

GIBBONS, Janie Moore, M.A (Alabama). Instructor in Marketing, 1957.

GIBBONS, Jean D., A.B., M.A. (Duke), Ph.D. (VPI). Professor of Business Statistics, 1970; Chair of Statistics and Quantitative Methods, 1971; Board of Visitors Research Professor of Statistics, 1975; Russell Professor of Statistics, 1989.

GILL, John, M.A. (Alabama), Ph.D. (Texas). Professor and Head of Business Statistics, 1960; Professor Emeritus, 1975.

GILL, John, A.B., M.A (Alabama). Assistant in Commercial Mathematics, 1932; Instructor, 1935; Instructor in Statistics, 1942; Assistant Professor and Statistician, Bureau of Business Research, 1945.

GILSTER, John E., Jr., M.B.A. (Harvard), Ph.D. (Michigan). Associate Professor of Finance, 1985.

GLOVER, Lee, B.S. in C&BA (Alabama). Instructor in Accounting, 1925.

GOING, James W., B.S. (Furman), M.S. (Alabama). Teaching Assistant in Accounting, 1930; Instructor in Accounting, 1932.

GORDON, Anyan A., M.B.A. (Alabama). Director, Commerce Extension Services and Lecturer in Management, 1962; Director of Continuing Business Education, 1979; Director Emeritus, 1983.

GRAY, J.Brian, B.S. (UAB), M.S., Ph.D. (Clemson). Associate Professor of Statistics, 1990.

GREGORY, Paul M., M.A., Ph.D. (Clark). Associate Professor of Economics, 1948; Professor, 1957.

GRIFFIN, Marvin A., M.S.E. (Alabama), D. Eng. (Johns Hopkins), P.E. (Alabama). Professor of Management Science and Operations Management; Area Chair of Management Science, Operations Management, Statistics, and Quantitative Methods, 1971.

GRIFFIN, Mary Claire, M.S. (Tennessee). Instructor in Secretarial Studies, 1949; Assistant Professor of Secretarial Administration, 1957; Associate Professor, 1961.

GRINER, Emmett H., B.A., M.B.A. (University of Arkansas), Ph.D. (Maryland), C.P.A. (Maryland). Assistant Professor of Accounting, 1990.

GUNTHER, William D., B.A., M.A. (Kent State), Ph.D. (Kentucky). Lecturer in Economics, 1968; Assistant Professor, 1969; Associate Professor, 1971; Professor, 1976; Associate Dean for Research and Service and Director, Center for Business and Economic Research, 1988.

GUP, Benton E., B.A., M.B.A., Ph.D. (Cincinnati). Alabama Bankers' Educational Foundation Banking Chair Professor, 1983; Robert Hunt Cochrane/Alabama Bankers' Association Chair of Banking, 1989.

GWINNER, Robert F., Ph.D. (Arkansas). Assistant Professor of Marketing, 1964.

HADAWAY, Samuel C., M.B.A., Ph.D. (Texas). Assistant Professor of Finance, 1975.

HAM, William Dunn, B.S., LL.B. (Illinois), LL.M. (Harvard). Instructor in Business Law, 1941.

HAMMER, Thomas J., B.S. (Illinois). Instructor in Commercial English, 1924.

HARRIS, Calvin, B.S. (Livingston State College), M.S. (Alabama). Temporary Instructor in Secretarial Administration, 1957; Assistant Professor, 1959.

HARRISON, M. Leigh, A.B., LL.B., LL.M. (Alabama), LL.M. (Harvard). Professor of Law, 1944.

HARRISON, Volney V., M.B.A. (Alabama), C.P.A. (Alabama). Assistant Professor of Accounting, 1956.

HARWOOD, Robert, A.B., LL.B. (Alabama). Instructor in Law, 1929.

HAVARD, Jesse Boyd, M.A. (Alabama). Instructor in Commercial Mathematics, 1939.

HAVENS, Ralph M., M.B.A. (Kansas), Ph.D. (Duke). Associate Professor of Economics, 1946; Professor, 1952; Head, Department of Economics, 1954; Professor Emeritus, 1970.

HAWLEY, Langston T., B.S., M.S. (Alabama), Ph.D. (North Carolina). Laboratory Assistant in Accounting, 1930; Teaching Assistant, 1932; Instructor, 1934; Associate Professor of Management, 1946; Professor, 1950; Head, Department of Management, 1966; Professor Emeritus, 1974.

HEFLIN, Wilson L., M.A. (Vanderbilt). Instructor in Business English, 1937.

HEILMAN, S. Earl, A.B. (DePauw), J.D. (Indiana). Assistant Professor of Business Law, 1942.

HELMS, Billy P., B.S., M.S. (Auburn), Ph.D. (Tennessee). Assistant Professor of Finance, 1973; Associate Professor, 1977; Professor, 1984; Head, Department of Economics, Finance, and Legal Studies, 1988.

HENDERSON, John S., M.A. (North Carolina), Ph.D. (Louisiana State). Associate Professor of Economics, 1949; Professor, 1957.

HERNANDEZ, Jose, B.S. (Peabody). Instructor in Commercial Spanish, 1930.

HEWETT, Wendell, M.B.A., D.B.A. (Texas Tech). Associate Professor of Marketing, 1970.

HEWITT, Charles M., LL.B., M.B.A. (Alabama). Assistant Professor of Business Law, 1950; Assistant to the Dean, 1952.

HICKS, Samuel A. Jr., M.B.A., Ph. D. (Wisconsin), C.P.A. (Tennessee). Lecturer in Accounting and Information Systems, 1975; Assistant Professor, 1976.

HILDRETH, Rodger P., M.Ed. (Montevallo), M.B.A. (Auburn), Ph.D. (UAB). Assistant Professor of Health Care Management, 1981.

HILL, John S., B.S. (University of Aston, England), M.A. (Lancaster, England), Ph.D. (Georgia). Assistant Professor of Marketing, 1982; Associate Professor, 1985; Professor of International Business, 1991.

HILLE, Stanley J., M.B.A., Ph.D. (Minnesota). Alabama Truckers' Association Chair of Transportation Professor, 1974.

HILTON, Chadwick B., A.B. (North Carolina), M.A. (North Carolina State—Raleigh), Ph.D. (Tennessee). Assistant Professor of Managerial Communication, 1986; Associate Professor, 1992.

HIMES, Samuel H. Jr., M.A. (Florida), D.B.A. (Florida State). Lecturer in Marketing, 1969; Assistant Professor and Executive Assistant to the Dean of the School of Communication, 1973.

HINCKLEY, Frank O., M.S. (George Washington). Lecturer and Coordinator of Health Care Management Program, 1973.

HINES, Mary Alice, M.S. (Indiana), Ph.D. (Ohio State). Associate Professor of Real Estate and Finance, 1974; Professor, 1977.

HODGES, Leroy S., M.A. (Alabama).
Instructor in Commercial English, 1922.

HOFFMAN, George A., M.A.
(Northwestern). Instructor in Business
English, 1927.

HOLLADAY, James, M.S. (Illinois), Ph.D.
(Iowa). Professor of Economics, 1927; Head,
Department of Finance, 1946; Professor
Emeritus, 1963.

HOLLADAY, William A., M.S. (Wyoming),
Ph.D. (Texas). Lecturer in Management,
1965; Associate Professor, 1966.

HOLLAND, Thomas, M.S. (Tennessee),
Ph.D. (Duke). Assistant Professor of
Economics, 1963; Associate Professor, 1964.

HOLLOWELL, Ralph, B.A. (Iowa).
Instructor in Business Administration, 1922.

HOOKS, Donald L., B.A., Ph.D. (Texas
A&M). Assistant Professor of Economics,
1971; Associate Professor, 1974.

HORNER, Seward L., A.B. (University of
Michigan). Instructor in Accounting, 1920.

HOUSTON, Franklin S., M.B.A. (Indiana),
Ph.D. (Purdue). Associate Professor of
Marketing, 1982; Professor, 1986.

HOWARD, Thomas P., B.S.B.A. (Drake
University), M.B.A., Ph.D. (Arizona State).
Director, Culverhouse School of
Accountancy and Professor of Accounting,
1992.

HOWE, Edmund Grant, M.A. (Harvard).
Assistant Professor of Political Science,
1920; Professor of Political Science, 1927;
taught courses on Public Finance and
Investments for several years.

HRUSKA, Robert, B.S. (City College of
New York). Instructor in Business Statistics,
1947.

HUDDLESTON, Paul F., B.A., M.A.
(Indiana University). Temporary Instructor
in Management, 1956; Instructor, 1959.

HUDNALL, Jarrett, B.B.A., M.B.A.
(University of Texas). Temporary Instructor
in Marketing, 1958; Instructor, 1959.

HUMBLE, Thomas N., M.B.A. (Louisiana),
Ph.D. (Texas), C.P.A. (Louisiana). Associate
Professor of Accounting, 1948; Professor,
1965; Professor Emeritus, 1978.

HUMMEL, Paul Matthew, B.A., M.A.,
Ph.D. (Ohio State). Instructor of
Mathematics, 1935; Assistant Professor,
1939; Associate Professor of Business
Statistics, 1946; Professor, 1948; Acting
Head of Department, 1959.

INGRAM, Robert W., B.A. (Eastern New
Mexico), M.A. (Abilene Christian), Ph.D.
(Texas Tech), C.P.A. (Texas). Ernst and
Whinney Professor of Accounting, 1985;
Director, School of Accountancy, 1987;
Steven J. Ross—Hugh F. Culverhouse
Professor of Accountancy, 1992.

JAMES, Louis J., A.B. (Missouri), M.A.,
Ph.D. (Kansas). Assistant Professor of
Finance, 1971.

JAMES, William L., M.S., Ph.D. (Purdue).
Instructor in Marketing,1977; Assistant
Professor, 1981; Associate Professor, 1983.

JANES, Harold D., B.B.A., M.B.A.
(University of Miami), Ph.D.(Alabama).
Instructor in Management, 1958; Assistant
Professor, 1961; Associate Professor, 1962;
Professor, 1966; Professor Emeritus, 1984.

JEAN, William H., B.S., M.A. (Kansas),
Ph.D. (Purdue). Professor of Finance, 1973.

JEANBLANC, Lindsey R., A.B., J.D.
(Illinois), LL.M. (Columbia). Associate
Professor of Business Law, 1938.

JOHNSON, Harry L., B.A. (Emory and
Henry College), M.A., Ph.D. (Virginia).
Associate Professor of Finance, 1960;
Professor of Finance, 1961.

JOHNSON, Mark R., B.S. (California
Institute of Technology), M.A., C.Phil.,
Ph.D. (California—San Diego). Assistant
Professor of Economics, 1989.

JOHNSON, Russell E., M.A. (Minnesota).
Instructor in Economics, 1937; Business
Analyst, Bureau of Business Research, 1940.

KARSON, Marvin J., M.A. (Johns Hopkins), Ph.D. (North Carolina State). Associate Professor of Statistics and Quantitative Methods, 1972; Professor and Acting Chair, Management Science, Operations Management, and Statistics, 1975.

KEE, Robert C., B.S. (Union), B. A., M.B.A. (South Florida), Ph.D. (Florida State), C.M.A. Assistant Professor of Accounting, 1979; Associate Professor, 1984.

KEELER, James P., B.B.A. (Ohio), Ph.D. (Indiana). Instructor in Economics, 1979; Assistant Professor, 1981.

KIM, Myung J., B.A. (Hanyang—Korea), M.A., Ph.D. (Washington). Assistant Professor of Economics, 1989.

KIRKHAM, Edward James, M.S. in Accountancy (Illinois). Instructor in Accounting, 1940.

KITTRELL, Edward R., M.A. (Virginia), Ph.D. (Chicago). Associate Professor of Economics, 1964.

KLAGES, Walter, M.A. (Munich), Ph.D. (Alabama). Temporary Instructor in Economics, 1965; Assistant Professor, 1967.

KLERSEY, George F. Jr., B.S.B.A., M.B.A. (Florida), Ph.D. (Southern California), C.P.A. (California). Assistant Professor of Accounting, 1988.

KNIGHT, Chester Howard, B.S. (Alabama), M.A. (Chicago), C.P.A. (Alabama). Instructor in Accounting, 1923; Assistant Professor, 1927; Head, Department of Accounting, 1934; Associate Professor, 1937; Professor, 1939; Veterans' Representative, 1944.

KNIGHT, Fred J., M.B.A., Ph.D. (Northwestern). Visiting Associate Professor of Management, 1967; Associate Professor, 1968; Associate Professor Emeritus, 1977.

KNOBLAUCH, Vicki I., B.A. (Wisconsin—Madison), M.A., Ph.D. (Wisconsin—Milwaukee). Assistant Professor of Economics, 1991.

KRUEGER, Paul F., M.A. (Missouri). Instructor in Commercial Math, 1930.

KRUGER, Daniel H., M.A., Ph.D. (Wisconsin). Assistant Professor of Management and Director, Commerce Extension Service, 1954; Associate Professor, 1956.

KURKJIAN, Badrig M., M.S. (George Washington), Ph.D. (American University). Professor of Statistics, 1976; Chair, Programs in Industrial Management and Statistics, 1978; Professor Emeritus, 1989.

KWON, Young–June, Ph.D. (Pennsylvania). Assistant Professor of Finance, 1986.

LAFFERTY, George W., M.B.A. (Pennsylvania), C.P.A. (Texas). Associate Professor of Accounting, 1946.

LAGRONE, Paul G., M.B.A. (Denver). Instructor in Accounting and Economics, 1953.

LAMBERT, Eugene W. Jr., B.S. (Arkansas), M.B.A. (Texas), Ph.D. (Alabama). Temporary Instructor of Finance, 1961; Assistant Professor, 1962.

LAMONT, Douglas, M.B.A. (Tulane), Ph.D. (Alabama). Associate Professor of International Business, 1967.

LANE, Joseph Ernest, M.B.A. (Pennsylvania), LL.B. (Alabama), C.P.A. (Tennessee, Alabama). Assistant Professor of Accounting, 1949; Associate Professor, 1953; Professor, 1957; Professor Emeritus, 1984.

LARCOM, Russell C., M.B.A. (Harvard), Ph.D. (Johns Hopkins), C.P.A. (Alabama, Mississippi, Texas). Associate Professor of Economics, 1942; Professor of Finance, 1947.

LEATHERS, Charles G., B.A. (Central State), M.A., Ph.D. (Oklahoma). Assistant Professor of Economics, 1968; Associate Professor, 1971; Professor, 1975.

LEE, Thomas A., C. A. (University of Edinburgh and Institute of Chartered Accountants of Scotland), M.Sc., D.Litt (Strathclyde, Scotland). Hugh F. Culverhouse Professor of Accounting, 1990.

LEEPER, James D., Ph.D. (Iowa). Assistant Professor of Industrial Management and Statistics, 1977; Associate Professor of Community Medicine (Statistics), 1982.

LEITCH, Robert A., M.S.J.A. (Carnegie Mellon), Ph.D. (Tennessee), C.P.A. (Tennessee). Director, School of Accountancy and Hugh Culverhouse Professor of Accounting, 1985.

LEMAISTRE, George, J.D. (Alabama). Alabama Bankers' Educational Foundation Banking Chair Professor, 1978; Professor Emeritus, 1983.

LESLIE, Henry A., B.S., LL.B. (Alabama). Assistant Professor of Business Law, 1948; Associate Professor, 1953.

LIGON, James A., B.S., J.D. (Illinois), Ph.D. (Pennsylvania). Assistant Professor of Finance, 1991.

LINDLEY, James T., Ph.D. (Georgia). Assistant Professor of Finance, 1982; Associate Professor, 1985.

LIPSEY, William, M.B.A. (Syracuse). Lecturer in Finance and Assistant to the Dean, 1981; Instructor Emeritus of Finance, 1987.

LIPSON, Harry Aaron Jr., M.B.A. (Northwestern), Ph.D. (Pennsylvania). Instructor of Economics, 1941; Assistant Professor of Marketing, 1948; Associate Professor, 1953; Professor, 1957; Head, Department of Marketing, 1960; Professor Emeritus, 1981.

LLOYD, Lee B., B.S., LL.B. (Alabama). Instructor in Business Law, 1948; Assistant Professor of Business Law, 1948; Associate Professor, 1954.

LOCKE, Miriam A., A.B. (Alabama), Ph.D. (Northwestern). Assistant in Business English, 1929; Instructor, 1931.

LOOMIS, Betty, B.A. (Winthrop College), M.A. (Florida State). Temporary Instructor in Marketing, 1966; Instructor, 1972; Assistant Professor of Written Business Communication, 1977.

LORD, Alan T., B.S.B.A., M.A., M.Acc., M.B.A. (Ohio State), Ph.D. (Case Western Reserve), C.P.A. (Ohio). Assistant Professor of Accounting, 1989.

LORENZ, Robert, Diploma in Economics (University of Breslau). Instructor in Economics, 1939.

LUCAS, William, M.A., Ph.D. (Alabama), C.P.A. (Louisiana). Associate Professor of Accounting, 1968.

LYNGBY, Alfred Robert, B.S., LL.B. (Alabama). Assistant in Commerce, 1937; Instructor in Economics, 1940.

MADOR, Sheldon A., B.S. (Massachusetts State College). Instructor in Accounting, 1947.

MANN, Howard W., M.A. (Iowa). Instructor in Accounting, 1937.

MANSFIELD, Edward R., B.A. (St. Mary's University [Texas]), M.S., Ph.D. (SMU). Assistant Professor of Statistics, 1975; Associate Professor, 1979; Professor, 1985.

MARSH, Gene A., B.S., M.S. (Ohio State), J.D. (Washington and Lee). Assistant Professor of Legal Studies, 1981; Associate Professor, 1985; Director, University Honors Program, 1989.

MARTELL, Terrence F., B.A. (Iona), Ph.D. (Pennsylvania State). Lecturer in Finance, 1972; Assistant Professor of Finance, 1973; Associate Professor, 1976; Professor, 1981.

MASON, J. Barry, B.S. (Louisiana Polytechnic Institute), M.A., Ph.D. (Alabama). Assistant Professor of Marketing, 1967; Associate Professor, 1969; Professor, 1971; Chair, Programs in Manpower, Industrial Relations, and Organizational Behavior and Programs in Marketing, Communications, and Logistics, 1974; Board of Visitors Research Professor of Marketing, 1978; Russell Professor of Business Management, 1983; Dean, 1988.

MASON, John O., Jr., B.S., M.S. (LSU), Ph.D. (Missouri), C.P.A. (Alabama, Louisiana). Assistant Professor of Accounting, 1968; Associate Professor, 1971; Professor, 1977.

MATTHEIS, Theodore H., B.S., M.B.A.
(Wayne State), D.B.A. (Maryland).
Associate Professor of Management Science
and Chair, Programs in Production and
Operations Management, Management
Science, and Statistics, 1976; Professor, 1980.

MAYER, Morris L., B.S. (Alabama), M.S.
(NYU), Ph.D. (Ohio State). Acting
Assistant Professor of Marketing, 1955;
Assistant Professor, 1960; Associate
Professor of Marketing, 1961; Professor,
1964; Head, Department of Marketing,
1969; Bruno Professor of Marketing, 1986;
Director, Hess Institute for Retailing
Development, 1984; Bruno Professor
Emeritus of Marketing, 1992.

McCABE, George M., M.B.A. (Michigan),
Ph.D. (Pennsylvania). Associate Professor of
Finance, 1978.

McCOY, Whitley P., A.B. (Dartmouth),
LL.B. (George Washington University).
Professor of Law, 1921; taught commercial
law.

McDOUGAL, Meredith Verson, A.B.
(Rice), Ph.D. (Johns Hopkins). Instructor in
Economics, 1935.

McGEE, M. Clinton, B.S., LL.B. (Alabama).
Assistant Professor of Business Law, 1946.

McLEOD, Robert W., B.S.B.A., M.B.A.
(Southern Mississippi), Ph.D. (Texas),
C.F.P., C.F.A. Assistant Professor of
Finance, 1978; Associate Professor, 1982.

McMAHON, James P., B.A., M.B.A.
(Texas). Assistant Professor of Economics,
1924.

McMILLAN, James B., B.S. (API), M.A.
(North Carolina), Ph.D. (Chicago).
Instructor in Business English, 1931;
Assistant Professor, 1937; Associate
Professor; Director of Instruction, Army Air
Forces College, and Acting Director, Bureau
of Business Research, 1943.

MECIMORE, Charles, Ph.D. (Alabama).
Assistant Professor of Accounting, 1966.

MEHR, Robert Irwen, M.S. (Alabama).
Assistant in Commerce and Economics,
1938; Instructor, 1939.

MELLICHAMP, Joseph M., B.I.E. (Georgia
Tech), Ph.D. (Clemson). Assistant Professor
of Management, 1969; Associate Professor of
Management Science, 1973; Professor, 1979;
Acting Head, Department of Management
Science and Statistics, 1981; Board of
Visitors Research Professor of Management
Science, 1989; Professor Emeritus, 1994.

MENNING, Dorothy Colby, B.J. (Illinois),
M.A. (Alabama). Instructor in Marketing,
1952; Temporary Instructor, 1954; Assistant
Professor of Written Business
Communication, 1976; Assistant Professor
Emerita, 1980.

MENNING, Jack Harwood, M.B.A. (Texas).
Associate Professor of Marketing, 1948;
Professor, 1953; Professor Emeritus, 1973.

MEYER, David G., M.B.A. (Concordia),
Ph.D. (Michigan). Assistant Professor of
Management, 1983.

MILES, Minnie Cadell, M.B.A.
(Northwestern), Ph.D. (Purdue). Instructor
in Commerce, 1942; Assistant Professor of
Management, 1947; Associate Professor,
1953; Professor, 1964; Professor Emerita,
1978.

MILLER, David M., B.S. (Alabama), M.S.,
Ph.D. (Georgia Tech). Associate Professor of
Management Science, 1983; Professor, 1985.

MILLER, Mrs. D. A., M.A. (Vanderbilt).
Part–time Instructor in Business English,
1938; Instructor, 1939.

MILLS, Donald, B.S. (Alabama), LL.B.
(West Virginia), Ph.D. (Alabama).
Temporary Instructor in Accounting, 1953;
Instructor in Accounting and Economics,
1956; Assistant Professor of Accounting and
Economics, 1957; Associate Professor, 1961;
Professor, 1971; Professor Emeritus, 1983.

MILLS, Mable D., M.S. (Alabama).
Instructor of Statistics and Assistant
Statistician, Bureau of Business Research,
1945.

MISIOLEK, Walter S., B.A., M.A. (Miami),
Ph.D. (Cornell). Instructor in Economics,
1975; Assistant Professor, 1976; Associate
Professor, 1981; Professor, 1987; Senior
Associate Dean and Director of Graduate
Programs, 1988.

MITCHELL, H. H., M.S. (Alabama), Ph.D. (North Carolina). Professor of Finance and Dean, 1981; Dean and Professor Emeritus, 1986.

MITCHELL, Harry Victor, B.S., M.A. (Alabama). Teaching Assistant in Accounting, 1928; Instructor, 1929.

MOELLER, John, B.S., LL.B. (Alabama), Certificate in International Law (London). Temporary Assistant Professor of Business Law, 1966; Assistant Professor and Acting Head, Department of Business Law 1967; Head, 1968; Associate Professor, 1969; Professor, 1976; Professor Emeritus, 1983.

MOORE, Albert B., M.A., Ph.D. (Chicago). Professor of History, 1923; taught economic history courses.

MOORE, Charles North, M.B.A. (Alabama), Ph.D. (Michigan). Instructor in Business Statistics, 1948; Assistant Professor, 1953; Associate Professor, 1962.

MOORE, Charles Tom, M.B.A. (Indiana), D.B.A. (Indiana). Associate Professor of Marketing, 1962; Professor, 1964; Vice-president for Academic Affairs, 1969; Assistant Vice-president, Medical Planning, 1971.

MOORE, Henry B., M.B.A. (Harvard). Professor of Economics and Director, Bureau of Business Research, 1951.

MOORE, Thomas David, B.B.A., M.B.A., Ph.D. (Mississippi). Assistant Professor of Economics, 1965; Associate Professor, 1967; Professor, 1969; Professor of Management, 1975; Assistant Vice- president for Program Development, 1979; Director, Alumni and Corporate Relations, 1990; Professor Emeritus, 1994.

MORGAN, Robert M., B.S. (Kansas), M.B.A. (Dallas), Ph.D. (Texas Tech). Assistant Professor of Marketing, 1991.

MORLEY, Burton Raymond, M.A., Ph.D. (Pennsylvania). Professor of Economics and Director, Bureau of Personnel and Placement, 1931; Head, Department of Management, 1946; Professor Emeritus, 1968.

MORRIS, James H., Ph.D. (Oregon). Assistant Professor of Organizational Behavior, 1977.

MORTON, James R., M.B.A., D.B.A. (Southern California), C.P.A. (California). Assistant Professor of Accounting and Information Systems, 1973; Associate Professor, 1975.

MOSES, Walter L., M.A. (North Carolina). Instructor in Business English, 1941.

MOTES, William H., B.S.B.A. (West Georgia College), M.B.A. (Georgia), Ph.D. (South Carolina). Assistant Professor of Marketing, 1981; Board of Visitors Research Associate Professor of Marketing, 1986; Board of Visitors Research Professor of Marketing, 1986.

MULVIHILL, Donald Ferguson, M.A. (Chicago), M.S. (Illinois), Ph.D. (Chicago). Instructor in Business English, 1941; Instructor in Economics, 1945; Assistant Professor of Marketing, 1946; Associate Professor, 1953; Professor, 1957.

MUNRO, Douglas R., M.A., Ph.D. (Ohio State). Assistant Professor of Economics, 1976.

NATIONS, Leroy J., A.B. (Illinois), M.A. (Columbia). Instructor in Business English, 1926; Assistant Professor, 1927; Associate Professor, 1938; Assistant to the Executive Secretary, 1941; Professor of Advertising and Business English, 1943; Professor of Marketing, 1946.

NEWMAN, Maurice S., M.B.A., Ph.D. (NYU), C.P.A. (Alabama, New York). Board of Visitors Research Professor of Accounting, 1977; Professor Emeritus, 1987.

NEWTON, Grant W., M.A. (Alabama), Ph.D. (NYU), C.P.A. (Tennessee), C.M.A. Lecturer in Accounting and Information Systems, 1973; Assistant Professor, 1974.

NICHOLS, Leonard D., B.S. (Pittsburgh), M.S. (Columbia). Assistant Professor of Economics, 1942.

NORRBIN, Stefan, M.S., Ph.D. (Arizona State). Assistant Professor of Economics, 1986.

ODEWAHN, Charles A., B.S., M.B.A.
(Louisville), Ph.D. (Kentucky). Assistant
Professor of Manpower, Industrial Relations,
and Organizational Behavior, 1971;
Associate Professor; Director, Graduate
School of Business; and Chair,
Interdisciplinary Programs, 1974; Professor
of Management and Director, Management
Institute, 1978.

OGILVIE, Walter, M.S. (Alabama).
Assistant Professor of Marketing, 1961.

OLSON, Richard E., M.S., Ph.D.
(Nebraska). Associate Professor of Finance
and Transportation, 1968; Alabama
Truckers' Association Chair of
Transportation Professor, 1979.

O'NEIL, Michael T., Ph.D. (Florida).
Assistant Professor of Written Business
Communication, 1977.

OTT, Roy, B.S. (Hendrix), M.A., Ph.D.
(Vanderbilt). Associate Professor of Finance,
1963.

OVERMEYER, Philip Henry, M.S.
(Oregon), Ph.D. (Minnesota). Instructor in
Commerce, 1939; Assistant Professor of
Economic History, 1940.

PAGE, Frank H., Jr., Ph.D. (Illinois).
Assistant Professor of Finance, 1991;
Associate Professor, 1992.

PARR, Johnstone, M.A. (Alabama).
Instructor in Business English, 1938.

PATTERSON, Ernest F., M.A., Ph.D.
(Texas). Assistant Professor of Economics,
1950; Associate Professor, 1955.

PAUSTIAN, Paul W., M.A., Ph.D.
(Columbia). Professor of Economics, 1947;
Acting Director, Bureau of Business
Research, 1959; Professor Emeritus, 1967.

PEARCY, George Etzel, M.A., Ph.D.
(Clark). Instructor in Commerce, 1939;
Assistant Professor of Economic Geography,
1940.

PENZ, A. J., M.B.A. (Northwestern), M.A.
(Western Reserve), Ph.D. (Ohio State).
Associate Professor of Accounting, 1947;
Professor of Accounting and Head,
Department of Accounting, 1953; Professor
Emeritus, 1971.

PETERSEN, Russell J., M.S. (Oregon),
Ph.D. (Washington), C.P.A. (Oregon).
Professor of Accounting and Dean, 1986.

PETTY, Mickey M., B.S. (Alabama), M.S.,
Ph.D. (Tennessee). Assistant Professor of
Organizational Behavior, 1972; Associate
Professor of Human Resources Management
and Director of Research and Evaluation,
Management Institute, 1975; Assistant to
the President of the University, 1977;
Professor of Management, 1978.

PHILLIPS, J. Donald, M.S. (Georgia Tech),
Ph.D. (Alabama). Temporary Instructor in
Business Statistics, 1965; Temporary
Assistant Professor, 1966; Assistant Professor
of Management, 1967; Associate Professor,
1969; Chairman of Management Science
and Operations Management, 1971;
Professor, 1979; Professor Emeritus, 1989.

PHIPPS, David W., M.B.A. (Denver),
C.P.A. (Colorado). University Professor of
Accounting, 1975; Professor Emeritus, 1988.

PLANCHON, John M., Ph.D. (Alabama).
Assistant Professor of Advertising and Public
Relations, 1981.
POPE, J. Bland, M.B.A., Ph.D. (Texas),
C.P.A. (Texas). Associate Professor of
Accounting, 1946.

POPE, Thomas R., M.S., D.B.A.
(Kentucky), C.P.A. (Kentucky). Assistant
Professor of Accounting and Information
Systems, 1976.

POSEY, J. M., M.B.A., Ph.D., C.P.A.
(Alabama, Arkansas). Assistant Professor of
Accounting, 1965; Associate Professor, 1969.

PRESCOTT, Joseph, M.A. (Harvard).
Instructor in Business English, 1939.

PREVITS, Gary J., M.Acc. (Ohio State),
Ph.D. (Florida), C.P.A. (Ohio). Assistant
Professor of Accounting and Information
Systems, 1973; Associate Professor, 1976.

PREWITT, Lena, B.S. (Stillman College), M.S., Ed.D. (Indiana). Associate Professor of General Business, 1970; Associate Professor of Manpower and Industrial Relations, 1971; Professor of Behavioral Studies, 1975; Professor Emerita, 1994.

PROPES, Ernest A., M.A. (Alabama). Instructor in Commercial Mathematics, 1939.

PRUITT, Clarence M., M.A. (Indiana). Associate Professor of Natural Science Education, 1929; taught economic geography courses.

RASP, John, M.S., Ph.D. (Florida State). Assistant Professor of Statistics, 1984.

RAYBURN, Frank R., Ph.D. (Alabama), C.P.A. (North Carolina), C.M.A. Assistant Professor of Accounting and Information Systems, 1974; Associate Professor, 1976; Professor, 1981; Acting Director, School of Accountancy, 1983; Arthur Young Distinguished Accounting Fellow, 1984.

REESE, Harold L., M.A. (Northwestern). Instructor in Business English, 1939.

REEVES, L. T., Jr., M.B.A., Ph.D. (Northwestern). Professor of Finance, 1967.

REEVES, Lorenzo, M.B.A. (Northwestern). Assistant Professor of Marketing, 1957.
RIGBY, Paul Herbert, Ph.D. (Texas). Assistant Professor of Marketing, 1952.

ROBBINS, Walter A., B.S.B.A. (Steed College), M.Acc. (VPI), D.B.A. (Tennessee), C.P.A. (Tennessee, Virginia). Assistant Professor of Accounting, 1981; Associate Professor, 1986.

ROBERTS, Michael L., B.B.A., M.Acc., J.D. (Georgia), Ph.D. (Georgia State), C.P.A. (Arkansas). Assistant Professor of Accounting, 1987; Associate Professor, 1992.

ROBICHEAUX, Robert A., B.S., M.B.A., Ph.D. (LSU). Associate Professor of Marketing, 1977; Professor and Director, Hess Institute for Retailing Development, 1993.

ROBINSON, Michael A., M.A. (Alabama). Instructor in Accounting, 1980; Assistant Professor, 1981.

ROCHE, John E., M.S., Ph.D. (Texas). Professor of Business Statistics, 1963.

ROCHESTER, David P., M.E. (North Carolina State), Ph.D. (Georgia). Lecturer in Finance, 1973; Assistant Professor, 1974.

RODGERS, Sarah Haughton, M.A. (Alabama). Instructor of Mathematics, 1930; Instructor of Business Statistics, 1946; Assistant Professor of Business Statistics, 1947; Assistant Professor Emerita, 1971.

ROLLISON, W. D., LL.D. (Indiana). Assistant Professor of Law, 1922; taught business law courses.

ROSS, Brett, M.B.A. (Ohio State). Instructor in Accounting, 1956.

RUDD, Judson, M.A. (Kansas). Instructor in Economics, 1927.

RUDOLPH, Patricia M., B.A. (Maryland—Baltimore County), Ph.D. (North Carolina). Assistant Professor of Finance, 1976; Associate Professor, 1982; Board of Visitors Research Professor of Finance, 1988.

RUSSELL, Ralph C., M.B.A. (Texas), C.P.A. (Texas, Mississippi). Assistant Professor of Accounting, 1945; Associate Professor, 1946.

RYAN, Michael J., M.B.A. (Xavier), Ph.D. (Kentucky). Assistant Professor of Marketing and Physical Distribution, 1974.

RYERSON, Frank E., M.A., Ph.D. (Iowa). Associate Professor of Marketing, 1962; Professor, 1965; Professor Emeritus, 1986.

SAILORS, J. Franklin, Ph.D. (Georgia). Instructor in Accounting and Information Systems, 1977; Assistant Professor, 1977.

SAMSON, William D., B.A. (VMI), M.B.A. (Old Dominion), Ph.D. (North Carolina), C.P.A. (North Carolina), C.M.A. Associate Professor of Accounting, 1984; Professor, 1992.

SANDERS, William A., B.S. (Athens College), B.S., J.D. (Alabama). Assistant Professor of Business Law, 1969; Associate Professor, 1976.

SCHATZ, Paul J. L., B.S., M.S. (Alabama). Teaching Assistant in Commerce, 1934; Instructor in Accounting, 1935.

SCHLESINGER, Harris, B.A., M.A. (SUNY College—Potsdam), M.S., Ph.D. (Illinois). Professor of Finance and Frank P. Samford Chair of Insurance, 1987.

SCHMIDT, Charles P., B.A., M.B.A., Ph.D. (Chicago). Assistant Professor of Management Science, 1984; Associate Professor, 1987.

SCHNEE, Edward J., B.B.A. (City College of New York), M.B.A., Ph.D. (Michigan State), C.P.A. (Kentucky). Professor of Accounting, 1982.

SCHUL, Patrick L., M.B.A. (Texas), Ph.D. (Texas A&M). Assistant Professor of Marketing, 1980.

SCHUTTE, David P., M.S. (Texas), Ph.D. (Minnesota). Associate Professor of Economics, 1985.

SCOTT, Charles R. Jr., M.S. (Cornell). Associate Professor of Management, 1949; Professor, 1957; Professor Emeritus, 1980.

SCOTT, Clyde J., B.A. (Pennsylvania State), M.A., Ph.D. (Minnesota). Instructor of Human Resources Management, 1981; Associate Professor, 1989.

SEEBECK, Charles Louis Jr., M.A. (Harvard), Ph.D. (North Carolina). Instructor of Commercial Mathematics, 1939; Assistant Professor, 1943.

SEERS, Anson, B.S., M.S. (Illinois), Ph.D. (Cincinnati). Assistant Professor of Human Resources Management, 1980; Associate Professor of Management, 1993.

SENDERLING, Ellwood Wesley, M.A., Ph.D. (Ohio State). Assistant Professor of Psychology, 1939; taught business psychology.

SHAFFER, Harry G., A.M. (New York). Instructor in Economics, 1950.

SHARMA, Subhash, M.S. (California State—San Jose), Ph.D. (Texas). Assistant Professor of Marketing, 1978.

SHARPE, R. Shane, B.S. (Kansas), M.B.A. (Dallas), Ph.D. (Texas Tech). Assistant Professor of Management Information Systems, 1991.

SHELBY, Annette, Ph.D. (Louisiana State). Assistant Professor of Written Business Communication, 1977; Associate Professor, 1979.

SHEPHERD, C. Wayne, B.S., Ph.D. (Kentucky). Associate Professor of Legal Studies, 1975; Professor, 1979.

SHOENHAIR, John D., M.S. (VPI). Instructor in Economics, 1979.

SILVER, J. Lew, B.S., M.A. (Delaware), Ph.D. (Duke). Associate Professor of Economics, 1990.

SIMS, Verner M., Ph.D. (Yale). Associate Professor of Psychology, 1928; Professor, 1929; taught business psychology.

SMART, George Kenneth, A.B. (Alabama), M.A. (Harvard). Instructor in Business English, 1935.

SMITH, Clarence D., Ph.D. (Iowa). Associate Professor of Business Statistics, 1947; Professor, 1953; Professor Emeritus, 1962.

SMITH, Edward, M.S. (North Carolina), Ph.D. (Alabama). Lecturer in Marketing, 1964; Associate Professor, 1965; Professor, 1970; Chairman of Interdisciplinary Programs, 1971; Associate Dean, 1974; Interim Dean, 1979.

SMITH, Frances Allene, M.B.A. (Northwestern). Instructor in Statistics and Acting Statistician, Bureau of Business Research, 1943.

SMITH, Howard L., M.S. (UCLA), Ph.D. (Washington). Assistant Professor of Health Care Management, 1979.

SMITH (Pettit), Martha C., M.A. (Peabody). Instructor in Secretarial Studies, 1945; Assistant Professor, 1956; Assistant Professor Emerita, 1969.

SNEDEKER, Everett Holmes, M.A., LL.B. (Columbia). Instructor in Business Law, 1940.

SNYDER, Robert A., Ph.D. (Maryland). Assistant Professor of Organizational Behavior, 1976.

SPEER, Arthur J., B.S. (Clemson). Professor of Economics, 1937.

SPEH, Thomas W., M.B.A. (Ohio—Miami), Ph.D. (Michigan State). Assistant Professor of Marketing and Physical Distribution, 1974.

SPENCER, Clarence A. Jr., B.S. (John B. Stetson University), M.S. (Tennessee), Ph.D. (Alabama). Temporary Instructor in Finance, 1957; Instructor, 1959; Assistant Professor, 1967; Associate Professor, 1970; Associate Professor Emeritus, 1990.

SPRITZER, Allan D., M.S. (Illinois), Ph.D. (Cornell). Lecturer in Management, 1968; Assistant Professor, 1971; Associate Professor and Coordinator, Manpower and Industrial Relations Institute, 1973; Professor and Assistant Dean, 1979.

STANFEL, Larry E., B.S. (Illinois Institute of Technology), M.S., Ph.D. (Northwestern). Professor of Computer–Based Management Systems, 1988.

STANTON, William John, Jr., M.B.A. (Northwestern). Instructor in Accounting, 1941.

STERLING, Jay U., B.A. (DePauw), Ph.D. (Michigan State). Assistant Professor of Marketing, 1984; Associate Professor, 1988.

STEVENSON, Holly W., A.B. (Georgetown), M.B.A. (Harvard). Assistant Professor of Business Administration, 1923.

STONE, Mary, B.A., M.S. (Central Florida University), Ph.D. (Illinois), C.P.A. (Florida). Assistant Professor of Accounting, 1981; Associate Professor, 1986; Board of Visitors Professor of Accounting, 1991; Ernst and Young Professor of Accounting, 1993.

STONE, Robert N., Ph.D. (University of Illinois). Assistant Professor of Marketing, 1984.

STRIBLING, Herman A., Jr., M.S. (Alabama). Lecturer in Economics, 1957; Instructor in Economics, 1958.

STRICKLAND, A. J., III, B.S. (Georgia), M.S. (Georgia Tech), Ph.D. (Georgia State). Assistant Professor of Management, 1969; Associate Professor of General Business, 1974; Professor of Managerial Policy, 1981; Coordinator of the M.B.A. Program, 1982.

SUCHAN, James E., M.A. (State University of New York), Ph.D. (Illinois). Assistant Professor of Written Business Communication, 1981.

SWEENEY, Robert B., M.B.A. (Texas), Ph.D. (Texas), C.P.A. (Texas). Associate Professor of Accounting, 1960; Professor, 1964; Head, Department of Accounting, 1970.

SWEET, Franklyn H., B.S., C.P.A. (Alabama). Assistant Professor of Accounting, 1946.

TAYLOR, James L., B.S. (Sam Houston), M.B.A., Ph.D. (South Carolina). Assistant Professor of Marketing, 1978; Associate Professor, 1982.

TAYLOR, Walton, R.L., Ph.D. (Pennsylvania State). Assistant Professor of Finance, 1973; Associate Professor, 1976.

TEEL, Jesse E., Jr., Ph.D. (North Carolina). Assistant Professor of Marketing, 1976.

THISTLE, Paul D., M.S., Ph.D. (Texas A&M). Assistant Professor of Economics, 1982.

THOMAS, John Ramsden, B.S. (Alabama). Instructor in Accounting, 1927.

THOMAS, M. B., M.A. (North Carolina). Instructor in Business English, 1934.

THOMAS, William Paul, B.S., LL.B. (Alabama), C.P.A. (Georgia, Alabama). Associate Professor of Accounting, 1947.

THOMPSON, Arthur A., Ph.D. (Tennessee). Associate Professor of Economics, 1967; Professor, 1969; Miller Professor of Business Policy and Strategy, 1983; Professor Emeritus, 1991.

TOPPING, L. Sharon, M.B.A. (Pennsylvania State), D.B.A. (Florida State). Assistant Professor of Management, 1983.

TREWATHA, R. L., Ph.D. (Arkansas).
Associate Professor of Management, 1965.

TURNER, Charles T., B.S. (Alabama),
M.S.H.A. (UAB). Assistant Professor of
Health Care Management, 1984.

UPGREN, Arthur R., A.B. (Wisconsin).
Instructor in Business Administration, 1921;
Assistant Professor, 1922.

VADEN, Andrew C., B.S. (Tennessee).
Instructor in Economics, 1937.

VALLERY, J. F. Jr., Ph.D. (Tennessee).
Lecturer in Economics, 1966; Assistant
Professor, 1967; Associate Professor, 1969;
Professor, 1979; Professor Emeritus, 1989.

VAN DER WESTHUYZEN, Johannes M.,
B.A. (London), F.C.I. Professor and Head,
Department of Accounting; Instructor in
Salesmanship, 1920.

VAN HOOSE, David D., B.A. (Indiana),
Ph.D. (North Carolina). Associate Professor
of Economics, 1990.

VAN VOORHIS, Robert Henry, Ph.D.
(Duke), C.P.A. (North Carolina). Associate
Professor of Accounting, 1949.

VINSON, Charles E., M.B.A. (Texas
Christian), Ph.D. (North Texas State).
Assistant Professor of Finance, 1969.

WADDELL, Sue, M.A. (Tennessee), C.P.S.
(National). Acting Assistant Professor of
Secretarial Administration, 1959; Assistant
Professor, 1962.

WADE, Bernard J., B.S., M.S. (Alabama).
Instructor in Accounting, 1947; Instructor
Emeritus, 1975.

WALLACE, Robert M., A.B. (Wofford),
M.A. (North Carolina). Instructor in
Business English, 1935.

WASHBURN, Horace Hanson, M.A.
(Iowa), Ph.D. (Wisconsin). Associate
Professor of Finance, 1948; Professor, 1961;
Professor Emeritus, 1972.

WATKINS, John C. Jr., B.S., LL.B.
(Alabama), M.S. (Florida State), LL.M.
(Northwestern). Temporary Assistant
Professor of Business Law, 1965; Acting
Head, Department of Business Law, 1966;
Assistant Professor, 1968.

WEAVER, Jerry R., B.S., M.A. (Alabama),
Ph.D. (Tennessee). Assistant Professor of
Management Science, 1980; Associate
Professor, 1986.

WEAVER, K. Mark, B.S., Ph.D.
(Louisiana). Associate Professor of
Management Policy, 1976.

WEBB, Darryl, B.S., J.D. (Samford). Assistant Professor of Business Law, 1971; Associate Professor of Legal Studies, 1979;
Assistant to the Dean, 1981.

WEBER, Alma B., M.A. (Columbia,
Alabama). Secretary–Registrar and Lecturer
in Economics, 1955; Instructor, 1957;
Instructor Emerita, 1971.

WEBSTER, F. A., M.B.A., Ph.D.
(California—Berkeley). Associate Professor
of Marketing, Communications, and
Logistics, 1973.

WHELESS, Deborah, M.A., Ph.D.
(Georgia). Instructor in Accountancy, 1980;
Assistant Professor, 1981.

WHITE, Phillip, M.B.A. (Oklahoma State),
Ph.D. (Texas). Assistant Professor of
Marketing, 1975.

WHITMAN, Marcus, M.A., Ph.D.
(Wisconsin). Associate Professor of
Economics, 1927; Professor of Finance,
1937; Chair, Department of Finance, 1963;
Professor Emeritus, 1972.

WHITNEY, William H., M.A. (Western
Reserve), C.P.A. (Alabama, Ohio).
Associate Professor of Accounting, 1946;
Professor, 1948; Professor Emeritus, 1963.

WHITTINGTON, William, M.B.A.
(Texas), Ph.D. (Illinois), C.P.A. (Texas).
Professor of Accounting, 1962.

WIEGAND, Richard, B.A. (Colorado), M.A. (North Carolina), Ph.D. (Florida State). Professor of Written Business Communication, Executive Assistant to the Dean for Continuing Education, and Assistant to the Dean for Management Development, 1978.

WILKINSON, Clyde, M.A. (Texas), Ph.D. (Illinois). Professor of Written Business Communication, 1975.

WILLIAMS, Miller, A.B. (Michigan). Assistant Professor of Accounting, 1924.

WILLIAMS, Robert H., Ph.D. (Utah). Assistant Professor of Marketing, 1976.

WILSON, Winfred Percy, M.B.A. (Michigan). Instructor in Statistics, 1939.

WITTNER, Sheldon, B.S., LL.B. (Alabama). Temporary Assistant Professor of Business Law, 1967; Assistant Professor, 1968.

WOEBER, Mary Agnes, M.A. (Iowa). Instructor in Secretarial Studies, 1940; Assistant Professor of Secretarial Studies, 1947.

WOOD, Richard H., Ph.D. (Princeton). Professor of General Business Administration, 1969.

WOODALL, William H., B.S. (Millsaps College), M.S., Ph.D. (VPI & SU). Associate Professor of Statistics, 1989; Professor, 1992.

WRIGHT, Gordon E. P., B.S. (Carnegie Tech.). Lecturer in Management and Director, Commerce Extension Services, 1957.

WU, Hsiu–Kwang, A.B. (Princeton), M.B.A., Ph.D. (Pennsylvania). Professor of Finance and Economics and Chair, Programs in Economics, Finance, and Business Law, 1972; Alabama Bankers' Educational Foundation Banking Chair Professor, 1973; Lee Bidgood Professor of Finance and Economics, 1978.

YEARGAN, Percy B., B.A. (Howard), M.S., Ph.D. (Alabama). Assistant and Part Time Instructor in Accounting, 1954; Assistant Professor, 1957; Associate Professor, 1959; Professor, 1963.

YLITALO, J. Raymond, M.B.A. (Northwestern). Instructor in Commerce, 1938; Instructor in Economic Geography, 1940.

YOUNGSON, Cecil M., B.S., J.D. (Alabama). Acting Assistant Professor of Business Law, 1955; Assistant Professor of Business Law, 1957; Associate Professor of Legal Studies, 1979; Associate Professor Emeritus, 1980.

ZEBDA, Awni, M.B.S. (Ain Shans—Egypt), Ph.D. (VPI). Instructor in Accounting, 1980; Assistant Professor, 1982.

ZHAO, Liming, B.A. (Wuhan Institute of Technology), M.A. (Beijing Polytechnic University), M.B.A. (Northeastern), Ph.D. (Case Western Reserve). Assistant Professor of Management, 1991.

ZUMPANO, Leonard, B.A. (Iona College), M.A., Ph.D. (Pennsylvania State). Instructor in Finance and Real Estate, 1975; Assistant Professor of Real Estate, 1976; Associate Professor, 1981; Professor and Chair of Real Estate, 1988.

Appendix F

Oral History Interviewees

Alumni
(alphabetically, by decade of attendance at the University)

1920s: Elizabeth Bates, Mortimer A. Cohen, Jefferson J. Coleman, Clinton Jackson Coley, J. Clemson Duckworth, William L. Jessup Sr., Harvey "Red" Terrell

1930s: William Edward Bertkau, Young Boozer, Iris Carmack, Harmon B. Looney, V. Hugo Marx Jr., Gerald Permutt, Max Sokol, Osie P. Spencer, Edward Turner

1940s: Raymon J. Baker, Allene S. Burbank (nee Smith), Margaret Carpenter, Laura G. Cooper, Morris L. Mayer, Catherine Miles

1950s: Frank Bromberg, Jack Brunson, Emory Folmar, Lowell Friedman, Wallace Malone Jr.

1960s: Toppy Ezell, Mickey Gee, Wayne Gillis, Dot Martin, Tim Parker Jr., Jon Rotenstreich, Pat Saik, Alma Sanders, Eddie Terrell, Tommy Tillman

1970s: Owen Aronov, Tom Canterbury, Ryan deGraffenreid, Mike Thompson

1980s: Marcus Bruchis, Shirley Maksoud Darr, Gena Hawkins Johnson, Wiley Mullins

1990s: Kristy Ellis, Chapel Hill, Kelly Nunnelly Litford

Former and Current Deans

John (Jack) Fielden, Paul Garner, Barry Mason, H. H. (Bill) Mitchell

Faculty Emeriti

Eric Baklanoff, Bill Bennett, John Bickley, Murray Havens, Miriam Locke, Morris Mayer, James McMillan, Minnie Miles, Art Thompson

Active Faculty
(as of 1993–94 academic year)

Trevor Bain, Hutton Barron, Ron Dulek, Toppy Ezell, Mary Fish, John Formby, Bill Gunther, Billy Helms, Tom Howard, Rob Ingram, John Mason, Rae Mellichamp, Walt Misiolek, Chuck Odewahn, Tom Moore, Lena Prewitt, Bob Robicheaux, Lonnie Strickland

Former Staff

Billie Gleisberg, Lillian Hinton, June Montgomery, Jean Warren

Appendix G

Endowed Chairs and Professorships

CHAIRS

Lee Bidgood Chair of Finance and Economics

Robert H. Cochrane / Alabama Bankers Chair of Banking

Hugh Culverhouse Endowed Chair of Accountancy

Real Estate Chair

Steven J. Ross–Hugh F. Culverhouse Chair of Accountancy

Frank Park Samford Chair of Insurance

PROFESSORSHIPS

Board of Visitors Fellows

Bruno Professor of Retail Marketing

Appendix H

Enrollment Figures for C&BA (1919 to 1991)

Figures from 1919 through 1973 are from the University catalogs. Figures from 1974 to 1991 are from the University of Alabama *Fact Books*.

	Men	Women	Total
1919–20	71	0	71
1920–21	165	2	167
1921–22	226	6	232
1922–23	330	5	335
1923–24	377	10	387
1924–25	71	6	77
1925–26	422	9	431
1926–27	501	12	513
1927–28	496	8	504
1928–29	635	13	648
1929–30	681	25	706
1930–31	756	39	795
1931–32	786	57	843
1932–33	692	35	727
1933–34	670	68	738
1934–35	797	88	885
1935–36	901	106	1007
1936–37	910	124	1034
1937–38	1036	173	1209
1938–39	1088	144	1232
1939–40	1057	137	1194
1940–41	943	170	1113
1941–42	767	192	959
1942–43	613	199	812
1943–44	144	216	360
1944–45	175	270	445
1945–46	1022	299	1321
1946–47	2151	319	2470
Graduate Enrollment	10	62	72
1947–48	2102	232	2334
	75	11	86
1948–49	2206	191	2397
	101	11	112
1949–50	1719	169	1888
	128	11	139
1950–51	1222	131	1353
	81	5	86
1951–52	949	136	1085
	59	1	60
1952–53	987	147	1134
	51	4	55
1953–54	1117	142	1259
	46	3	49

	Men	Women	Total
1954–55	1264	151	1415
	78	4	82
1955–56	1489	163	1652
	97	3	100
1956–57	1541	180	1721
	105	6	111
1957–58	1605	175	1780
	73	4	77
1958–59	1614	170	1784
	84	3	87
1959–60	1692	163	1855
	108	6	114
1960–61	1657	154	1811
	102	8	110
1961–62	1676	153	1829
	116	5	121
1962–63	1628	152	1780
	122	9	131
1963–64	1706	143	1849
	146	9	155
1964–65	1913	181	2094
	183	8	191
1965–66	2187	218	2405
	251	11	262
1966–67	2464	220	2684
	278	10	288
1967–68	2685	236	2921
	302	17	319
1968–69	2939	263	3202
	289	14	303
1969–70	3008	288	3296
	302	20	322
1970–71	2850	310	3160
	337	19	356
1971–72	2572	310	2882
	307	16	323
1972–73	2475	302	2777
	287	24	311
1973–74	2319	339	2658
	237	24	261
1974–75	2174	370	2544
	222	27	249
1975–76	2142	482	2624
	230	36	266
1976–77	2054	577	2631
	223	45	268
1977–78	2176	774	2950
	246	56	302
1978–79	2408	1025	3433
	215	57	272

	Men	Women	Total
1979–80	2601	1349	3950
	205	58	263
1980–81	2669	1529	4198
	168	71	239
1981–82	2409	1507	3916
	149	59	208
1982–83	2130	1448	3578
	133	56	189
1983–84	1900	1332	3232
	156	68	224
1984–85	1833	1299	3132
	164	74	238
1985–86	1913	1294	3207
	203	73	276
1986–87	2088	1441	3529
	220	83	303
1987–88	2299	1559	3858
	247	104	351
1988–89	2633	1649	4282
	236	85	321
1989–90	2724	1662	4386
	199	95	294
1990–91	2697	1572	4269
	239	103	342
1991–92	2442	1460	3902
	263	98	361

Index of Names

Numbers in bold refer to text in sidebars. Numbers in italics refer to illustrations

Photographic Support

Typeset in Goudy Old Style with Bookman and Amazone display.

Output service by Craftsmen, Inc. of Tuscaloosa, Alabama.

Printed and bound by Thomson-Shore,

Dexter, Michigan on Moistrite text.

Jacket printed by Alabama Press of Birmingham, Alabama.

Book and jacket designed by Sherry Lynn O'Brien.